Melbourne born and educated, Richard Champion de Crespigny got his first taste of a future flying career as a fourteen year old when his father took him on a tour of the Royal Australian Air Force (RAAF) Academy at Point Cook in Victoria.

In 1975, aged seventeen, he joined the RAAF. One year later, he started flying. During his eleven years with the RAAF, he was seconded as Aide-de-Camp to two Australian Governors-General – Sir Zelman Cowen and Sir Ninian Stephen. Richard remained with the RAAF until 1986 when he joined Qantas.

Richard and his wife, Coral, have two children, Alexander and Sophia.

For more information, please visit http://QF32.Aero

QF32

RICHARD DE CRESPIGNY

MACMILLAN
Pan Macmillan Australia

First published 2012 in Macmillan by Pan Macmillan Australia Pty Limited
1 Market Street, Sydney

Reprinted 2012 (three times)

National Library of Australia
Cataloguing-in-Publication data:

de Crespigny, Richard.

QF32 / Richard de Crespigny with Mark Abernethy.

9781742611174 (pbk.)

Airplanes—Collision avoidance.
Aircraft accidents.

Other Authors/Contributors: Abernethy, Mark.

363.12416

Typeset in Sabon 11.5/18 pt by Midland Typesetters, Australia
Printed by McPherson's Printing Group

This book is for everyone who played a role in QF32.
To all of you, I am proud of you.
Thank you.

To wonderful Coral.
You are the wind beneath my wings.

To my son, Alexander, and daughter, Sophia,
who keep my feet firmly on the ground!

To Dad – thank you for the RAAF Academy tour!

With thanks to Mark Abernethy,
my collaborator, who was integral
to this story being told.

Contents

GENERAL DECLARATION

The Pilot-in-Command is responsible for completing the General Declaration. The General Declaration that I completed for QF32 is reproduced below. This document is necessary for international flights, and includes details of the crew, aircraft registration and itinerary. Copies are provided for airport authorities and customs at the departure and destination airports.

Owner of Operator: Qantas Airways Limited
Registration: VH-OQA   Marks: 'Nancy-Bird Walton'
Flight number: QF32   Date: 04 November 2010
Departure from: Singapore   Arrival at: Sydney, Australia
I declare that the following crew operated the QF32 Flight from Singapore to Sydney on 04 November 2010.

CPT Champion de Crespigny	Richard	CFA Zemek	Sarah
F/O Hicks	Matthew	CFA de Mario Henry	Simone
S/O Johnson	Mark	CFA Hayward	Jay
		CFA Bax	Craig
S/N CPT Evans	David	CFA Jasaragic	Vahid
S/N CPT Wubben	Harry	A/C Bergnofer	Deborah
		A/C Beynon	Claire
CSM Von Reth	Klaus	A/C Lee	Jordan
C/S Hyland	Mark	A/C Lawler	Patrick
CFA Morton	Paul	A/C Lam	Sandy
CFA Hart	Julie Ann	A/C Murray	Simon
CFA Monte	Alfred	A/C Spowart	Michelle
CFA Madison	Ian	A/C Sireilles	Nicole
CFA Teres	Emma	A/C Jurkans	Trentan
CFA Calleja	Aldo	S/N Jostsons	Annie
		S/N Wason	Paul

Signature
Richard Champion de Crespigny
Pilot-in-Command
CSM – Customer Service Manager   A/C – Air Chef
C/S – Cabin Supervisor   S/N – Supernumerary
CFA – Chief Flight Attendant

CHAPTER 1

First Flight

4 February 1976. It was a rare day over southern Victoria, with the sky so clear you could look upwards and see blue receding forever into white. I remember it well because I was at the controls of a Royal Australian Air Force (RAAF) A-85 Winjeel and beside me, in the instructor's seat, was a legend of the Air Force, Flight Lieutenant Bill Evans.

It is the mark of a small air force that the best of the best are called on to teach the novices, and so Evans was spending time away from flying Mirage III fighters to instruct new RAAF trainee pilots in the propeller-driven Winjeel. An aircraft first designed in 1949, the Winjeel was a bit like a Caterpillar D6 bulldozer with wings – it didn't look like it belonged in the air.

The nine-cylinder, 13-litre Pratt & Whitney radial engine produced a deafening roar as we chugged away from the Point Cook Air Force Base to our cruising altitude of 5000 feet. The heavy Winjeel's performance was not helped by the fact its tail fin had been moved significantly forward along the airframe for the sole purpose of making the aircraft less stable and easier to 'flick' into a violent spin.

Trimming the aircraft to fly 'hands-off' at cruise altitude and heading across the Bellarine Peninsula aiming for Tasmania, I was happy the engine had lost its coughing roar and found its comfort level, more like a sleeping alsatian than an angry attacking bear. This was my first instructional flight and it seemed pretty straightforward. Responding to Evans's tour of the flight controls and his instructions to 'feel' the stick in my hands and the rudder pedals at my feet, I gave the thumbs-up.

I relaxed as we settled in, cruising at around 140 knots. The sky seemed to sparkle with sugar crystals and the green of Victoria gleamed like a jewel. It was a beautiful day to fly, a great day to be alive. As I was starting to enjoy myself, Evans's voice crackled in my ears: 'Throttle back – let her slow down, hold your height and give her some left rudder.'

I eased the throttle back. As the speed slowed I felt the stick pull forward as the heavy nose wanted to drop. I pulled back to maintain the altitude, pushed slightly on the left rudder pedal to twist or yaw the aircraft to the left, then put a bit of right stick to stop the aircraft rolling left wing down.

'Back off some more,' Evans said, 'and give me some more left rudder.'

I did as I was told, feeling the big engine in front of me

quietening. Even at full throttle the old Pratt & Whitney radials only turn at around 3000 RPM, and backing off the throttle at 5000 feet sounded like the whole engine was about to shut down. The Winjeel didn't just look like something that shouldn't fly, it also felt like it, and I worried that too much pulling back on the throttle would put us into a stall. As the speed slowed I had to pull back harder, and adding rudder meant I needed even more right stick to stop the aircraft rolling left.

We must have slowed to about 70 knots by the time Bill Evans's voice jumped into my headset again. 'Take more off the throttle – and give it more rudder!'

Less throttle, more rudder, more back stick, more crossed aileron input – suddenly the Winjeel flipped right wing over the left. The nose dived for the ground – it must have looked like the footage you see of aircraft breaking away from a forma- tion, except we were flying at about 60 knots and corkscrewing straight down to the ground in a tight spiral.

Every one of my senses was in overload. I remember my mouth hung open in a mask of terror as the aeroplane spun downwards with continuous roll, yaw and pitch forces I had never felt before. I knew the theory of an aircraft spinning, but never imagined it to be so physically stressful. Sitting on my parachute and held in tight by my harness, I turned towards the fighter ace for guidance.

Flight Lieutenant Bill Evans was sitting back, looking at me with a smile on his face and his arms crossed smugly over his chest. He winked and pointed at me: here I was frozen with terror and the instructor wasn't going to help! It was my plane. I turned back to face the fast-approaching farmlands and gripped my hands around the joystick.

I was eighteen years old and I was in a full and potentially deadly spin. It was terrifying. It isn't just the terror of racing towards the ground that fills your mind with panic, but the physical spinning that pushes your head sideways against the canopy, disorienting you, making it hard to think and even harder to make good decisions.

I gathered my senses and pushed the stick forward – which is counterintuitive – gave full opposite rudder and set the throttle to idle. When the plane stopped spinning and stabilised I was able to throttle up, pull the plane out of its dive and fly the aircraft again under my control. None of it thanks to Bill Evans who didn't touch a thing. He let me handle the whole emergency on my own and made me realise I should *never* permit myself to be too relaxed while flying. *Ever!*

Thirty-four years later, on 4 November 2010, four minutes after a routine take-off from Changi Airport in Singapore, the Qantas 'QF32' A380 that I was in command of, climbing out at 7400 feet, bound for Sydney with 469 people on board, experienced a massive explosion in Engine 2. This engine was mounted closest to the fuselage (and passengers), and projected 6 metres proud from the leading edge of the left wing.

The huge Rolls-Royce Trent 900 engine was destroyed. The extent of damage was unprecedented in Airbus's history. Two heavy chunks tore through the wing, travelling at approximately two times the speed of sound. The fan blades and chunks acted like the explosive core of a hand grenade, ripping wing panels into shrapnel that sprayed like missile fragments over the fuselage as far as the massive tail sections. One chunk also ripped through the aircraft's belly, severing hundreds of wires.

Over 600 wires were cut causing almost every aircraft system to become degraded. I think one of the aircraft's two backbone networks failed, confusing both flight warning computers. The hydraulics, electrics, brakes, fuel, flight controls and landing gear systems were all compromised. No Airbus aircraft had ever suffered so much damage to so many systems.

I am proud of the impeccable performance of the other four pilots on the flight deck and the 24 Qantas cabin crew who managed to bring QF32 back into Changi after the catastrophic engine explosion, with no deaths or injuries. I also appreciate the enormous and critical support provided by Singapore's air traffic controllers, as well as the firefighters, police and Qantas ground and crisis management staff who assisted us. Then there were the 440 passengers. Their contribution was priceless, helping to ensure a safe outcome. Following the accident, many passengers became evangelists for Qantas and their kind words are humbling. It's not every day a crew is praised by strangers for simply doing their job.

The decisions I made on QF32 were influenced by my earliest flying lessons, beginning at the RAAF Academy with my first flight in that Winjeel, through 35 years of training in aviation to the day before our fateful flight. Every lesson is valuable.

When Bill Evans directed me into the spin at the controls of the Winjeel, back in 1976, he was forcing me to confront some of the raw physical forces that act on all aircraft at all times. In a few terrifying seconds he shook me out of a contented world of stable flight and the romance of air travel, and brought me face to face with gravity, velocity, weight and catastrophic forces that, if not handled correctly, result in death.

In that first flight, I learned two lessons about flying that I would never forget.

The first is that the overriding job of any pilot is to *fly* the plane – to *aviate*! There is no computer, manual, autopilot or carefully crafted standard operating procedure that will ever replace that key responsibility: to keep the aircraft in the air in one piece. As the pilot-in-command in the flight deck, you can delegate the navigation and you can ask someone else to work the radio, but you can never delegate your responsibility to aviate.

The second lesson is to never, ever become complacent about aviation. The pilot-in-command has absolute and final authority over the crew and passengers. From the simplest act of signing for the amount of fuel loaded into the aircraft to the most complex reaction to a mid-air catastrophe, the captain carries this responsibility on his own shoulders: legally, professionally and personally. If he's lucky he gets to spread the load by delegating tasks to competent pilots, but he can never outsource the fact the passengers he signs for are the passengers he is expected to return safely to ground. He also signs for the aircraft – but that is of secondary importance. Evans taught me that when something happens up there, you're on your own and you had better fix it – fast.

I must have learned that lesson quickly because when I encountered Bill Evans again in 2011 he reminded me of that first flight and then burst into uncontrolled laughter. When I asked what was so funny, he said, 'The look on your face when we started spinning.'

Indeed, that was my wake-up call – a lesson I would carry with me for the rest of my life.

CHAPTER 2

Planes, Balloons and Duels

Flying was always going to exert an influence on my life.

My great-uncle, Air Vice Marshal H.V. 'Vivian' Champion de Crespigny, was a Melbourne boy who volunteered for service in the First World War when just eighteen years old. He enlisted in the British Army as a flying officer in the Special Reserve and became the commanding officer of 29 Squadron in France at Poperinghe and La Lovie. Under his command 29 Squadron flew reconnaissance over, and conducted raids on, the German lines around the battlegrounds known as Passchendaele.

Vivian was awarded a Military Cross and many other honours. The citation in the *London Gazette* on 3 December 1918 for his Distinguished Flying Cross reads:

A brilliant and gallant officer who displays high initiative in night flying . . . flying a machine unsuitable for night duty, and in face of adverse weather conditions, he reached, and successfully bombed, his objective. A fine performance, calling for cool courage and determination.

Years later, Vivian was promoted to the rank of air vice marshal when he was the air officer commanding the Allied headquarters in Iraq and Persia. He was among the first and only generation of pilots who carried out air-to-air combat with pistols and hand-held guns.

Another great-uncle, Air Commodore Claude Champion de Crespigny, followed his brother Vivian to England during the First World War and joined the Royal Air Force (RAF). Claude would then command Blenheim bomber raids over Europe during the Second World War before becoming commanding officer of RAF operations in Singapore.

My uncle, Squadron Leader Humphrey Champion de Crespigny, joined the RAAF during the Second World War, flying Wirraways out of Darwin to defend Australia's front line from attack by Japanese fighters and bombers. He was discharged in 1945 and continued flying. He owned a Cessna 210 and then a twin-engine Cessna 310, but stopped flying in 1974 when his aircraft was destroyed in a fatal accident. (A pilot chartered

Humphrey's aircraft on 2 April, became disoriented in thunderstorms then lost control. The tail plane separated from the fuselage and was later found over 550 metres from the main wreckage.)

My father, Peter Champion de Crespigny, always harboured an obsession for flying. He was a boarder at Geelong Grammar and would craft Spitfire fighters from blocks of wood. He used to play truant from the dorms at night and ride his bicycle across the paddocks to Lara Airport where the RAAF conducted night-flying training. When the aircraft stopped at the end of the runway to do their pre-take-off checks, Dad would open the rear door and climb in. He'd then move forward, taking his 'seat' behind the two pilots – sitting on the bare wing spar and holding onto the fuselage with both hands. The pilots knew it was wrong to take Dad flying but they had never seen a boy so keen, so off they would go, bouncing down the grass runway then spearing into the black sky as they flew around Victoria.

Dad would sneak back into school early in the morning, but eventually he was busted and my grandfather, Frank Champion de Crespigny, a well-respected doctor from the country town of Ararat, received a letter from the headmaster of Geelong Grammar informing him of Dad's aberrant behaviour. Dad was also skipping classes during the day to test-fly Airspeed Oxfords from the International Harvester Works at Corio, but the headmaster thought that passion expressed by a young man should be encouraged, not beaten out of him, and suggested that, if Frank approved of Dad's flying, the school would not interfere. My grandfather agreed and Dad continued to fly.

When he was just out of school, Dad joined the Royal Australian Air Force (RAAF) for wartime service, on his eighteenth birthday in May 1944. He commenced the pilots' course, but when the Japanese surrendered in 1945 Dad was discharged along with about 15,000 other Australian pilots who were now surplus to the RAAF's needs. He wanted to continue as a pilot in the aviation industry but lacked sufficient experience to compete with all the pilots coming home from the war, so he joined Australian National Airways (ANA) on the administration side.

Under the leadership of one of its founders, Sir Ivan Holyman, ANA was growing rapidly. Sir Ivan formed a management course to groom future leaders and Dad was one of the first chosen. Travelling the world visiting major cities and socialising with royalty, politicians and the foreign service at cocktail parties and the opera, Dad learned to appreciate how aviation would cross oceans, flatten borders and unite economies. After two years, he returned home and introduced an innovative ticketing system that was used Australia-wide.

After eleven years, Dad's time at ANA came to a voluntary end after a disagreement with Sir Ivan. Dad had suspended Sir Ivan's nephew for being absent from work when an incident occurred at Perth Airport. Dad had a lot of power and influence at ANA, but it didn't extend to being able to suspend a Holyman. To his extraordinary credit, and as a measure of his integrity, Dad refused to have his decision overruled and so resigned from the job he loved dearly.

ANA would make other mistakes. The Australian Government approached Sir Ivan about nationalising ANA and making it Australia's sole domestic airline. Sir Ivan, a staunch believer of private enterprise, refused the offer. Another offer was made to a smaller airline – Queensland and Northern Territory Aerial Services – an offer that was accepted by its founder Sir Hudson Fysh. Qantas was turbo-charged into the form we know today and ANA would find itself 'kneecapped' by the government, which set up a domestic competitor (TAA) and restricted the aircraft ANA could purchase. After Sir Ivan Holyman's death, ANA's steady demise continued until it was sold to Sir Reginald Ansett, who then rebadged the airline as Ansett–ANA.

As for Dad, he went to work for his father-in-law at his newsagency for a time and then started a furniture business called StyleCraft, which became successful.

Dad finally got to fly. When I started pilot training in the RAAF, Dad bought a Piper Turbo Arrow aircraft (registration VH-SOI) and started his flying lessons again on the same day that I started my flying in the RAAF.

Patricia Champion de Crespigny, my wonderful mother, died unexpectedly when I was in my final year at school. Mum had dedicated her life to bringing up four over-energetic sons and forwent so many of life's pleasures – she never travelled overseas. I left home to join the RAAF and Dad later married Mariea, another wonderful woman 22 years his junior who has been a loving wife to Dad and a wonderful mentor to me. Although Mariea is only nine years older than I am, I introduce her to my friends as my 'Wicked Stepmother'. Recipients show surprise at this introduction, but I figure, all stories with stepmothers present them being wicked and feeding poisoned apples to their children – so why should my stepmother be any different? I enjoy the process as everyone who meets Mariea quickly comes to love her and appreciate the wonderful partner she is to Dad. I call her my WSM and she proudly signs her letters to me just the same.

Dad is still a legend and inspiration to us all. He's 86 years young now, runs an Alpaca farm, keeps his flying licence current, flying his Piper Turbo Arrow aircraft every few days and swims a kilometre three times a week. My wife Coral and I spend ten days every year to go powder skiing in America with him and Mariea.

Finally, the Champion de Crespigny surname needs an explanation.

The Champion family were good Roman Catholics in Normandy, France, until 1617, when Richard Champion changed his religion in order to marry Marguerite, the daughter of a wealthy Huguenot. From her father they acquired the property called Crespigny near Vire.

Their son Claude did even better. Claude took the more aristocratic name of Champion de Crespigny and he persuaded the government that he had noble ancestry and so did not have to pay the *Taille* tax which was levied on commoners. He then married the Countess of Vierville and they lived in his wife's manor at Vierville-sur-Mer, on the coast near Caen. Their fine family chateau survives today. It was at the centre for the D-Day landings of 1944, yet survived the bombardment. It can be seen today at the top of the peaceful winding road that climbs away from Omaha Beach, and a plaque on the front gate explains that the house was spared so it could serve as Allied headquarters after the invasion.

Unfortunately, however, King Louis XIV took a dislike to Huguenots. In 1685 he revoked the 'Edict of Nantes' which had granted them tolerance, and Claude and his family were forced to flee to England. They were at first very poor there, but they adapted remarkably well and became respected citizens. The gravestone of Claude and Marie is still preserved and displayed in the churchyard of Marylebone in the centre of London.

Our formal surname 'Champion de Crespigny' is often shortened to 'de Crespigny'. However, both names are synonymous and history abounds with interesting tales from my ancestors and relatives who gained notoriety from living outside the square.

In 1805, the grandson of Claude and Marie, also called Claude, was appointed a Baronet, a hereditary title.

The Baronet's grandson, the Reverend Heaton de Crespigny was one of the last Englishmen to take part in a duel. The scene was set in 1828 on the beach at Calais after Mr Long Wellesley (a failed politician and nephew of the Duke of Wellington) had publicly insulted Sir William de Crespigny (Heaton's paralysed father). Wellesley refused Heaton's demand for a retraction, so Heaton 'called out' Wellesley to a duel: 'You think I have only got a black coat,' he said to Wellesley, 'you are wrong: I've a shooting one as well.' Soon afterwards, facing each other on the French sands, both men faced off at ten paces, then fired at each other. Both missed. (Heaton was a clergyman, hence the 'black coat'. He was later defrocked and died in the Australian goldfields.)

In 1847, the great-great-grandson of Claude and Marie (and great-nephew of Heaton) was born and as you probably would have guessed now, was also called Claude. On the death of his father in 1868, he assumed the title to become the fourth Baronet, Sir Claude Champion de Crespigny.

Sir Claude led a remarkable and eccentric life, full of adventure and danger. His escapades are encapsulated in his book, *Forty Years of a Sportsman's Life*. He spent time in the Royal Navy (in India) and the British Army with the Limerick Artillery in Ireland. He still believed that duels fulfilled a method to restore a savaged dignity, writing 'should a man be challenged, he is bound, if a gentleman, to go out.' Nevertheless, Sir Claude was more a sportsman than a fighter.

Sir Claude lived to experience the genesis of electrical power and was the first member of the family to have a passion for aviation, though this period was well before the advent of handy communication devices such as the radio. He took a keen interest in ballooning and is remembered for many epic flights. During one short flight he unfortunately launched into a strong wind that drove him and his basket into a brick wall – breaking his leg. Being more adventurous, he broke another leg on 11 June 1882, when attempting to cross the English Channel from Maldon France to England. Unperturbed by injuries, our intrepid Sir Claude tried the opposite direction. So at noon on a mild and sunny English day in June 1883, Sir Claude set off in a balloon made of 'India rubber and bird lime' in an attempt to cross the English Channel from England to France. Meteorology was not the science it is today, and so Sir Claude soon found himself above cloud and after rising in a thermal to an altitude of 17,000 feet, wisely decided to descend before nightfall. He and his fellow balloonist crash landed in Holland, and that is how they accidentally become the first people to cross the North Sea in a balloon. Sir Claude won the Ballooning Society's Gold Medal for this achievement. Sir Claude's eccentricities had no bounds. In 1886, much to his wife's chagrin, he became the assistant executioner in Essex under the 'nom de noose' of Charles Maldon. He remarkably died of natural causes in 1935 but his name persisted through all five sons whom he called 'Claude'!

Another interesting relation was Colonel David de Crespigny Smiley, the son of Valerie de Crespigny (and Sir Claude's grandson). David was a British Special Forces and Intelligence Officer in Europe and Persia during the Second World War. It's thought that the author John le Carré moulded David's character into 'George Smiley' in his 1974 spy novel 'Tinker Tailor Soldier Spy' (now a movie). David was also a noted sportsman, holding the record for the most broken bones accrued in a season of skeleton sledding at the famous Cresta Run at the St Moritz Tobogganing Club. My son Alexander completed his first Cresta Run in Saint Moritz in 2008 and he's been accorded the honour of being the Tower Boy at the Cresta at the end of 2012. I hope he's not targeting Smiley's record!

The 'flying bug' gene will probably continue through the de Crespigny line. I have the 'flying bug' gene, and Coral inherited the same courtesy of her father, Roy Ford who was also a RAAF pilot flying Avro Ansons at 15 Squadron SFTS, Canada during the Second World War. This answers Alexander's curiosity as to why his dreams are replete with the touch of a wing, the taste of an oxygen mask, the sound of the radial, the smell of kerosene and the sight of women in uniform.

*

Even though flying was in my blood, it wasn't really an obsession for me before my teen years. My first love was engineering and motorbikes. Growing up in Melbourne's inner-city Toorak and going to a school like Melbourne Grammar was always a bit stifling for my three very active brothers and me. It was a case of too much testosterone and no place to burn it off. We were often in trouble around the neighbourhood – not for any criminal reasons but just because we were always getting bored and would easily fall into making mischief.

My father was aware his four sons were a handful and that we needed room to let off steam, so he bought 5 hectares of wild bushland fronting the King Parrot Creek near Flowerdale, 70 kilometres north of Melbourne, with 400 square miles of national park surrounding it. We called the property 'The Ponderosa', after the American TV show *Bonanza*, and Dad commissioned the builder of the Australian Alpine Club ski lodges to build a very basic timber house on the property. There was no electricity, so we plumbed our own gas lights, heating and water.

From when I was about nine years old until my early twenties, this bushland was where we'd spend most weekends. I was the second youngest son, and it was a classic role-play: the oldest, Michael, was sensible; the middle son, Simon, was a rascal; and the third – me – was spoiled. Christopher, the youngest, was a very cute toddler.

One day Simon found an old motorbike in a ditch beside a road – the original owner had nearly died in an accident and had left the bike at the scene. The 1930 model Ariel Red Hunter is a large, very heavy British motorbike with a 'live tail' (no rear suspension) and a dry clutch. It had the hallmark of everything British-made at that time – it leaked oil and broke down. To start the 500 cc single cylinder motor, you had to move a lever to retard the ignition, another lever to engage the decompression valve, then slowly press down on the kick-starter to position the piston up to TDC (top dead centre) after the compression stroke. Finally, you closed the choke butterfly valve then kick-started the beast into action. Miss any of these steps and you risked a kick-back that would either bruise your leg or eject you over the bike. But no one told any of us this. Michael and Simon had to discover how to fix the bike then get it back into working condition. For me, it was the first motorbike I knew, so I assumed they were all heavy, loud, unmuffled and had leg-breaking torque.

We used to ride the bike up into the forest. On one occasion, the clutch sprang apart, disgorging the rotating clutch plates onto the ground – they then found traction and accelerated away in front of us! We were stranded 10 kilometres away from home on a rough dirt road in a quiet forest with a broken-down bike. We could have panicked, but there was no point – there was no one else to help. I remember fumbling around, finding the springs, screws and clutch plates, reassembling the mess and then riding home. It was a confidence-building experience.

I was ten years old by the time I could ride the Ariel, but I was not tall enough to touch the ground, so to get it going we would rotate the bike back up onto its rear stand so the rear wheel was off the ground, start the bike, put it into gear, get the wheel spinning in second gear, then rev the engine slightly. Simon would then slowly ease the 150-kilogram bike forward off the stand. I can still clearly remember the sound of the thumping engine dropping a few revs as the enormous knobby tyre engaged with the sodden grass, throwing a thick rooster tail of mud 6 metres into the air as we slowly accelerated away – leaving behind a snaking 3 inch–deep trench – magic!

But four kids can't ride one bike. So I scraped together $15 and bought an old broken Lambretta motor scooter. We would go screaming through the forests exploring, jumping creeks and having a ball. I owned four motorbikes during my teen years.

There were so many injuries then, and today I still feel guilt and remorse for the anguish I caused my mother. Before I left home I broke my leg four times – once skiing, and the other three times on motorbikes. The time I broke it skiing I was six and Mum had just given birth to Christopher. Dad had been planning a family skiing holiday, and after Chris was born we left Mum behind in the hospital and travelled to Falls Creek. Unfortunately I broke my leg on the first day, so Dad drove for five hours to take me back to Richmond hospital – the same hospital where Mum was staying with Christopher. I remember Dad having to ask the staff not to tell Mum her son was in the next ward having his leg set in plaster.

I've got a few scars to show for the spills, but not as many as my brothers. Michael broke his legs a few times and lost half his calf muscle when his leg scraped up against the cooling fan on an engine's fly wheel. Christopher had a particularly nasty compound fracture deep in the bush (we needed a bulldozer to access the site and extract him), and he required plastic surgery to stitch up his abdomen when it was punctured by a set of handlebars.

But Mum was stoic and met all our misdemeanours with extraordinary resilience. I remember one time, when I was fourteen, I took my motorbike to my friend's parents' property. Although the property stretched over 100 hectares, it was clearly too small to hold our interest when compared to the Ponderosa's forests, so we rode into Bendigo to get a milkshake. The police were not amused. We spent a few hours in the police station and I faced five charges: underage riding; riding without a licence; no registration; stealing; and displaying false plates. (I'd taken them off a wrecked bike I'd found in the bush.) Fortunately for me, my friend's father invited the police officers to the farm for a picnic and all charges were eventually dropped. When Mum found out she just laughed – there wasn't anything else to say.

Not all of my injuries were sustained in the bush or on the slopes. When I was eleven, I was riding my bicycle to school one morning and was going very fast down Glenferrie Road, a busy street in Melbourne, when a woman opened her car door without looking behind. I collided headfirst with the door then fell to the street in front of the busy peak-hour traffic. I lost some front teeth and there was blood everywhere. My father was summoned, and he took one look and rushed me to the dentist. 'Where's his teeth?' the dentist asked. Dad returned to the scene and found my teeth lying at the bottom of the tram tracks in the middle of the road. The teeth were re-planted, and I was told I would have to wear a denture if the teeth were knocked out again. So that was it for football and other contact sports. For the rest of my schooling I rowed and played tennis.

Our family's numerous injuries came at great financial cost, and the suspicions of the medical insurance company were eventually aroused. The tipping point came when Dad and three of his four boys were all laid up in bed at the same time claiming for different injuries – the insurance agent visited us personally to verify the claims were legitimate.

School didn't really excite me in my middle years and I was an average academic performer and not too naughty, perhaps having one detention per year. But to the great surprise of my friends, I joined the St John's Church choir, not because of my singing abilities or religious fervour, but because my brother Michael had joined, found a beautiful girlfriend and announced that that's where the pretty girls were. My other brother Simon had quickly joined too, and also found a girlfriend. So I joined and found a girlfriend too. Michael was right – that's where the pretty girls were hiding.

While I wasn't bad academically, I just wasn't fully motivated. My interests were motorbikes, engineering and electrics. I had extensively reworked the 240-volt wiring in my room with automatic timers for fans and lights. I now appreciate that I owe my survival to the excellent retention properties of the electrical tape that held the wiring mess together and saved me from electrocution most of the time. I loved the mechanics class that met once a week, where we rebuilt a VW beetle – tuning the engine by ear only. I could strip down and rebuild a bike or a car engine and get it working again. This wasn't such an extraordinary skill back in the early 1970s; if you wanted to ride bikes you had to understand every part of the machine to build, fix and maintain it – all on your own and on a tiny budget.

The time bashing around on those bikes and fixing them gave me a respect for machinery that I took into my aviation career. Years later, my bottom-up approach would frustrate my instructors and peers when I would try to learn how each plane I flew actually worked. I believe the foundation for safety is an appreciation of the limitations of your environment, the machinery you're operating and yourself, so you can recognise when you are inside those limits and feel confident to operate there.

My background often put me into situations where I had to come to grips physically with power, velocity, mass and gravity, and most of the confidence I later had with large planes originated on motorbikes in the bush behind the Ponderosa.

As I got to the end of my schooling at Melbourne Grammar, I could easily have settled down into a career as an (electrical) engineer. However, by the time I was seventeen I realised enough about myself to know I needed a robust physical challenge to go with the mental. I would not waste my life behind a desk. I needed fast machinery in my life, but I also wanted intellectual stimulation.

If you need a fast ride and lots of homework, there's only one way to go: the RAAF.

CHAPTER 3

With Wings as Eagles

The idea to join the Royal Australian Air Force (RAAF) Academy didn't come out of nowhere. In 1972, three years before the end of school, we went to our bush property for the weekend. When we arrived at the Ponderosa we found the property had been carved up: huge bulldozer tracks cut deep into the soft soil, fences had been flattened, trees toppled, and there were charcoal burns on the grass from campfires. It appeared to be a wanton act of vandalism, although whoever did it had left our house alone.

Dad asked around. It turned out the destruction was the result of the RAAF conducting a local bivouac. While looking for their training site, the group had become lost and camped on the wrong property.

Dad tracked the guilty parties down and had a chat with the base commander responsible. The Air Force was highly apologetic and offered to pay for any damages. Dad still had great memories of the RAAF in 1944, so he suggested that, instead of financial compensation, the RAAF could make amends by taking two of his sons (Simon and me) on a tour of the RAAF Academy at Point Cook Air Force Base (now combined with Laverton and called RAAF Williams). Dad knew I was interested in flying because my uncle Humphrey had recently taken me for a flight over Melbourne in his Cessna and I'd come home raving about it. The base commander agreed to Dad's request, and I remember that tour very clearly.

The RAAF Academy had extraordinarily manicured grounds, a modern overarching graduation hall and mess halls, and spectacular lecture theatres and labs for chemistry, computers, electronics, engineering and aerodynamics. Jet engines, subsonic and supersonic wind tunnels – you name it, if there was leading-edge aviation technology in Australia you'd find it at the Academy. There was even a full-size aircraft hangar fitted out with tools, spray painters, welders, presses and sheet iron for the Academy cadets' exclusive use. There was also a strong sense of history about Point Cook. It was the site of the original Australian Flying Corps – before it became the Royal Australian Air Force after the First World War – and its aerodrome is still the longest continuously operating military aerodrome in the world.

The Academy was the most remarkable institution I had ever seen – and I immediately wanted to be a part of it. This would be the career that combined my love of technology with my need for physical challenge. I would gain an education, learn extraordinary skills and be pushed to my limits. I decided there and then I had to go flying – I had to join the Academy. But there was a problem. I needed to graduate in the top 5 per cent of the state to be accepted. At that stage I was probably in the top 40 per cent. I now had a new target.

My dogged determination to excel at school increased another notch in 1974, my last year of school. Back in 1973 Mum became sick, a sickness that would persist for two years and see her in hospital many times. Both of her kidneys had failed. In late 1973, after six months on the waiting list, she was finally put on dialysis. She'd visit hospital two times a week for the procedure and was beginning to feel well again. It was great to have her back with us, relatively healthy and happy, and wanting only for a kidney transplant. Our lives were returning to normal.

Three months later, in February of 1974, Mum visited hospital for her dialysis session, but there was a problem. The dialysis machine's thermostat malfunctioned and failed to regulate her blood temperature. Her cleansed blood was too hot when it re-entered her body. The dialysis machine had a warning system, which would emit an aural warning and illuminate a warning light when an overheat is detected, but the nurse tasked to monitor the machines was absent. Mum effectively died on the dialysis machine that day.

The grey matter in Mum's brain had been overheated and destroyed. All that remained were the autonomic reflexes of breathing, heart rate and the semblance of an intellect no more advanced than that of a newborn child. The mother we knew and loved was gone. I would go and see her in hospital, hold her hand and talk to her, hoping the way her eyes followed me around the room was a sign there was awareness within. But for visit after visit there was no improvement, and we began to realise her reactions were no more than basal reactions – like a baby's eyes following a moving object above its cot. Mum would never recover.

On 22 May 1974 – the middle of the school holidays – my best friends and I were riding our motorbikes at the Ponderosa when Dad turned up unexpectedly to tell us Mum had died. It seemed so unfair for Mum, especially when I thought of how tough we, her sons, had been on her. She had sacrificed and endured so much, and now – just when her quality of life should have been improving – she was gone. Dad, my brothers and I suffered for a long time – we never properly grieved her loss and it took me more than 30 years to revisit those memories and confront the pain.

When Mum died, I was in the middle of my last year at school. I was not a bright student, but I could work hard. I remember thinking to myself that I could not bring Mum back and nor could I make up for all the grief I had caused her. But I could do something that would have made her proud – I would work day and night to get into the top 5 per cent of the state, to get accepted to the RAAF Academy. Nothing would stop me now.

In order to apply for the RAAF Academy I had to matriculate in English, chemistry, physics, and the tougher pure mathematics and applied mathematics. The maths courses ran over two years; for the first year (fourth form) I had been in the lower class of general mathematics and so Melbourne Grammar wouldn't let me switch across because they said I wasn't smart enough. The school thought I should follow a career with my hands, like watch-making. But if I was to join the RAAF I had to do pure and applied maths, so I gave the school no option: 'I'm turning up for pure and applied maths, so you'd better schedule my classes.' Dad received a letter warning there could be adverse effects from my taking on subjects beyond my ability, but the school later relaxed and put me into the lowest of the three graded pure and applied maths classes.

I was bottom of the class in maths when I started fifth form, but it's amazing the difference ambition and motivation can make. Four thousand would apply for the 28th RAAF Academy course and only 44 would be accepted, so I didn't just have to pass my subjects, I had to excel. Through grunt, determination and the help of my extraordinary teachers, I did so well in the final year that I could have been accepted into medicine at Melbourne University. It was an extraordinary time in my life and I was very proud of what I achieved.

My advice for all young, aspiring students is simple. Find your passion; develop and work hard at it, and you will be rewarded. Better still, if your work is your passion, you'll never have to 'go to work'. John Bartels, the captain of the QF30 aircraft in July 2008 that suffered an explosive decompression after an oxygen bottle exploded, expressed these thoughts even better: 'The harder I work the luckier I get.'

These days I look back on myself during those intermediate years at Melbourne Grammar and I can clearly see a directionless kid who just needed to find motivation. I thank Dad who, when faced with a bad event (the RAAF damaging the Ponderosa), turned the problem into an opportunity (the RAAF Academy tour) that changed my life. We all face situations like this and we should always strive to think outside the box to get the best results.

When I applied for the RAAF, after evaluating me they said there were few openings in the RAAF for pilots but plenty for engineers and navigators. They offered to accept me immediately for the engineering and navigation courses, and advised that if I passed up those opportunities I might later miss out on the pilots' course and therefore lose my chance at a career with the RAAF altogether. My decision was easy: 'It's the Academy and flying – or nothing.' They then told me they could accept me as a direct-entry pilot, which meant they'd throw me straight into pilot training. But there is little security in being a pilot. I wanted a backstop, a safeguard in case I failed the pilots' course or lost my aircrew medical. So I said, 'No, I want the science degree from the Academy and then training to be a pilot.'

On 22 January 1975 I joined number 28 Academy course with 43 other cadets. My earlier interest in electrics morphed into a passion for electronics, and I particularly enjoyed the engineering and electronics–related studies. I built a 'music chaser' – a device for pulsing coloured lights in synchrony to musical sounds. The three-channel lights used triacs (electronic switches) that were designed to have their 'base' at the active (240 volts) potential. Most people find this hard to understand, and so did I because one day I accidentally touched a triac with one hand and the kit chassis with the other. I remember the scorching pain running up my arms and meeting at my chest – I could hear and feel the hum of my chest vibrating at 50 hertz. My legs kicked hard and I found myself thrown 2 metres back, lying on the floor. Like anyone who has been electrocuted or injured, I ran through a checklist of my body to see if anything had been damaged: toes, feet, chest, arms, fingers, neck – all okay. I was lucky I had learned a valuable lesson without being hurt.

I made life-long friends at the Academy. When joining the RAAF, the orientation course had simple ambitions: to shred every recruit down to their basic being, then rebuild them with the standard military substrate. We lost all our personal rights; we were challenged as a group and we discovered we would only survive if we functioned as a team. Over four years you end up knowing many intimate details about each other, and you develop a close friendship and trust. By the time you graduate you share an esprit de corps with your course mates, and many become part of your extended family for the rest of your life.

*

Even though I was now at the RAAF I still had very little flying experience. Commercial flying was a very privileged and expensive activity. When my mother died at the age of 43 she had never travelled overseas. I was eighteen years old when I first left my home state of Victoria. I fitted earplugs, then walked up the ramp into the back of a very noisy 'A' model RAAF Hercules that would transport me from Laverton, Victoria, to the Richmond Air Force Base outside of Sydney, New South Wales.

The Hercules is a transport aircraft devoid of passenger comforts. I can still remember the cocktail of screeching noises: hydraulics, pneumatics and engines. The noisy propellers generated a highpitched scream and a painful 'beat'. The 'beat' is a cyclic noise, created when the propellers rotated at slightly different RPMs, enough to make the pressure on your ears ramp up and down every few seconds. Having no other experience, I assumed all large aircraft were just as noisy.

A year later, I was nineteen and on my first commercial aircraft flight, a DC9 from Melbourne to Sydney. As we taxied towards the runway, I noticed the low hum that indicated the auxiliary power unit (APU) was running. I wondered when the pilots were going to start the engines prior to take-off. It was only after we charged down the runway and launched into the sky that I realised what I thought had been the APU's noise was actually the sound of the engines, the engines had been running for the last fifteen minutes, and I wasn't even wearing earplugs! It might seem naïve to have expected that commercial jets were as noisy as Hercules, but in the 1970s air travel wasn't as common as it is now.

For the four years I spent at the Academy I often looked across the road to the airfield where the direct-entry cadets were learning to fly – and I was envious. Conversely, the direct-entry pilots looked down at us in our lecture rooms and thought we were nerds. At the start of the second year we flew twenty hours in Winjeels, which was provided to boost our motivation and morale.

In the fourth year of the course each of us spent one month visiting the squadron of our choice, to participate in their operations and lifestyle. I wanted to experience the latest and best technology, so there was only one choice – F-111s. The F-111 was a strategic long-range bomber capable of delivering conventional or nuclear weapons with pinpoint accuracy in bad weather, day or night. I spent one month at 6 Squadron attending briefings, researching the aircraft and mixing with the pilots. It was a remarkable time – I had one three-hour flight where I experienced my first supersonic cruise, and then low flying with terrain following radar (TFR). TFR was unique to the F-111, permitting it to fly at high speed under the radar detection heights. The pilot selected the ground clearance (down to 100 feet) and the ride (soft, medium or hard), and the computers did the rest. A typical mission profile was a high-altitude transit followed by low-level interdiction at 480 knots (890 kph), just 100 feet above the ground and under the radar – and the F-111 could do all of this in cloud or at night. It was remarkable to fly through a valley at night and see nothing except the short flash of ground illuminated by the wingtip strobe lights. After this experience I was convinced about my flying career – I had to fly F-111s!

The Academy years were difficult but rewarding. I graduated in December 1978 with a Bachelor of Science (majoring in physics and maths) and a Graduate Diploma in Military Aviation. I also graduated as an RAAF commissioned officer – presented by His Excellency Sir Zelman Cowen, the governor-general. I had become a flying officer yet I had very little flying experience.

The RAAF Academy trained many more officers than would ever get their wings. Like most armed forces around the world, the majority of Academy cadets are ultimately destined for management positions, liaison and diplomatic postings – they're more likely to be sponsored through officer promotion and executive MBA courses than through multiple expensive aircraft conversions. The reality was the Academy did not want to invest four years of education in a young man so he could go kill himself in a damn plane. It was a dreadful irony that those who duxed RAAF Academy – being the best – won a poisoned chalice. For it was the dux pilots who disproportionately lost their lives in aircraft accidents.

I nearly considered resigning from the RAAF one week before my graduation day. If I graduated from the Academy and accepted a commission I would become bonded to the Air Force for another five years. But only 25 to 35 per cent of pilots pass the one-year pilots' course. The odds were against me. I told my father I was thinking of resigning because I couldn't stand the thought of being stuck in the RAAF at a desk job. He said, 'Rich, flying is your dream. Nothing's easy, and taking risks brings rewards, so take a risk and try your hardest.'

My great friend Adrian Wischer was more direct: 'Security is a swear word; there is never security, you make your own luck.'

I graduated from the RAAF Academy, then entered number 107 Pilots' Course flying CT4 (piston) aircraft and Macchi jets. This twelve-month course was exciting – the risks were high but the rewards were breathtaking. I joined a strict training path where every flight had goals and requirements, and I was generally too busy concentrating to enjoy myself. We were always only three fail rides away from being scrubbed – the first flight, the retry flight and then a scrub ride with the chief instructor. Our training covered a diverse range of skills, from navigation, aerobatics and low flying through to formation and instrument flying. Instrument flying tripped up the most pilots. I think all those years of manhandling and fixing motorbikes at the Ponderosa helped me through my pilot training. Being unafraid to aggressively manoeuvre aircraft was an asset when chasing my instructor around the skies, trying to stay on his tail. Appreciating machinery and knowing my body's capabilities also helped me to stay relaxed and fly smoothly in stressful situations.

The basic flying techniques drilled into me during formation flying helped me 30 years later when converting to Airbus aircraft with Qantas. Aircraft fly in formations to maximise the number of aircraft that can manoeuvre in a limited airspace, and air controllers treat a formation of aircraft the same as they treat a single aircraft. So aircraft in formation must fly very close to each other – close enough that the wingman never loses sight of his leader. The wingtip-to-wingtip separation reduces, getting down below 2 metres when penetrating the thickest cloud.

It's hard learning to fly in formation. Just when you think you have nudged up close enough to your wingman your instructor berates you for being too distant and out of position. You respond by pushing in closer to your wingman, but your primitive survival instinct takes over and your hand moves subconsciously to fly you apart. You consciously push in closer; your body subconsciously pulls away – in, out, in, out, in, out. It's very frustrating – your conscious and subconscious minds are at war with each other. Learning to fly in formation is the classic tracking exercise where pilots often over-control and, in the worst case, enter an oscillating (in-out) behaviour called a pilot-induced oscillation (PIO). It was 'Stork' who had a wonderful remedy that corrected my PIO tendencies.

All RAAF pilots are given an alias name that sticks for their entire career. I had two – 'Dick' and 'Gino'. Most pilots take animal names for aliases – such as 'Dog', 'Rat', 'Snake', 'Beetle' – and 'Stork' was no exception. At 6 foot 3 inches tall and wafer thin, 'Stork' was an exceptional instructor who guided me through my Macchi pilots' course. During one formation flight, I was trying to keep close-in beside my manoeuvring leader. I was becoming tired and tense – my hand was squeezing the top out of the joystick – and I was starting to get the wobbles. I knew I was tense, but I couldn't relax and I was tending towards another PIO. Stork's suggestion broke through my concentration and fixed my problem.

'Dick,' he said, 'you're too tense on the joystick – you're grabbing it too firmly. Imagine the aircraft is your girlfriend and the joystick is your girlfriend's nipple. Don't grab it with a clenched fist! Hold it gently between your thumb and finger. Now fly the aircraft by bending the nipple, gently – just as she would like it. Fly the nipple!'

I've never forgotten Stork's remarks. My formation flying improved, and this technique works a dream on the A380!

I finished close to the top in my course, so I could have my first preference for the squadron I'd be assigned to. There were no vacancies at 6 Squadron on F-111s, so I planned to make my next bid to go to Mirage fighters instead.

I had struck up a great friendship with Stork. When he discovered my second preference was to fly the Mirage fighters – another elite aircraft in the RAAF – he warned me against it. He said, given my personality, I'd get bored in the fighters because all they do is shoot bullets and drop bombs. Also, the waiting list to get a command on a C-130 Hercules – the planes that do most of the interesting foreign assignments – was too long. He said I should apply for 38 Squadron, flying Caribous.

The Caribou is a medium-sized, twin radial engine, propeller-driven STOL transport aircraft. (STOL means 'short take-off and landing'.) They can carry a large load and they have remarkably complex flight controls enabling them to take off and land on 300 metre–long runways – very short in aviation terms. The Caribou's large tyres can be deflated to 20 psi, which means that if a four-wheel-drive vehicle can drive over a surface the Caribou can land on it! It's for all these reasons that the

Caribou was the Australian Army aircraft of choice for the front lines of Vietnam and for the untamed jungles of New Guinea.

Stork said, 'Caribous are exciting – you'll work the aircraft to its limits. The flying is diverse and fascinating, and you'll have your command within six months.'

I applied for F-111s but there were still no slots. So I said, 'I'll take Caribous.'

CHAPTER 4

Wombat Airlines

The de Havilland Canada DHC-4 Caribou is a Canadian 'tactical' transport plane that first saw service in the Australian military in 1964, in Vietnam. Its 4-tonne payload permitted these aircraft to carry two large Army Land Rovers or an equivalent weight of artillery pieces, but, during my time, the Caribou was mostly used in tactical roles such as carrying supplies to remote villages in New Guinea and supporting Australia's Special Forces.

The Australian armed forces loved the Caribous; they were strong and enjoyed a dignified career. When I undertook my Caribou conversion course in 1980, there were plans back then to retire the aircraft and find a replacement, but a capable replacement was never found and the aircraft served for another 30 years. Of the initial 29 Caribous that entered RAAF service during the Vietnam War, eleven were still in service when they were decommissioned in 2010.

The Caribou was powered by two 1450-horsepower Pratt & Whitney radial piston engines. These were classic engines that proved to be powerful, reliable and simple to maintain. But like all supercharged engines, they needed to be treated with great respect. So the Caribou conversion course included lots of theory about engine design and operation – radial engines contain many heavy rotating parts that could be damaged by under-boosting just as much as over-boosting. The engine start was just as critical. Three long-stemmed switches needed to be 'tickled' in the correct timing sequence to start the cranking, fuel pump and ignition – get it wrong and everyone within 200 metres would hear the explosion and see the flames. I have very fond memories of the P&W engines, and I think I am wiser for the experience because the principles we learned then can be applied to any engine, even jet engines.

The Caribou had remarkably impressive performance. The high wing allowed for operation on narrow and makeshift runways while the high tail section meant an easy-access cargo door could be lowered at the rear of the aircraft, whether on the ground or airborne. This 15,400-kilogram aircraft could take off and land on 300 metres of unprepared strip (a standard Boeing 737 or Airbus A320 requires a minimum take-off and landing distance of 1700 and 1400 metres respectively). Some of the places I operated into during my years with 38 Squadron tested this famous STOL capacity to its limits. We were trained to operate into these runways at night using only six runway lights: two at each threshold and two along the left side of the runway. In reality there were few runways we operated into that were 300 metres short, but we were trained for the worst case so we never felt stressed when operating into limiting airfields.

Unlike most aircraft, the propellers on the Caribou's engines could be put into reverse. This feature is used to reverse the aircraft on the tarmac, but its main benefit is to reduce stopping distances. It also reduced airflow and lift on the main wing. You might engage the propellers into reverse during landing if you find yourself 'floating' down the runway and unable to put it down on the ground quickly – but you have to be mindful of the effects: you would drop like a brick if the wheels were higher than two feet above the ground.

For such a basic plane, the Caribou had very complex flight controls. But once you were airborne it had an effective operational ceiling of just 10,000 feet because the cabin wasn't pressurised. The super-charged engines could have powered us higher, but on those occasions where we did 'push the envelope' and climbed up to 20,000 feet, the cold limited our enthusiasm – our fingers and feet froze, and everyone needed oxygen masks.

The Caribou was a fabulous machine to develop 'hands-on' flying skills. It had no radar, so we couldn't see embedded thunderstorms in front of us, and it had no autopilot to fly us through turbulence. We 'rigged for rough running'

– disconnecting the HF aerial from the receiver and tying everything down for the ensuing roller coaster ride – whenever we thought we might be about to enter the 'twilight zone' in a thunderstorm. We also had primitive navigation equipment. When outside the range of our radio navigational aids, we navigated over water by flying at 100 feet and used the Beaufort scale to calculate wind speed. Over the desert, we calculated our drift angle by pressing a soft pencil to the window to track an object abeam us on the horizon. It doesn't get any simpler than that!

New Guinea was the theatre in which the Caribou and its pilots' skills were proved. Many of our landings were onto short, soft runways carved out of the jungle and the hillside. We could land and take off from any runway, but if we suffered an engine failure the remaining engine provided insufficient performance to climb out of the valleys and over the 14,000 foot-high mountains. The safety height to clear all obstacles was up to 15,000 feet, well above our single-engine performance ceiling. So for most of our flying in New Guinea, we had to stay under the cloud – and therein lay the challenge. Anyone who's lived in Papua New Guinea will tell you that to fly under cloud in the interior of that mountainous country means flying through narrowing valleys and finding saddles that you can either leap over or you have to evade. We had to know our aircraft's evasive 180-degree turn potential – get this wrong and you'd be dead.

Our navigation in New Guinea was completely visual, the co-pilot thumbing his way along a topographical strip map as we traversed valleys, always below the cloud base. To enter cloud would be to enter a no-man's land of zero visibility, and those who did would have sweated, knowing that sighting a tree in the fog would be an ominous warning that you had seconds to live before slamming into the side of a mountain.

One of the most challenging and rewarding runways we operated into was Tarpini. Located in the middle of the New Guinea Highlands at 8000 feet above sea level, Tarpini was a native village with no access roads and no telephone or electricity. It's just an isolated village with an undulating boggy grass runway cut out of the jungle into the side of a sticky red clay mountain.

We operated Caribous in Tarpini using performance standards and procedures that would never be permitted by civil regulators. The mixture of high altitude, low performance, short runways and high temperatures meant we had to operate with extreme rules if we were to operate at all. At 2000 feet (660 metres), Tarpini's runway was long enough, but the Caribou's engine performance in the tropics at 8000 feet, particularly on one engine, was appalling.

We created our own flight plans, maps and instructions to get to Tarpini. These were surprisingly simple, just showing Tarpini as a cross on a hillside. To land at Tarpini we navigated under the cloud – along the valleys, over the saddles to the 'entry point' where we met, then followed, a descending goat track along an escarpment off our right wing. At the point where the goat track diverged, we'd bank hard left, fly around a ridge, and only then would we expect to see Tarpini a short distance ahead. Descending with the goat track put us at the right height; turning at the goat track marker put us on the runway centreline. No radios, no electronic guidance, no air traffic control clearances. The challenge didn't end when we touched down – the runway dipped down initially then climbed at a 15 per cent gradient up to the far end of the runway. So after touchdown we had to put on a lot of power to drive up the steep slope to the end of the runway, quickly do a 90-degree turn to stop sideways, then shut down. Magic!

The take-off at Tarpini was more dramatic – a 600-metre dash downhill initially, then uphill for the last part of the runway, then over a cliff, at which point we became airborne as the ground disappeared below. A quick turn down-valley and we're looking down thousands of feet to the valley floor. That's if everything went perfectly.

The Caribou's performance at take-off was a remarkable learning curve, something that I still appreciate today. For us, the biggest challenge was the 'dead zone' – a portion of the runway from where (if an engine fails on take-off) there's not enough runway remaining to continue to accelerate on one engine and take off, and not enough to brake and stop before the end of the runway. How did we handle it? The captain's take-off brief included: 'If we have an engine failure between tree number 1 [pointing to it] and tree number 2 [pointing to it], then we can't stop on the remaining runway and we can't continue a take-off on one engine. So in this case I'll steer the aircraft into that ditch or drive it between those two trees to rip the wings off and stop us.' The dangers of flying Caribous in New Guinea were very real and in the time they operated there, there were two crashes, one fatal.

As well as our operations in New Guinea, we supported the Special Air Service (SAS), who were based at Swanbourne Barracks in Western Australia. Our assignment was to take them out to Corrigin in the Western Australian interior and then support them in their low-altitude parachute runs. The lowest height a parachutist can open their chute is about 500 feet, which is too high for a stealth approach (under radar and enemy fire) to a drop zone. So we'd practise flying over the treetops at 100 feet, finishing with a perfectly timed 2-G pull-up, and followed by an almost zero-G 'bunt-over'. The loadmaster then helped the soldiers get out through the rear cargo door as fast as possible. The pull-up had to be managed precisely as the heavily laden soldiers, who were standing ready for their jump, couldn't handle more than 2-Gs of acceleration. Too much G during the pull-up and they'd collapse to the floor. The bunt-over at the top of the ascent also had to be flown carefully because the soldiers would become almost weightless. If we pushed our control column forward too aggressively, then there would be too little G in the bunt and they'd float weightlessly into a position that would be impossible to recover from when the G came back on – nasty!

I learned some valuable lessons in terms of leadership and responsibility during my operations with the SAS. The flying was exhilarating, and a good example of how the services (Army and Air Force) have to coordinate and work very closely with one another. When you start your flying career you are focused only on the aeroplane – keeping it in the air, getting the take-offs and landings right, and navigating correctly. But once you transition to an operational squadron your focus broadens. It is assumed you can fly your aircraft well – indeed you are expected to fly it to its limits – and you're expected to bring the aircraft back in one piece, but the aircraft is now just a tool, a means to an end. In the military it's all about the mission – you have to deliver. You're responsible for the aircraft, the passengers and the task. The SAS put their ultimate trust in you and expected you to fly the right path and profile to support their low-altitude jumps. It's your job to dovetail their requirements with the aircraft's capabilities to keep the operation safe.

I was 22 years old, and that was young to be taking charge of the lives of 30 SAS jumpers and their instructors in a tactical environment. I loved it! Perhaps the RAAF psychologists knew more about me then than I knew about myself.

We had some great times relaxing as well. One afternoon when we'd been in the bush with the SAS for almost two weeks, the other guys in my crew wanted to go further east for the weekend, to a gymkhana on a property a few hundred miles away in the desert south of Kalgoorlie. I wanted the detachment to relax at this rodeo near Kalgoorlie – where there'd be plenty of entertainment and fun – so I suggested to the SAS commander, 'I'd love to give the guys a break, but how can we achieve this?'

He smiled and replied, 'I think we need to do some more practice jumps in the desert, it's the perfect training terrain.'

So we flew to the property, spent Saturday doing parachute drops, then let the boys enjoy the gymkhana for the rest of the weekend.

The RAAF crews contained a lot of characters. Light-hearted times were important in order to balance the confronting reality of life in both the army and the air force. We were often reminded how small the gap between life and death was. Dave 'Cass' Cassebohm deserves an honourable mention as an RAAF legend for his remarkable escape from an aircraft crash. On 19 March 1968, Cass was in a Sabre fighter armed with rockets taking off from Butterworth airport in Malaysia. He was passing the end of the runway at 50 feet when the engine failed. He flew under 30,000 volt power wires then ploughed into the paddy field in front and stopped in an irrigation ditch. The jet was engulfed by fire. All the evidence suggested that he should have died from impact forces and the post-crash fire.

As fate would have it, Cass had been in a special safety briefing immediately before his crash. The briefing discussed a new technique for minimising body overshoots during car and aircraft crashes. When a severe impact was imminent, the theory recommended the victims put their feet up high, and then bury their faces into their hands, and their hands against their knees. An hour later as Cass's fighter skidded off the runway, he jammed his feet hard against the rudder pedals and pushed his forearms against the instrument panel. He then braced for impact by burying his head into his arms. The plane slammed into the paddy field; Cass took one look up during the deceleration to see mud and grass flying overhead the canopy. The missiles disappeared down into the mud.

The aircraft was destroyed. The deceleration forces were extraordinary: the aircraft's oxygen cylinder tore free from its metal mounts, punctured the fuselage then ended up 30 metres in front of the wreck. Cass survived uninjured. He was able to extract himself through the small gap in the canopy only after taking his helmet off, and then escaped to safety.

Cass's Sabre crash was the first time the hands and feet technique was used, and proven successful. The professor who had given that briefing became an internationally recognised expert in crash survival. His theory and Cass's experience became the reference points for the crash survival techniques that are taught today. Every time you fly, think of Cass when you observe the 'brace' instructions as part of the cabin crew's pre-flight safety announcement and hope you don't have to use them.

Many people don't realise the extent to which aviation safety relies on experience being passed person-to-person in a crew room or over a beer. In an age where planes run on autopilot and flight computer systems, the interaction of peers and mentors is still one of the most important learning tools.

CHAPTER 5

Aide-de-Camp

After eighteen months flying Caribous and having the time of my life, I was promoted to flight lieutenant.

Nonetheless, I was starting to get frustrated with my career progression. The Caribou flying was great but I didn't want to continue flying it for too long – the technology was getting old and I was still not getting any closer to flying the aircraft of my dreams – the F-111. There was also a lot of bureaucracy for pilots in the RAAF – paperwork, reports, secondary duties – and I wanted to stretch myself more. I wanted more responsibility and more authority. I figured if I couldn't get this through a conventional flying posting I'd get it by jumping the queue and mixing with the crème de la crème of the bureaucracy. So I decided to be an aide-de-camp (ADC). Two positions were available at the time – the ADC to the chief of the Defence Force or the ADC to the governor-general. The decision was easy.

In the middle of 1981 I made an appointment with Ian Mallett, my postings officer at Canberra. I had a long chat with Ian, telling him I wanted a greater challenge. I still wanted to fly the F-111, but if this was not possible then I wanted to be an ADC.

Ian said: 'You mean ADC to the chief of the Defence Force?' And I said, 'No, ADC to the governor-general. It's the governor-general or nothing.'

Ian was surprised. Few if any pilots ever show an interest in being an ADC. They mostly regard the position as a useless ground job, full of ceremony. Ian was also slightly reluctant about my request. He was supposed to talk to me about options and 'broadening horizons' – all that excellent career stuff – but his job, to a large extent, was really to ensure that people who'd been put through the multimillion-dollar RAAF Academy and pilot training were kept busy in the profession for which they'd been equipped, which, for me, was flying the SAS around in a Caribou.

Nonetheless, the RAAF relented and I was dispatched to Government House in Canberra as one of three candidates. The other two were close friends and we worked out very quickly, while waiting in the anteroom, that I was the only one who really wanted the job (one friend pulled out when he discovered the job was so busy you had to remain single for the duration). After a day of interviews with the governor-general, Sir Zelman Cowen, and the other official staff, I was offered the position of being the Air Force ADC to the governor-general.

I reported to Government House in February 1982 armed with a new wardrobe – uniforms with aiguillettes, business suits, white mess dress, black tie and tails – ready and eager to take my career in an entirely new direction. Each of the armed services provided an ADC, so the Army and Navy ADCs and I planned the schedules of the governor-general and accompanied him on all engagements. We had 'high-tech' equipment in 1982: a telephone pager and a first-generation fax machine.

I served during the terms of Sir Zelman Cowen and Sir Ninian Stephen, two remarkable yet very different people who had reached the pinnacle of their careers. It was an honour to work with two such distinguished governors-general.

The three ADCs lived with the governor-general's family at Government House overlooking the serene Lake Burley-Griffin in Canberra. The ADCs had breakfast by ourselves but attended nearly all lunches and dinners with Their Excellencies. At the age of 25, it was the opportunity of a lifetime to be involved in the extraordinary conversations that took place over lunch and dinner. After a private game of tennis with Sir Zelman one Sunday, I remember asking him how he had reached such a prominent position. I was reassured by his response. 'It was all hard work and dedication,' Sir Zelman said. 'I never aimed for greatness and I certainly never thought Anna and I would end up living here at Yarralumla.' Sir Ninian gave a very similar reply. Although they probably never realised it, I considered Sirs Zelman and Ninian mentors.

The ADC's job had its perks. We wanted for nothing. We had cooks, footmen, housemaids and secretaries to assist us. We could order anything to eat or drink, which is how I ended up one night enjoying lasagne and thinking, 'What a rather excellent wine.' I'd asked for a glass of red and they brought up a bottle of Grange Hermitage.

It was a busy and strange life with a frantic schedule, and the three ADCs were required to cope with the unrelenting workload. We often worked sixteen-hour days, were on call 24 hours a day and only averaged one day off each month. The daily dress for the duty ADC was military 'number ones', and we had to be immaculate, from trim haircuts right down to our spit-polished shoes. Sir Zelman averaged two public events per day in any one of Australia's six states and two territories; so many events that his nickname was 'Can-O-Mat', after an innovative kitchen device that would 'open anything'. The ADCs organised all the functions, liaising with the organisers, special service security and transport. We ensured the hosts understood and complied with vice-regal protocols. We produced an 'order' for every event comprising timings to the nearest minute, greeting lines, seating plans and summaries of all attending guests. It was our job to check the list of attendees for sensitive people and groups, and to ensure the required protocol was being attended to and the office of the governor-general was protected.

I met the most extraordinary people during my time as an ADC: prime ministers, politicians, diplomats and business leaders. The Queen, Prince Philip, Prince Charles and Princess Diana all toured during my shift.

There were many memorable functions. I remember a Yugoslavian function where we discovered that 1500 Serbs and Croatians would be meeting together under one roof. Over the previous two years the Serbs and Croats had been conducting private wars in Melbourne, bombing offices in South Yarra and shooting each other on motorbikes. We were very concerned at the possibility of violence at the event, but the organisers promised that all guests would be well behaved for Sir Ninian. Indeed, both sides had agreed that no knives would be brought to the event! Security was set to an all-time high and over 100 plain-clothed federal policemen were in attendance, just in case.

Working with the governor-general gave me insights into politics and personalities. For instance, one of my specified jobs was to organise the governor-general's travel, which meant scheduling the Air Force VIP jets. This was an interesting task because in Commonwealth protocol the governor-general has first dibs on the VIP jets over the prime minister. It wasn't that there was only one plane – there were two – but, of course, the first choice for any person of importance was the larger BAC 1-11, rather than the smaller executive jet-sized Mystere. On the BAC 1-11 (about the size of a Boeing 737), the VIP could travel with a large retinue and stretch out with a lot of space. The Mystere was cramped and you had to duck to enter it.

This discrepancy in VIP jets was made more interesting by the fact that Malcolm Fraser, the prime minister of the day, was a very tall man who hated the Mystere because he had to move around it like Quasimodo. Fraser was not a tolerant man and made it very clear through his staff's dealings with Government House that life would be much better for everyone if Sir Zelman simply accepted the Mystere – which Sir Zelman rarely did, because Sir Zelman also liked the BAC 1-11.

Sir Zelman was a much-loved public figure. He had become Australia's nineteenth governor-general after the famous 1975 dismissal by the previous governor-general, Sir John Kerr, of the serving prime minister, Gough Whitlam. A great proportion of Australians disagreed with Kerr's actions. The reputation of the governor-general, and even the need for a monarch, was questioned. When Sir Zelman became governor-general, he was acutely aware of the tenuous state of the vice-regal office he had just inherited. He knew he had a tough battle in front of him but he worked tirelessly, healing the wounds of the past and earning the Australian people's respect and loyalty.

Sir Ninian Stephen was also a remarkable governor-general. At work or around the house, Sir Ninian and Lady Stephen were the most capable, compassionate, caring, friendly and relaxed couple you would ever want to meet. They had the rare ability to engage with a king or a cleaner and make them both feel equally important and at ease.

The 3rd of February 1983 was a fascinating day at Government House. Sir Ninian Stephen was home at Yarralumla, Bill Hayden was the leader of the opposition Labor Party, and Malcolm Fraser was prime minister. The press had speculated that Fraser was going to call an early election to capitalise on Hayden and the Labor Party's weakness at the polls.

On this morning, Malcolm Fraser had apparently got wind of a meeting in Queensland between Hayden and Labor shadow minister Bob Hawke, and that a press conference was to be held by them later that morning. Fraser's intelligence was correct: Hayden would announce he would relinquish his leadership of the Labor Party and pass it on to Hawke. Fraser had other plans. If he could dissolve both houses of parliament before Hawke took over the opposition leadership, the opposition leadership would effectively be frozen with Hayden at the helm. Fraser's head of the Department of the Prime Minister and Cabinet rang the official secretary to the governor-general at 9.00 am to enquire about the governor-general's engagements that day. He was told Sir Ninian would be spending most of the day at his desk and that his only official engagement was a farewell meeting at 12.45 pm with the departing Polish ambassador and his wife, who would stay for lunch.

The first that we in the ADC office knew about any of this was when two bells went off in The House at about 12.30 pm. One bell going off meant you had to go to the official portico entrance because there was a visitor who had to be greeted. When three bells went off, the governor-general was arriving at the private entrance and had to be greeted. When two bells sounded, it signalled the prime minister had passed the gate-house and was on his way to the private entrance – a courtesy extended to the prime minister.

Two bells! The other two aides and I looked at one another in the office. I was the duty ADC, so I was in my uniform and I had to greet the prime minister. We hurriedly looked through the daily schedule we produced for the governor-general and the 70 Government House staff, but could see nothing special. The secretary had also heard the bells and, in disbelief, thumbed through his diary and schedule. There were no entries for a meeting between the prime minister and the governor-general, and unannounced meetings between these two constitutional pivots of the Australian system have never occurred in living memory.

As we were looking at each other, wondering who among us had missed the prime minister's appointment, we saw the prime ministerial white car flashing past outside our window, screaming down the narrow drive towards the private entrance.

Any chance of my gracefully receiving the prime minister at the side door vanished as the white car disappeared out of view, now very close to the private entrance. I grabbed my jacket and ran for the private entrance, wondering how I was going to handle this. No one was expecting the prime minister and there was no time for me to warn the governor-general, so I turned back and asked the other ADCs to warn the staff. Sir Ninian was in his office, reading and relaxing with a cup of tea. He wasn't ready for a meeting with the prime minister, so it was my job to protect the governor-general and ensure the prime minister adhered to protocol.

The race was on. By the time I got near, Fraser had beaten me to the private entrance. He hadn't even knocked and waited. As I rounded the corner into the private entrance foyer, his towering form had charged though the patio door and he had advanced inside Government House. I moved to greet him but he walked around me, not even bothering to acknowledge me, and charged straight for the governor-general's study.

I ran around Fraser, stood in front of him and blocked his entrance to Sir Ninian's study. I'm almost the same height as Fraser and I probably looked young and fit, but it didn't faze him. He looked me in the eye and simply said, 'I'm here to see the governor-general.'

I told him I'd announce him to Sir Ninian. He eye-balled me. I asked him to take a seat in the morning room. He sized me up and down slowly, and then turned reluctantly for the morning room. It was most unpleasant.

I ducked into Sir Ninian's study. He was reclined in his chair reading with a pipe in his mouth and his feet up, shoes off, on his immaculate leather-covered desk. I told him the prime minister was here and demanding to see him.

Sir Ninian looked confused. 'What does he want?'

'I don't know,' I said. 'But he's awfully determined and in a hurry.'

Sir Ninian thought about this and then said, 'Okay – give me 30 seconds and then show him in.'

When I showed Malcolm Fraser into Sir Ninian's study, he almost ran into the office.

After meeting with Fraser, Sir Ninian and Lady Stephen hosted a lunch to farewell the departing Polish ambassador and his wife. I was attending the lunch and it was an awkward time. We could all see Sir Ninian's mind was distracted and he apologised for only staying at the lunch for 45 minutes before retiring to his study. He did at least say that 'something unusual' had arisen and that we'd all know about it from the press within a few hours. We subsequently learned that the prime minister had handed the governor-general a 39-page document.

The gossip around Yarralumla was that Fraser had turned up at Government House that morning to demand an immediate double dissolution. Indeed Fraser had supposedly organised a press conference for 1.00 pm Canberra time to announce the double dissolution, expecting it to lead the news of Hawke's ascendency. But Sir Ninian had told Fraser that he couldn't dissolve both houses of parliament without first studying the 39 pages that Fraser had just delivered. Sir Ninian promised to call Fraser at 3.30 that afternoon.

Fraser's plan had come unstuck. He'd left Yarralumla empty-handed and furious. The 1.00 pm press conference (noon Queensland time) would be cancelled. Not only had he not got his way, Fraser's dash to Government House had also been detected by the media and rumours were now rife of an imminent double dissolution and an early election.

Sir Ninian was back in his office by about 2.00 pm. True to his word, he called Fraser at 3.30 pm and asked for additional information to be provided. A letter containing that information was delivered to Sir Ninian at 4.45 pm. After reading this additional information Sir Ninian advised Fraser there were sufficient reasons to dissolve both houses of parliament. At 5.00 pm, Fraser announced at a press conference that both the House of Representatives and the Senate would be dissolved by the governor-general, and the government would be put into caretaker mode.

Fraser's timing was unfortunate. Having found out the governor-general's schedule was free for the entire morning, had he taken this opportunity to visit him earlier, perhaps the governor-general would have had sufficient time to read the 39-page document and grant the request for a double dissolution, all before Hayden's press conference, and Fraser would have achieved his ambition to go to an early election against Hayden.

But Hayden's press conference was delivered on time at about 1 pm Canberra time. Hawke was announced as the new leader of the Labor Party and Fraser was ensnared by his own trap. Fraser could have declined to give the governor-general any additional information, in which case the government would probably have continued through its normal term with an election much later. But such a reversal by Fraser would have probably exposed and weakened his reputation.

The double dissolution was actioned and an election ran in which Australians voted for Hawke in a decisive victory against Fraser. Fraser's mistake was to take too long to approach Government House that morning and expect the governor-general to immediately rubberstamp his request for a double dissolution. Sir Ninian's brilliance at managing a constitutional crisis was proven.

My experiences at Government House would serve to change my plans for my military career. When I joined the RAAF, my long-term aspiration was to ascend the ranks and end up at 'the top' as chief of the Air Force. But as my term as ADC progressed I began to question these plans. I had a privileged view of the lives, skills and personalities of Australia's political leaders, and I didn't like all I saw, and I wasn't alone.

Some of the politicians were at best appalling and many had scant knowledge of the industry or their responsibilities. I had an epiphany: if I remained in the military and became the chief of the Air Force I would have to serve and answer to incompetent politicians. I was not going to waste my career getting to the top of the RAAF only to end up answering to people I didn't respect. I saw no future for me in the RAAF – I had to find an alternate career.

After fifteen months of being ADC to two governors-general, I had two more years of payback owing to the RAAF until I was free to move on to newer challenges. In the Air Force the compensation for being an ADC is that you get your choice of posting. Here again was my chance to go to F-111s. This time it should work.

I had become close friends with Stuart McAllister, my old commanding officer for the Caribous at 38 Squadron in Richmond. He had watched my career progress and was now conveniently in charge of all RAAF officer postings. I could not have been more fortunate. I told Stu I wanted the F-111s again – I really wanted to fly the fastest and the best, and nothing in Australian aviation went faster or was more challenging than the F-111. Stuart said F-111s was possible but, acting as my mentor, he made a very good suggestion.

The problem with the F-111 was that it had never been used in operational conflict. The F-111 was Australia's most significant deterrent, but a deterrent like the F-111 is best protected if it is never actually deployed. Stuart explained if I went straight to F-111s I would finish that posting as a successful middle-ranked RAAF officer, but unfortunately an officer who has never experienced real operations at conflicts such as Vietnam or Korea. Stuart's suggestion was simple. I should take an operational posting overseas, then transfer to the F-111s. Such an opportunity existed.

The Iroquois helicopters were being deployed to Egypt as part of Australia's contribution to the Multinational Force and Observers (MFO). Here was an operational posting overseas where every pilot learns invaluable operational experiences. But I was worried.

'Stu, every pilot who transfers to helicopters gets stuck there,' I said. 'They never escape from the rotary world. I can't afford to be stuck on choppers for the rest of my career. I want F-111s!'

'Leave that to me,' said Stuart. 'I'll look after you.'

Here was a gamble and an opportunity. With Stuart McAllister's help, I'd be posted to Iroquois helicopters, get my operational command, then get posted to the Sinai to gain essential operational experience (a real leg-up in the Australian military), then finally be posted to F-111s. But there was the risk I'd be stuck in choppers for the rest of my career if Stu McAlister left the postings division or fell under a truck. All my friends thought I was crazy, but with risk comes reward and the opportunity was too extraordinary to pass up. So I went for it.

CHAPTER 6

The Road to Cairo

In the early 1980s, Australia contributed to the Multinational Force and Observers (MFO) in the Sinai Peninsula, an effort designed to keep the peace between Israel and Egypt.

I was posted to number 5 Squadron in Canberra to fly Iroquois. This would be my first experience in rotary-wing aircraft.

In a fixed-wing aircraft, such as a Caribou, the airframe is bolted firmly to the rigid wing set. When the pilot sets a flight path (we call it the 'attitude'), the inherent stability of the fixed-wing design keeps the attitude constant – you can even take your hands off the controls for a short time. Many flight control surfaces are used to change the attitude and control flight: the ailerons at the end of the wings provide a differential lift laterally, causing the aircraft to bank left or right; the slats and flaps along the forward and aft edge of the wings are used to alter the wing size and enable aircraft to take off and land on shorter runways; and the horizontal stabiliser and elevators provide a torque to rotate the aircraft into a nose high/low attitude.

Helicopters are different.

Helicopters are naturally unstable machines and they don't naturally want to fly. We look up and see helicopters looking smooth, elegant and controlled when they're flown by professionals, but this is an illusion. It all comes down to their complicated design. In a nutshell, helicopter pilots fly the rotor disc through the sky, expecting that the fuselage will follow after a short delay. You can never take your hands off the helicopter's controls – constant input is needed to maintain a steady attitude.

My helicopter conversion was eye-opening, a case of learning '101 ways to kill yourself without trying'. We trained for possibilities like engine and tail rotor failures. We couldn't train for the worst – a mast bump followed by a main rotor failure – because we would have died. The mast bump was particularly nasty, occurring when the machine's centre of gravity moves out of limits, or the pilot pushes too aggressively on the stick or pushes negative G. (Negative G force is the force you feel during a roller-coaster ride when your body hangs upside down, restrained only by the shoulder straps.) The results of a mast bump typically follow the same sequence: the main rotor blades fracture the hinge that connects them to the mast, the rotor disc wobbles, the left side slightly down, then a rotor blade penetrates the windscreen and slices the co-pilot in half at chest level. It was cheerfully related lessons such as this that made my 100 hours of basic instruction pass rather quickly.

Despite these potential failures, helicopter flying is great fun, and the best helicopter pilots are the ones trained to recognise the danger signs, and who are sensible enough to minimise the risks.

I remained at 5 Squadron for another six months to earn my operational command status before shipping out for the Sinai and the MFO.

*

I met a great girl while I was in Canberra. My friend Georgie Hyles had asked me to serve champagne at a fundraiser she was hosting for the premiere of the movie *Phar Lap*. At the end of the successful evening, the other 30 helpers and I decided to go to dinner at the Red Door restaurant just down the road.

'Can I please get a lift with someone?' I called out. My prized Datsun 260Z was being extensively repaired after I had hit two kangaroos on the main road leading out of town (luckily I missed the other three).

A beautiful girl with a beaming smile and waist-long hair replied, 'I'll take you.' It was such a long walk to Coral Ford's car that by the time we arrived at the restaurant the other 28 friends had been turned away.

'We can't take 28 people this late at night,' the waitress complained.

'Well, do you have a table for two?' I asked.

'Sure . . .'

And the rest is history!

*

Flying choppers taught me how to fly an aircraft at and beyond its limits – and not get too stressed. I had two memorable experiences.

My first loss-of-control experience occurred during a refuelling exercise. I was piloting one of two Iroquois flying in formation along Victoria's coastline, returning from a deployment, and was carrying extra fuel in long-range bladders inside the cabin. Our main fuel tank was getting low so I decided to land on the beach so we could transfer the fuel from the bladder into the main tanks. We were still quite heavy, but the engine was operating at about 35 psi, well below the maximum power limit of 50 psi. I made my approach into wind over an ocean estuary towards the beach. All was going well until we entered an unexpected strong downdraft that increased our descent rate. We were now descending so fast that we would hit the water short of the beach if I made no correction. I increased the power, but there was no dramatic improvement. We were still descending too fast. So I did the last thing I could do, other than over-stress the engine and gearbox and face a few days stranded on a coastal beach awaiting a maintenance rescue team. I increased the power to the limit – 50 psi – and held it exactly at that limit. We all braced and waited. The rate of descent slowed, but not enough. The Iroquois skids entered the salt water and then the aircraft belly settled into the water – only six inches down, but enough to lighten the weight and stop the descent. After what I thought was about ten seconds, the downdraft abated and the aircraft slowly recovered and pulled itself out of the water, enabling us to hover safely across to the beach.

We survived, but I was not happy. Back in Canberra, I went straight to the commanding officer and explained what had happened.

'What did I do wrong and how could I have handled it better?' I asked him.

'You did nothing wrong, Dick,' he said. 'Every helicopter pilot loses control of their helicopter sooner or later. It was just your turn that day. Don't worry about it.'

My second 'limited power' experience occurred during an army exercise in the tropics of northern Queensland. To take off, we had to ascend vertically inside a narrow circular clearing ringed by 100 foot–high trees before we could transition forward. We had risen about 75 feet up when we noticed our rate of climb decreasing and the power creeping up to 50 psi – our limit. We had no excess engine power and we were contained within the circle of trees.

I had to act quickly. We could not risk descending back down to the ground because we were close to the trees and the rotors might generate a dangerous vortex that would exacerbate the situation and might even have us 'settling with power' (an alternative expression for crash). There was no time to waste – I pushed the right pedal forward. This reduced the power to the tail rotor, so the tail rotor now had insufficient thrust to keep the helicopter pointing straight ahead, with the effect that the engine torque started rotating us clockwise. This was not a pleasant situation. However, reducing the power absorbed by the tail rotor enabled more power to be directed to the main rotor, to lift us up and away from the trees. We started spinning right, but we also started to climb. We corkscrewed our way up and out of the trees and to safety. It was a very uncomfortable experience; much like sitting in a car that is being spun about its tow bar.

I look back on these experiences now with two thoughts. First, I am not pleased that the events occurred at all. I'd always prefer never to face those types of situations, but pilots don't have the luxury not to address the dangers that confront them. If you want to be the best pilot, you have to be prepared for the unexpected. Secondly, I am grateful the RAAF taught us how to operate our aircraft to, and sometimes beyond, the limits to extract ourselves from such incidents, and to keep our cool in the process.

Twelve months after my conversion to helicopters I was on my way to the Sinai and the MFO. I was based at the MFO's North Base at El Gorah, Egypt, about 20 kilometres from the Israeli border and 40 kilometres from the Mediterranean Sea. Twelve contingents contributed to the MFO's massive patrol operations in the Sinai, from Norway, Fiji, the United States, France, Colombia, Australia and New Zealand. The French contingent provided twin-engine Transall fixed-wing aircraft.

The Australian and New Zealand contingents provided armour-plated Iroquois helicopters to fly the MFO in their orange coveralls around the Sinai Desert, allowing them to check the provisions of the peace accords between Israel and Egypt were carried out.

The Sinai is a 60,000 square–kilometre minefield. Since the First World War, different occupying forces had laid about 21 million anti-tank and anti-personnel mines in minefields across the desert. If the minefields were mapped, the maps had been lost. The safety fences that delineated the minefields were stolen by the Bedouins, who then sold them for scrap metal. Mosaic grids containing hundreds of mines get exposed, then slowly buried, then exposed again with the vicissitudes of the drifting sand dunes blown by desert winds and sandstorms.

I knew that if I put an Iroquois down on an anti-tank mine we would all be dead. If people jumped from the helicopter onto an anti-personnel mine, the last thing they would hear would be the 'click' as the small arming rod is pushed down to arm the mine. When pressure on the rod is released – boom – they would be dead.

The mines we could see were fine; it was the buried ones, even the half-rusted anti-tank mines, that were the problem. Six months before I arrived at El Gorah, the troops found an anti-personnel mine just 1 foot to the side of the entrance path to our briefing room. So we kept to the roads and trodden paths, and never ventured into uncleared areas.

The government was trying to clear the Sinai of mines. The mines-clearance teams used huge, armoured bulldozers with revolving drums with chains attached. As the drums spun in front of the bulldozer, the chains thrashed the ground and triggered the mines.

The local Bedouin handled the threat differently: they either knew where the local fields were or, when they traversed unknown terrain, the women were dispatched out front, to be followed by the camels and then the men. That puts a different spin on 'women and children first'!

Flying in the Sinai was exciting. We flew mostly at low level so we didn't advertise our position. The images are still clear in my mind: the Valley of Moses, across sandy ridges dotted with mines, and along the Mediterranean coast, the Suez Canal and the Red Sea, the carcasses of bombed, missiled and burnt-out wrecks and tanks still littering the landscape. The Israelis tethered a blimp at 25,000 feet that supported very capable look-down radar, watching every inch of the Israeli landscape to ground level. We would be intercepted by Israeli F-4 Phantom jets launched from underground runways if we strayed more than a few feet into Israeli territory.

During the sandstorm season, visibility sometimes reduced to 30 metres, posing a massive risk to operations. We couldn't fly above or around the sand, so we flew through it. The sand-blasted turbine blades degraded so fast that the operational engine life would be reduced by 70 per cent. Navigating was very challenging in 30 metres' visibility. You couldn't distinguish the road from the sandy desert; it was easy to get lost. The safest option was to find a truck going your way and then lock yourself 50 feet above and behind it. The trucks got used to this and knew we were navigating by counting the trees until the next turn.

I had a few scares during my stay. The Israelis accidentally bombed a Fijian lookout post (with a practice round), creating a flurry of activity for a day. On another occasion I was forced to make a precautionary landing in the desert one hour from El Gorah after an engine gave the warning signs it was about to fail. Five of us were stuck in this vast, empty desert, sitting in a dead Huey awaiting a rescue flight from El Gorah. It was dry and hot when, out of the mirage on the horizon, appeared a solitary Bedouin mounted on his camel, slowly tracking towards us. It took the Arab ten minutes to reach us, whereby he dismounted to set up a campfire and make us a cup of coffee. Bedouin coffee, for the uninitiated, is a black, tart amalgam served in a mug half filled with sugar syrup. Five Australians sat with our local host around the fire sipping coffee together. It was a priceless experience.

The final scare occurred during my last flight at El Gorah. Often the most dangerous flight a military pilot makes is their last flight for the posting: rules get broken, luck is stretched. I warned the other pilot, before the flight, that I wasn't going to do any fly-pasts or scare anyone. I just wanted this to be a safe, uneventful flight before I returned to Australia to fly F-111s. Luck was against me. Ten minutes after take-off the hydraulics that powered the flight controls failed. That meant the controls became very heavy, much like a car without power steering. It wasn't a life-threatening situation but I had to keep a cool head and not panic. We made a gentle and steady approach using slow and deliberate control inputs, and I survived my Sinai posting with an unblemished record.

A few other incidents of note occurred. The Fijians handled base security. While they were friendly to us, they were brutal to their own people. Whenever Fijian soldiers got out of line, they'd be taken out behind the buildings and beaten senseless. While I was there I became friends with Lieutenant Colonel Sitiveni (Steve) Rabuka, the commanding officer of the Fijians. He was a tall, powerful, proud and friendly man, and when he discovered I was a former ADC to the governor-general he gave me a calendar featuring him shaking hands with Sir Ninian Stephen. A few months later, Steve's father suddenly died at home in Fiji. Steve tried to leave to attend the funeral but the Fijian military command wouldn't release him. Steve went anyway. Relations between him and the military never recovered and, a short time later, I heard there was a bloodless coup in Suva. Sitiveni Rabuka would declare Fiji a Republic and sever ties with the British Monarchy.

*

The desert does strange things to people. For me, it brought out my romantic side. We had three weeks' leave over the duration of the deployment and I decided to plan my time off constructively by courting Coral. After we'd met in Canberra, where she was working for the directors of the construction company building the new Parliament House, Coral accepted an opportunity to work as a cost controller in the oil industry in Norway.

I called her before my leave and asked if she'd like to come down and spend a couple of weeks over Christmas in the Sinai Peninsula. She thought about it for a few seconds, then agreed.

Coral and I were both a bit nervous about our desert reunion. From our brief time together in Canberra we knew our relationship was special but for various reasons we hadn't spent a lot of time together before she left Australia for Norway. So as I drove to Tel Aviv Airport to collect Coral, I was concerned that after a year away, I might not recognise her. Would she still look the same? Did she still have beautiful waist-long hair and a beaming smile? Funnily enough Coral later told me that she had experienced similar reservations.

I remember the joy of instantly recognising Coral as she drifted out of the airport terminal. We locked eyes and the thirteen months of separation instantly vaporised. I had booked a great room in the best hotel in Jerusalem for our arrival early on Christmas Eve. After checking in at the hotel, I was shocked, when upon opening the door to our room, to discover two small single beds widely separated in front of us, not the king-size bed I had specifically requested. Of course I could not admit to Coral that the two single beds were a mistake but to my great surprise and delight Coral said: 'Quick! Let's push the beds together!'

We had two wonderfully romantic days celebrating Christmas in Jerusalem.

Life insurance was automatically provided to everyone at El Gorah, so when Coral arrived at the base she was able to participate in MFO activities. Once we had Coral briefed and in a flying suit, she joined us in the crew room and was welcome to accompany us on our operations. She sat in the jump seats flying with the French and the Aussies and Kiwis. Her best trip in the Transall was a low-level flight at 100 feet up along the Valley of Moses, the valley where legend has it that Moses tapped his stick against a rock and caused water to flow.

Having an intrepid spirit of adventure, Coral volunteered to be the target for winching practice. Winching activities are actually quite dangerous. In the case of an engine failure during the winch, there's no way to ensure the winchee is not killed by the descending fuselage or the rotating rotor blades. We would never be able to take these risks in Australia, but the MFO was a civilian exercise with insurance, so we had some fun. I flew Coral deep into the desert on a navigation exercise, low-flying to a random destination among the sand dunes. From a 120-foot hover, Coral was winched out and down onto the sand. We flew away, then low-level navigated our way back to her and winched her into the cabin. Coral was nervous but excited when she got back in the chopper. Ten minutes standing alone on the sand amid 21 million landmines was sufficient time to reflect on all the stories she had heard in the crew room.

For the last part of Coral's visit we took off for a week cruising up the Nile. I exceeded the limit of my American Express card trying to give her the best time possible on my meagre pay. I spent a year paying off that holiday, but it was the best investment I ever made.

Our fate would be decided at the conclusion of the MFO posting, when I took a few weeks' leave to visit Coral in

Norway before returning to Australia. Our relationship was still basking in the glow of the Sinai–Egypt holiday, but it was Coral's friend Harry Konterud who sealed our fate. When he heard of my imminent arrival at Oslo, Harry organised accommodation for Coral and me for a week, then drove us to a small wooden log cabin with a wood fire high in the Norwegian mountains. It was a week we will always be grateful to Harry for organising and one we'll never forget. I had fallen in love with Coral and we married about eighteen months later. Marrying her was the best decision I ever made.

*

My six-month posting to the MFO was coming to a close and I was returning to Australia. So I did what I had always wanted to do but had so far failed to achieve. I applied for F-111s again. And finally I received the posting I'd been waiting for.

CHAPTER 7

Twenty Minutes of Fame

My interest in F-111s had not waned over the seven years since my three-week visit to 6 Squadron in 1978, although I knew I needed a few bridging courses to transition from slow rotary aircraft to fast jets. I completed a jet familiarisation course at East Sale, Victoria, and then moved to Williamtown, north of Sydney, where I completed the introductory fighter course, learning basic fighter combat manoeuvres and the techniques fighter pilots would use to shoot my F-111 down.

I spent four months in Macchi jets learning the basics of fighter manoeuvres, combat flying, air-to-ground gunnery and bombing. After passing this course a pilot was deemed ready for F-111s.

Coral returned from Norway at about this time, and I remember this period as one of the happiest times I had in the RAAF. Each day after work, Coral would collect me from the base in the Datsun 260Z, and on the way home we would stop to have a jog and body surf along the 50 kilometre–long, 1 kilometre–wide Stockton Beach. We lived in an apartment on the shores of Nelson Bay; I can still remember having breakfast watching pods of dolphins swimming by.

I couldn't start an F-111 course until the previous F-111 conversions course had been completed, so I remained at 76 Squadron, Williamtown, in a holding pattern flying Fleet Support operations until 6 Squadron could receive me. During Fleet Support operations we flew formation air attacks against the Royal Australian Navy's ships off Nowra, practised our air combat manoeuvre (dogfighting) skills and joined in a few joint-service exercises.

Even though I was pursuing my dream of flying F-111s, I was becoming restless. I was growing tired of the ego-driven, macho and aggressive briefings/debriefings that epitomised jet-jock life. Missions were won or lost in the post-flight debrief with shouting matches about 'who "foxed" who' and who was out of place by a few metres. I didn't like this environment. Fighter pilots need super egos to match their fearlessness and aggression to take on high-risk missions, but my years flying transport operations had conditioned me to the pleasures of working in teams with other pilots and passengers. I didn't enjoy flying alone with no one to talk to, and I didn't want to finish my flying career in one- or two-pilot aircraft.

As I got closer to the F-111 posting, I became worried that perhaps I was getting too old for this game; that I was not the fighter pilot type. I was starting to doubt I would last long at Amberley AFB. Although I wanted to accomplish my dream of flying F-111s, I was also thinking about leaving.

Back in 1974 I had canvassed many aviation career options and I had applied to be a pilot for Qantas. Dad had also arranged me an interview with Peter Gibbs, the Chief Pilot of Ansett–ANA. At that time 30 per cent of Australian pilots were unemployed, so Peter recommended I spend 10 years in the Air Force and return to civil aviation when the market had recovered and was recruiting again.

Peter Gibbs was an ex-ANA pilot, Dad's friend and a rascal. One time his DC3 was cruising at 5000 feet when the hostess 'Bubbles' visited the flight deck to take drink orders. She noticed the window just beside each pilot. 'What would happen if you opened those windows in flight?' she asked. 'We would both be immediately sucked out through the window,' Peter replied tersely, angry that Bubbles had forgotten such basic safety information. Then when Bubbles went off to prepare the drinks, Peter opened his side window, engaged the auto-pilot and he and the first officer then unstrapped and moved back into the coat locker and closed the curtain. A minute later, Bubbles opened the door to the flight deck. The sound of the air roaring past the open window was only surpassed by her horror as she realised both pilots were missing and no one was flying the aircraft. Poor Bubbles dropped the tray of drinks and fainted.

I began corresponding with Qantas in 1984 while I was posted in the Sinai. Like most pilots, I was canvassing my options to see what the big airlines would pay me to switch. Qantas had told me they would look at me when I was back flying fixed wings – rotary hours didn't count. That was one of the reasons I'd happily put my hand up to fly any sortie against the Navy out of Nowra – to get my fixed-wing hours up again.

Before I could get any employment commitments from Qantas, I was given one week's notice to move to Amberley, Queensland, to start my F-111 conversion course. Stu McAlister's mentoring and influence had finally paid off and the RAAF was about to spend at least 4 million dollars converting me to the F-111 (each F-111 flying hour cost more than $20,000 in 1984). I decided to honour Stuart's commitment to me by completing at least one tour on F-111s.

Coral and I were now very much ensconced with each other. We moved to Brisbane and signed a lease on an apartment for one year. Coral secured a job on day one, working with the director of the largest jeweller in Queensland.

I was finally in Amberley at 6 Squadron. The first briefing, the Welcome Briefing, was at 8.00 am on Wednesday morning. Just twenty minutes into the one-hour brief I was called through to the commanding officer's (CO) office. He sat me down and said in a clear, deliberate voice: 'Dick, you're off the course.'

I was stunned. The CO told me they'd just lost two instructors to Qantas and so there were insufficient instructors to train everyone on the course. Since I was 28 years old, they were going to use the available instructors to train the younger guys.

After eleven years in the waiting, my F-111 posting lasted just 20 minutes – the shortest posting in RAAF history. My navigator resigned on the spot. To make it worse, I had just told Qantas I would be at F-111s for three years, and I also had another six months left to serve in the Air Force. Not to mention the fact that Coral had shifted north to be with me. Everything was up in the air.

I held my tongue and waited for offers. The RAAF postings division was shocked and offered me any posting to keep me happy. I told them I wanted VIP command on the B707 VIP jets. They said no because I didn't have enough fixed-wing hours. So I replied, 'Then give me Macchi jet instructor at Pearce, Western Australia.'

Having missed out on the F-111s, I knew I had still successfully negotiated a privileged career: Academy, Caribous, Government House, Iroquois helicopters and now Macchis. I was a jack of all trades, but I had learned a lot and was wiser for the broad experience. Very few other officers were as fortunate as I was.

So I was back at Central Flying School (CFS) in East Sale again, but this time for a four-month-long jet instructor's course. The CFS staff was sympathetic to my plight so made it easy for me to apply for jobs in the airlines. I approached Qantas, TAA, Ansett and Cathay-Pacific. I also digested *Handling the Big Jets* by D.P. Davies – the 'bible' for large jet pilots and the text you're expected to know backwards when the airlines interview you.

Cathay told me I had too many rotary hours and to come back in a year. Qantas asked me what I loved about the RAAF and I said the training. They asked me what I hated, and I said the alcohol culture where it was considered macho to drink heavily in the evening and go flying first thing in the morning. (I lost a friend in a Mirage accident that occurred the day after an intoxicating Dining-In night. I think the accident was preventable.)

Another incident involving booze that affected me deeply occurred in 1975, when I was in the first year of the Academy, I was taken for a tour of the RAAF base at Fairbairn in Canberra, and was having a drink at the officers' mess bar with a flight lieutenant I had met that day. A steward approached this officer to inform him his wife was waiting in the car park and was enquiring when he would be leaving the bar; she'd been there since 6.00 pm and it was now past seven. This senior officer waved the steward away, saying, 'Tell my wife I'll leave here when it suits me – when I've finished drinking with my mates.'

The Army had an unofficial motto: 'If we wanted a soldier to have a wife, then we would have issued him with one!' I didn't think the RAAF environment was any more enlightened. I never wanted to be like that officer, so from that day forward I vowed never to marry while I was in the RAAF.

Just one month before I graduated from the instructor course, Qantas offered me a job and I accepted. My marks were pretty good, so the commanding officer of CFS made me an extraordinary offer; he wanted me to complete the last month, graduate as an RAAF instructor, then join the CFS staff and teach the next jet instructor's course for my last two months.

It was a great honour to be recognised this way, but the RAAF tradition at that time was to punish pilots for resigning. The RAAF offered me a job in Canberra, answering phones, but the CO managed to negotiate a better deal. I'd stay at CFS and lecture in aerodynamics, and travel to the various Australian military bases looking for a suitable vintage aircraft that could be mounted at the East Sale gatehouse. I searched bases for Spitfires, DC3s, Meteors and Sabres, and ended up finding the '05' Winjeel that's still there today guarding the gate.

After eleven years, ten locations, thousands of stories and numerous lifelong friends, my beloved RAAF career was over. Sadly, many of my friends didn't make it. Chris Wylie, the dux of my year at the Academy, was killed in a Mirage mid-air crash; my friend Paul Carter died stalling – spinning in his Winjeel on base turn at Williamtown, just after I returned from the Sinai. Craig Mackelmann died in a Mirage just off the coast at Williamtown. Russell Page, my flatmate in Newcastle, died in a Macchi jet when pulling G – the wing snapped off and hit him in the head. Ross Fox, Rick Jeffreys – we lost four people from our seven-person Nelson Bay carpool. Coral knew many of them and was affected too. It was time for a change. I was happy to not only be starting a new career with Qantas, but to be going to a place where my friends and colleagues were definitely not going to die.

And one week after resigning from the RAAF, I proposed to Coral.

Wrapping up, my father says I was of more benefit to the RAAF after I resigned than while I was enlisted and I'd have to agree. I helped resolve two events that exposed shortcomings in the military. The first was that I wrote articles for *The Australian* newspaper addressing the disparity between military and civil salaries and that the high military wastage rate was not in Australia's interests. The damning numbers I published were never disputed, because they were true. The RAAF pilot salaries were increased dramatically a few months later. The second deficiency was researched and presented by my friend John Wasiliev in his financial magazine *The Smart Investor*. John's article exposed the illegality of the dreadful military pension scheme that existed at that time. A government senate enquiry was held and the pension was improved. I was the first in my Academy year to leave the RAAF and I did it with excitement, exactly five months over the six years of service I owed the RAAF.

CHAPTER 8

Steam Power

Coral and I moved into a one-bedroom apartment in Glenmore Road, Paddington, in Sydney's inner city. Coral got a job managing Joint Ventures for the Australian Petroleum Management Fund. Life was pretty simple then. I remember one night lying with Coral on the floor (we had no lounge furniture) watching flies land on the ceiling; how did they do it? Was it a loop or a barrel roll before touchdown?

Qantas pay scales were very low for entry-level pilots. I started on a second officer's salary of $3657 per 56 days (with $266 overseas pay), and I trained at Mascot on Boeing 747 Classic aircraft. This was 1986, when Qantas was still solely international and the only airline in the world to fly Jumbos exclusively. Murray Warfield, a fellow ex-RAAF pilot who also joined my course, had three young children at the time and he qualified for social security payments to supplement his meagre income.

There were four pilots on my 747 conversion course, but two of them left just before we started to join Cathay for a lot more money. Cathay called me about a year after that and offered me a job flying out of Hong Kong. I said, 'Double my salary and we'll talk.' I'm glad they didn't get back to me; I love Australia and I didn't want to be tempted to move countries simply for the money. Qantas replaced the two Cathay-bound pilots and we moved on. We trained in simulators, learning the aircraft and all the possible failures that could befall them, which meant going over and over the standard operating procedures (SOPs) and checklists.

The early generation Jumbos produced up until the late 1980s were given the affable title 'Classic'. These aircraft had no computer networks, so engineers were carried to manage the complex systems. The Classic Jumbo range comprised the early generation 100 and 200 series (with the short upperdeck bubble), and the 300 series (with the longer bubble). With hindsight, the 747 Classics were fairly simple 'steam-driven' aircraft, essentially like a Cessna except bigger, faster and with more thrust. They had very simple thrust control: long cables connected the thrust levers to each engine. You had four throttle levers in a row, and the aim was to carefully push them forward or pull them back in unison because the jet crabbed sideways if the levers were not aligned (the engines on one side would power up with more thrust than the engines on the other side).

The pilot of any light jet aircraft would have felt at home in the Classic Jumbo's cockpit. We had to manually compensate for the secondary effects of the controls (aileron, rudder). For example, when the ailerons are moved to roll the aircraft, the pilot must also pull back (move the elevators) to stop the nose dropping, and move the rudder pedals to stop the passengers slipping sideways in their seats – jobs done automatically these days.

Qantas had an exciting international network in the 1980s, servicing destinations in five of the seven continents. There were a lot of airports to get used to. My favourite airports were Hong Kong (Kai Tak), Tahiti, Los Angeles, Rome, Athens, Paris and London.

Kai Tak was one of the two most challenging airports I experienced in the Qantas network. When landing towards the south, pilots flew the infamous IGS dogleg approach as it avoided the 3300 foot–high mountains that prevented simpler straight-in approaches. The approach to runway 13 was a wonderful exercise in planning, using visual and instrument cues to fly, and crew support. It was even more challenging in conditions of poor visibility and strong crosswinds. We descended in cloud on the first part of the dogleg approach, aiming 47 degrees to the left of the airport. If we saw flashing strobes starting to appear through the cloud as we approached the minimum altitude, we could continue the approach visually and land (even though we couldn't see the airport or the runway). Once we made the decision to continue, it was a bit like the goat track approach at Tarpini – we had to keep descending, our only reference being the line of strobes as they led us into a right turn. At the end of the turn we would skim a few hundred feet over the tops of residential buildings while the locals nonchalantly hung their washing to dry on their roofs. The right turn finally finished as we passed 300-feet altitude with the runway straight in front of us. Here's the catch. If there was a strong tailwind on the first leg of the approach it would become a crosswind from the right after we had turned through the 47-degree right turn onto finals. That final turn is made so low that we only had time to make one wing-down followed by a wing-up movement to align with the runway – only one turn so we had to be precise.

A good co-pilot earns his pay on this approach. You could easily end up in a situation where it's unsafe to continue to land. Wise pilots who blew the approach 'went around' and tried again. One unwise pilot who continued with an unstable approach, in 1993, ended up over-running the end of the runway and parking ignominiously in Hong Kong's harbour.

I loved flying the Classic Jumbo. By the time I entered Qantas, the Classic had been in operation for almost eighteen years and Qantas was trying to get the final ounces of thrust from what was ageing engine technology. They injected 2400 kilograms of de-mineralised water into each engine during take-off to enable operations from hot, humid places, such as Cairns, with a full load. (The water reduced the internal engine temperatures, permitting more fuel to be introduced, and so more thrust. Steam also provided a thrust benefit.) The JT9 engines on the Classic could produce just 45,500 pounds of thrust (dry) and 47,000 pounds (wet) when the complicated water injection was used. These days, the new A380's Trent 900 engine has been tested up to 93,000 pounds of thrust, though Qantas only pushes it to 72,000 pounds.

The Classic Jumbo's technology was leading edge for its time, but is now regarded as primitive. The auto-landing system was a humble mechanical device, incorporating lots of servos and actuators that delivered mediocre performance and reliability, and needed to be checked regularly. In the 200- and 300-series Jumbos, some of the automated systems and warnings were retrofitted. There were switches and warning lights for everything, but there were no computers to monitor them. We had to continually scan the panels for failures, and every twenty minutes the engineer would record about 50 engine and system parameters in an A2-sized log book that would be returned to Sydney for plotting and analysis. There were no warning computers or electronic checklists, so even the simplest failures could take a long time to resolve. For example, in 1988, the leading edge slats failed to deploy when I was approaching to land at Melbourne airport. It took the three of us (two pilots and one engineer) 30 minutes to work through the emergency checklist – a procedure that would only take two pilots ten minutes today.

The navigation systems were good for their time, but there was no GPS technology. We used Inertial Navigation Systems (INS) technology developed from the aerospace programs that used mechanical gyroscopes and accelerometers. INSs were impressive back then; we could launch from Sydney, turn off all our radio aids and trust our navigation to three US$100,000 Litton INSs. Twelve hours later, as we approached Los Angeles airspace, we would be confident our position was accurate to within 72 kilometres (39 nautical miles). (GPS today would put us inside 3 metres – 23,000 times more accurate and at a fraction of the cost.)

All pilots on the flight deck were busy when we flew from Asia to Europe. On a flight to London we'd pick one route from a selection of about twenty. The route would have about 200 waypoints – positions on the ground provided by countries to control where aircraft enter, transit and leave their airspace. We would expect to be intercepted by fighters if we diverted from our cleared route. Each waypoint's position was defined by latitude and longitude references printed on our flight plan and navigation charts. Those 200 coordinates had to be input into the INS by a pilot on the flight deck – a slow, laborious job that is done automatically by data uplink these days. One by one, the support pilots would load successive (fifteen-character) coordinates into each of the INS's nine waypoint slots; it was all the INS could handle. The INS was then coupled to the auto-pilot and the aircraft would track to the next waypoint. It was a simple system that needed constant attention. In the days before 9/11, we'd welcome some passengers into the flight deck and show them how it all worked.

I remember one time over Russia in the middle of the night, I was entering my next sequence of nine coordinates into the machine and I must have been distracted because suddenly one of the waypoints was displayed to be 13,000 kilometres (7000 nautical miles) distant – the giveaway that I'd entered an incorrect character. The manual exercise of inputting these 135 characters, then methodically crosschecking the waypoints (by checking tracks and distances) sometimes occupied the entire focus of the support pilot. In Russia, where waypoints can be separated by one or two minutes, your efforts to pre-load the next nine INS waypoints would be in vain when the air traffic controller then cleared you to track from waypoint 1 direct to waypoint 9, and you'd have to go through your sequence and scrub out the ones now not needed then load new waypoints ahead again. It's worth noting that the generation of flyers before us thought we had it easy; up to the 1960s navigators used sextants and slide-rules – they could plot by the stars if they had to.

Radio communications were dreadful back then, nothing like the pleasant environment we share today. Very high frequency (VHF) radios are the preferred choice to deliver clear reception over short distances (up to 280 kilometres or 150 nautical miles). But last century many countries couldn't provide a VHF infrastructure so we used high frequency (HF) radios to communicate with the controllers. HF communications suffer from two problems: quality and interference. The controller's voice was often drowned out by the 'hiss' from noise and solar activity (flares) that charge up the Earth's ionosphere, and our HF transmissions were being constantly over-transmitted by multiple people.

The stress for today's crews flying from Asia into Europe has changed. The INS has been replaced by multiple flight management computers that upload or understand the world's routes. Pilot stress is reduced because clear VHF communications are now available in most countries. The Traffic Collision and Avoidance System (TCAS) was introduced in the mid-1990s and provided an extraordinarily successful last line of defence against mid-air collisions.

The Classic Jumbos were tough, reliable old planes. Bits would fall off and they'd still fly. One time I was flying from Sydney to Auckland and we were hit by a very strong bolt of lightning. As the aircraft became electrostatically charged, every particle of dust in that aircraft lifted up and hung in the air as if suspended. We lost one HF radio because the lightning vaporised the 4 millimetre–thick steel tube that was our HF antenna, but the plane barely reacted. It had been developed to be a military transport and it was tough.

Today, the stresses the Classic pilots had to endure have been reduced, but there are new problems to contend with – congestion, aircraft complexity, aircraft performance, aircraft automation, fatigue, complex airspace and complex air traffic control instructions. All of these factors steadily increase with time while the number of pilots in the cockpit decreases.

Pilots worked up to twenty-hour tours of duty and slept in bunks beside the cockpit, but it was more luxurious than the Air Force: all the accommodation, transportation, flight plans, fuel calculations and paperwork were organised for us by Qantas. When you shut down the engines you didn't have to secure the aircraft; you just walked away and climbed into a dedicated bus bound for the crew hotel.

It took some time to get used to flying with such a large flight crew on the Classics. The normal crew complement consisted of the captain, one first officer (FO), one second officer (SO) and one engineer. The SO relieved the pilots and the engineer in the cruise. On flights longer than twelve hours, we'd have an additional SO for inflight relief. With five technical crew members, the Classic's cockpit was congested on long-haul sectors, and sometimes the overcrowding produced interesting human dynamics.

Sometimes the additional pilots actioned activities outside their responsibility. In their minds they were trying to help, but instead they were interfering with the pilot and co-pilot's standard operating procedures (SOPs). In the worst cases, ego battles could erupt in the flight deck which, if not countered, could lead to anarchy. For example, during one approach into Los Angeles, when I was sitting behind the captain, I felt the shoulder of the other second officer crush between the engineer's and my shoulder as he pushed in front to change the active frequency on the captain's radio control panel. He was trying to fly from the back of the flight deck – an aggressive action that could be dangerous. I was surprised the captain did not rebuke the SO's actions as it should never have been tolerated.

This incident was the catalyst for my second career epiphany. I had to leave the Classic Jumbos and fly in a cockpit with fewer crew; the fewer the better as far as I was concerned. I wanted to move to an aircraft where the pilots' roles were clearly defined and where the pilots prioritised team performance over personal ego. I also promised myself that when I became a captain I would create a friendly environment where all pilots are encouraged to contribute in an efficient team that followed the SOPs.

I got wind of a new Boeing that Qantas was looking at buying: the 747–400. It was my ideal aircraft: new high technology, the best of the best, new challenges, an exciting introduction and fewer crew!

I started the first officer promotion course for the 747 Classic in early 1988, only eighteen months after joining Qantas. I had to fly circuits for a week at the very windy Avalon Airport in Melbourne. It must have cost Qantas $80,000 for each of us given that, for every 'touch and go', the landing fee is $2000, tyre wear would cost $500, and that's before the fuel bill for 8000 kilograms of kerosene per hour!

I also learned something about my eyesight. One windy night at Avalon, when we were practising landing in cross-winds, Malcolm Hatton-Ward, my instructor, told me to use the approach lights (TVASI) to help me get on the correct approach path. I couldn't see what he was talking about as RAAF airports didn't use these approach lights and so I had never given them high priority while at Qantas. Malcolm asked me if I could see them. I shook my head, and the other second officer I was with – Joel Gregory – took off his spectacles and offered them to me. It was like emerging in another world – everything was clear. I'd had no idea I had low-light myopia (night short-sightedness) and that I needed glasses.

I completed my first officer conversion course in early 1988 and sat in a holding pattern waiting for my position as an FO on our brand new 747–400s.

CHAPTER 9

747–400

Flying in civil aviation is all about seniority and pecking order. All Qantas pilots have a seniority number, which they are allotted the day they join the company. The most senior pilot has a seniority number of 1, the next senior, 2. So a pilot will start his employment with a seniority number that will get closer to 1 with every retirement or resignation. The seniority number determines who gets on the next promotional course for higher rank, who converts to a new aircraft type, and who flies a particular flight. The pilot with the seniority number closest to 1 gets preference if too many pilots are bidding for a course, flight or day off.

The pilot who joined recently will be assigned an activity no one wants.

I was fortunate. I bid for the 747 first officer (FO) promotion course as soon as I joined Qantas and completed it two years later. I was now trained to take the first officer's right-hand seat, but a temporary oversupply of FOs meant I would take the intermediate position of senior second officer until an FO's seat became free. The first officer has a fantastic job in aviation; you take almost all the benefits that come with command without the onerous legal responsibilities, you share the flying and you're in command while the captain is resting. So I spent six months as a senior second officer, keen to take a right-hand seat but blocked because of staffing levels.

My luck was about to change. As 1988 drew to a close, I learned more about the impending 747–400. Again, here was a revolutionary new design from Boeing – this was the biggest aircraft, the most advanced and the best – and just as I wanted to fly the F-111 in the Air Force, now I wanted to be part of the 747–400 operation at Qantas. The problem was that, as a new first officer, all the other first officers would surely beat me to the first 747–400 conversion courses. I might have to wait years to get to the 400.

Soon after, I was amazed to discover that none of the FOs were bidding for the 747–400, which meant the pecking order for the conversion course could drop all the way down to someone as junior as me. The pilots were reluctant to bid for new aircraft. I hadn't seen this in the Air Force. In the military, the pilots and the seagulls (pilots who didn't want to fly) sort themselves out pretty quickly – those keen to fly get lots of it. There was never a shortage of pilots vying to fly the latest and greatest aircraft. But in all the major international airlines, Qantas included, many captains and first officers avoid flying a new aircraft straight out of certification trials that has not been 'case hardened' or proven in extensive airline operations. There was always the worry that a problem that had not been detected during certification might pop up and cause an accident that would put the pilots at fault. The pilots also didn't want to fly an aircraft where the pay and conditions were unresolved.

I was never worried about the remuneration on the 747–400. Most of the pay scales in the airlines are constructed around the weight of the planes you fly and the number of passengers you carry. A380 pilots are paid more than 747 pilots, who are paid more than those flying 737s.

The 747–400 was the leading edge in technology; a revolutionary departure from the Classic. It had been talked about and was the subject of so many unfounded rumours that when positions opened for technical crew on the new 400s that would be delivered in 1989, I was one of only two first officers out of 300 who applied for the conversion. I was also the most junior. It was such a poor response that Qantas assigned pilots to the aircraft. The Pilots' Union got angry on the basis that you shouldn't force a pilot to fly a plane they don't want to, and won a reprieve that the new pilots could convert back to their previous aircraft after twelve months if they didn't like the 400.

Me? I just wanted to be on a 747–400. I had read about their new onboard computer systems and their revamped engines, and I assumed they would be the new industry standard for long-range flying, while the Classic – as nice as she was – would be phased out. I had bid before the security of pay and conditions for the 747–400 were agreed by Qantas, but I didn't care – you make your own luck. I knew Qantas ultimately had to provide competitive salaries for the new 747–400 or they would lose pilots to other airlines offering better conditions.

I also knew you could spend years preparing for an opportunity only to see it vaporise at the last minute – as I had learned with F-111s in the RAAF. There is no such thing as security. You have to be aware of your options and not be afraid of change or failure. In fact, change is vital – a company that is not changing and improving is going out of business. So, while some pilots are creatures of habit and don't like converting to new aircraft, I take the opposite approach and go for it – it's better than being made redundant.

I commenced the first officer's conversion course for the 747–400 in mid-1989. The older pilots thought only a lunatic would accept the 400 slot before pay and conditions were agreed, so I just pretended I had been assigned to the 400 and kept my mouth shut.

The 747–400 conversion took almost four months, which meant lots of time in simulators, studying manuals and sitting in front of Kodak carousel slide projectors.

I needed two licences to operate the 747–400, the first being a 'Command Instrument Rating' from the Australian Civil Aviation Safety Authority (CASA), which proves I know the aircraft and the instruments well enough to operate it privately, and the second a Qantas licence, which cleared me to operate as a first officer to fly a Boeing 747–400 on Qantas routes.

The other first officers who were converting to the 400 had already flown sectors as FOs in the right-hand seat on Classic Jumbos, but I hadn't. I'd been trapped in the limbo of senior second officer. I needed to fly a sector in the 400 before I would be granted my Qantas licence. One sector, anywhere. To my delight, I was tasked to fly an empty 747–400 for one sector. The captain asked me where I'd like to fly. 'Hobart sounds nice,' I replied. So the Melbourne–Hobart–Melbourne flight plan was submitted and off we went – just two of us and a brand new 747–400. There were a few engine problems climbing out that required us to return to Melbourne, but it was great fun. And I was then a first officer, rated for the 400-series Jumbo.

I was the inaugural first officer to 'check out' and fly the 747–400. My first operational sector in the 747–400 was from Sydney across the Pacific to Los Angeles with Geoff Westwood, an infamous senior captain who had been instrumental in forming the Pilots' Union in the late 1970s. The four-person flight crew met at Sydney's airport for a pre-flight briefing before we took off, and Geoff asked each of us what our experience was. Only one of us, Geoff included, had ever flown an operational sector in the 400 and that person was a second officer. We had a laugh; we were not exactly overconfident, but we were excited.

*

The 400 series was a wonderful plane, but in those early days its computers were not reliable and 50 per cent of our flights departed late. None of us were used to these new systems and booting up the aircraft from a cold state proved very challenging. The problem was determining in which order to start the 100 computer systems; the Boeing engineers had not produced a reliable sequence. If the engineers booted up the plane in a slightly different sequence, or missed one of the 100 steps, one computer would hang, which would, in turn, hang the rest of the process. In a notable case in Los Angeles, our problems began when we were in the flight deck trying to reboot an aircraft that had been shut down the previous night. It should have taken fifteen minutes to start the computers the next morning, but in our case it took four hours. The expensive fix for the next few months was to never de-power the aircraft. The auxiliary power unit (APU) would run continuously whenever the engines were shut down.

The computers were very glitchy on that first flight across the Pacific with Geoff Westwood. Just before we were cleared for take-off, after a 90-minute delay, I was going through the systems as we taxied and saw the computers had altered the cabin temperature of the plane to 2 degrees hotter than the Qantas settings. I was about to attempt a fix on it when Geoff said, 'Don't touch it! For God's sake, don't touch it!' So we flew all the way to Los Angeles with the passengers complaining about the heat.

Another time early in the 747–400's life, Captain Graeme Cant and I were climbing out from Los Angeles for San

Francisco when the flight management computers (FMCs) decided to switch from metric to imperial without prompting. The FMCs display the weight of the plane, which allows us to set the engine thrust, and calculate fuel usage and landing speeds, and so on. All we could see were astronomically large numbers displayed on the FMCs. Then the auto-thrust failed. A few bells and warning lights activated that added to the distractions. The FMCs weren't making any sense but the aircraft was flying beautifully, and that first commandment, 'Aviate', flashed to the front of our thoughts. Graeme and I looked at the thrust that had advanced uncommanded to the 'maximum continuous' setting. There were plenty of opportunities to be confused and to become distracted, but I'll never forget Graeme's response once we'd worked out the problem: 'Let's see what she'll do,' Graeme smirked as he rode the very light 747–400, climbing like a Saturn V rocket up into the heavens.

The 747–400 required no flight engineer as the job was taken by central maintenance, flight warning and reporting computers. Hundreds of other system computers communicated with each other to provide a level of automation that had never been experienced before.

Despite the challenging introduction to service, the airline, pilots and passengers loved the 747–400. It offered enhanced safety, efficiency and comfort. Once the glitches were ironed out, the computers worked superbly and seldom failed. The flight controls were also improved. A 'turn coordinator' was installed that automatically put in rudder deflection in a turn, the first step towards reducing the pilot inputs required during flight and the first hint of what fly-by-wire flight controls had to offer.

With the engineer gone, it was the job of EICAS (Engine Indication and Crew Alerting System) to notify the pilots of failures and the checklists needed to resolve the failures. EICAS displayed system failure and checklist messages on the pilots' central display. We'd go to the 747–400 QRH (quick reference handbook), which was a bible of 240 checklists for every conceivable failure on the plane.

The 400 marked the dawn of the period of 'automated' aircraft that people are so worried about today. You could fly all the way to LA without really touching too many controls: it had an excellent mechanical autopilot, and the flight management computer presented performance indices to warn the pilots of an impending stall and also to prevent flight into 'Coffin Corner' (a situation when flying above the aircraft's maximum altitude where engine and airframe limitations reduce the safety margins). The computers and automation were a great flying aid but they were not fool-proof. The pilots still needed to carefully read and interpret the computers and flight instrument displays.

I remember once on the way to London, we were in the 747–400 at 35,000 feet, very close to our maximum altitude. Meanwhile, a 747–400 from another airline came from behind and 4000 feet above us. Our instruments showed we were cruising with a speed margin of plus/minus 5 knots. We would get supersonic buffet if we sped up 5 knots, and we might stall in a turn if we slowed down 5 knots. We didn't know the performance of the 747–400 behind us, but we figured (since it was also flying from Asia to Europe) they were also heavy and so shouldn't be that high. They must have had no speed margin to play with. We then passed a waypoint where the route turned through a 40-degree angle, an unusually large change in direction. The G force came on as our aircraft banked into the turn, and our speed tapes showed the previous 5-knot margin was now pinched down to almost zero. The thrust increased to the maximum cruise limits and, bit by bit, we nudged our way through that turn. We were fine but the same was not true for the trailing 747–400 – they hit and then penetrated Coffin Corner. The speed tapes must have already shown little margin when they were flying straight. But now, in the turn, their speed margin reduced to zero and the engine thrust at the higher altitude was insufficient to counter the increased drag. With stalled wings and insufficient thrust they only had one place to go – down!

'PAN PAN PAN – [callsign] in an emergency descent to 35,000 feet.' They plummeted down through those 4000 feet in about 30 seconds.

It was a terrible example of airmanship. The engineer in a 747 Classic would have warned the pilots not to climb so high, but the engineer had been replaced by computers and the pilots didn't understand their jet's performance. They probably understood the yellow no-go speed zones on the speed tape, but they didn't know the autopilot would mindlessly bank the aircraft into a 20-degree banked turn at high altitude. They could have negotiated the turn more safely if they knew they could limit the bank angle, but they were clueless.

There's one potential problem with automation: that it will be accompanied by complacency and ignorance.

The 747–400 would consign the older Classic Jumbos to 'legacy' status, but at a cost to the industry. As the Classic drifted into history, it took with it the manufacturers' philosophy of building aircraft around the captain and engineer. The Classic's captain and engineer knew every part of their aircraft intimately: how it was designed, how to operate it. When the systems failed, these legacy crews knew how to diagnose the problem, apply a remedy and avert a disaster. Their legacy aircraft might have been simple, but the crews could save their jet whether it was stalled, spinning, inverted, falling apart or on fire.

Today, jet engines fail on average about once in every 300,000 engine hours. For a four-engine aircraft, that means one in every three and a half pilots will ever see an engine failure in their entire career. Well, that's the theory. In practice the die rolled differently for me. I've experienced three engine failures while I've been in the seat and two engine failures when passengering. Surely I must be protecting the odds for others!

The first engine failure I experienced was a textbook example. It was on 1 October 1993 and I was flying out of Frankfurt for Bangkok with Captain John Pickhaver – a gentle man, a great mentor and a fantastic pilot – and Second Officer Des Howson. John's son John and daughter Anne were both on the flight deck observing the sector. We had taken off at our maximum take-off weight of 397 tonnes; the autopilot had levelled the aircraft at 6000 feet while waiting for aircraft to pass above us. All of a sudden, an EICAS message 'ENG 2 – LOW OIL PRESS' displayed on our centre console. This message was not normal, but it was also not alarming.

As Des read through the QRH checklist, I felt my yoke (steering wheel) start to rotate – the autopilot had inadvertently wound in about half of the aileron roll control. This was unusual! We looked at the engine instruments closer and then it dawned upon us. Engine 2 had failed at an idle thrust! The failure was so gentle neither John nor I had detected it – even when we were at maximum take-off weight. John was cool; there was no rush. We continued on towards Munich, trying twice to restart the engine but without success. We then spent an hour dumping 100 tonnes of fuel to get our weight back down to our maximum landing weight before we made our approach and landed back at Frankfurt.

John and Anne were amazed. They watched their father and me take our time and methodically go through all the processes to try and restart the engine before we decided to give the flight away and return to the airport. It was a controlled, zero-stress flight, and it was a delight to have experienced this under John Pickhaver's excellent command.

My second engine failure was not so pleasant.

It was January 1994 and Captain Warwick Tainton and I were at Bangkok airport about to fly a 747–400 to Sydney. When we arrived at the aircraft in the afternoon we discovered it was unserviceable. Engine 4 had two 30 foot-long fire loops that surround the engine to detect an overheat condition between the engine and the engine nacelle (cover). We could depart with one fire loop failed, but on that day both fire loops had failed and the aircraft was grounded, awaiting spare parts. There were no spare fire loops in Bangkok, and so the aircraft would be delayed five hours awaiting the replacement parts to be flown in from Singapore.

While Warwick was talking to the passengers in the airport lounges, I watched over the aircraft. Over a period of two hours I reviewed the flight history of the aircraft, both in the technical log and in the history files stored in the central maintenance computer (CMC). What I found alarmed me. The CMC had been logging continual exceedances for the past 20 hours. The vibration sensor for the high-speed rotor in Engine 4 was recording the maximum value. What made the research more distressing was that the two fire loops that had failed in Bangkok had failed during the previous sector in Frankfurt, and the aircraft had been delayed a few hours while replacement loops were found in Europe.

I was very uncomfortable! I went down to see the engineers at the engine and asked to view the failed fire loops. Along its 30-foot length, both loops had fractured side by side. I asked the engineer: 'Does this look like a vibration fracture to you?' He answered, 'Perhaps.' I added: 'Well I don't want to fly this aircraft, because the vibration sensor shows a full-scale deflection even at idle RPM and the engine is clearly showing signs of distress. It's trying to tell us something.'

I went to see Warwick and told him of my concerns. We talked to the engineers and agreed that after the loops were replaced we would start Engine 4 and then make a decision.

A few hours later, we started Engine 4 with the new fire loops installed. I'll never forget it. The engine sounded like a lawnmower with an angry 'buzz saw' type growl. The vibration sensors for the engine went to full-scale deflection. We refused to take the aircraft, but pushed the thrust up slightly to 20 per cent to enable the CMC and the aircraft logging systems to record the engine parameters.

We had only had the engine at 20 per cent thrust for about ten seconds when . . . KABOOM!

A compressor blade in the high-pressure compressor fractured. Flames shot out of the engine, reaching as far forward as the cockpit. The flash that night illuminated the precincts at Bangkok airport. We now needed a new engine, which was a challenge to the Boeing 747 fleet worldwide as no one had ever ferried (fifth podded) a spare 747–400 engine before on the wing of a 747–400. We were stranded in Bangkok for five days before the replacement engine could be installed and enable us to return to Sydney.

The lessons from this incident were obvious. I had followed my instincts, tempered by years of study, training and experience.

I was confident and sure of my decisions. We were the last line of defence to protect the passengers from threat. Be prepared, be confident and don't compromise.

And I'll be extra careful the next time I hear an engine sounding like a lawnmower!

CHAPTER 10

The Far Side

Many commercial pilots have backup skills and qualifications that they nurture should the day ever arise when they don't want to fly anymore, or they fail their licence checks or annual medical.

My interest in personal computers developed through my military career. I ordered the very first Compaq Portable PC in 1984 while I was on assignment in the Sinai Peninsula. The name 'portable' was tenuous since it weighed 30 kilograms, was as big as a suitcase and had no battery backup – but it did have a handle!

I read piles of books on software development and was soon able to write computer programs for the RAAF in my spare time. Once I joined Qantas, I visited the offices of a leading software company in Sydney to see about a part-time job as a programmer and started writing code for them.

Coral and I started Aeronaut Industries in 1985 to manufacture 'The Flying Kneepad' for fighter pilots in the RAAF and, later, civilian pilots. In 1987 we decided to expand Aeronaut into a software company. The next three years were very enjoyable. I spent time off at home and overseas writing code.

We'd always wanted to have an extra stream of income as a backup should something go wrong at Qantas. We'd already had our first child, Alexander, born in July 1989 and, although we always planned to have two kids close together, the next pregnancy six months later was a wonderful surprise. There is nothing like children to focus your mind on financial security.

It became clear the future lay in importing, distributing, supporting and supplying training tools for software developers, and we realised I'd need a year off flying to make it work. Economists declared Australia was going into recession and Qantas requested pilots to take leave of absence. What an opportunity! I got my leave and included a new requirement that Qantas would keep my simulator checks going and my licence current so I could return after the break and slip straight back into the seat. Qantas agreed.

The business grew so fast I needed a second year off to get things under control. We were selling to some large organisations and the word was spreading: we had great tools and offered good advice.

In 1990, to stay current for my Qantas licence I not only had to do the 747–400 simulators every six months, but I also had to do an annual route check. A route check is when you fly a sector and a check pilot sits behind you, remaining silent, and assesses you on how well you fly, manage the aircraft and your crew, and comply with SOPs. If you fail the route check, your pay stops and you cease flying for Qantas.

So in September 1990, after having taken six months off, I flew to Singapore to do my route check. I was to land at Changi, go to the hotel for a sleep, and then fly back to Sydney the next day. The whole sector would be 36 hours. Our daughter was due at this time, but Coral said, 'Go, I'm not close.'

But when I arrived at the hotel in Singapore, Coral called me from the hospital delivery room. She continued to call me between contractions, until the fourth call when she cried and told me we had a daughter, Sophia. Talk about lousy timing! I had set aside just 36 hours in an entire year to do my route check, and that's when my daughter was born.

I remember announcing this to the passengers as I flew out of Changi on Father's Day, 1990.

Coral began working with me full-time in the business at Aeronaut. I found the technical side easy, but I was useless at the back office accounting, clerical and marketing side. I needed Coral and we made a fabulous business team.

Aeronaut grew rapidly with Coral at the helm. To this day, Australia's largest retailer and half of Australia's hotels run on our databases. We'd built ourselves a secondary source of income, we gave ourselves a very good standard of living and were able to send the kids to good schools and take them skiing every year. It was fun to be in the computer business, but Coral had taken over and I needed a physical challenge. I wanted to get back to flying and Qantas was expecting me to return.

In 1992 I returned as a first officer on 747–400s, and it suited me to stay in that position. When on long layovers in overseas ports, I took every opportunity to meet with the leaders at the best software companies – an opportunity I wouldn't have had if I was stranded behind a desk in Australia – and I'm sure most of the IT executives I spoke with had no idea I was a Qantas pilot fronting for my wife's company back home.

My plan was to remain as a first officer on the 747–400 until I had sufficient seniority to get a 747–400 command course. I loved the 400 and didn't want to operate any smaller, low-tech alternatives. I also didn't want to fly short sectors within Australia. So I let pass the opportunities for 737 and 767 command, and flew the more challenging long-haul routes to US and European destinations. All was going to plan: Qantas was expanding, I had been cleared to commence command training and I expected to start my training in 2004. These plans would be thrown to the wolves when Qantas blocked 'vertical promotion on the 747–400'.

The block was to stop people flying the 747s as a first officer and then captain. There was a worry that complacent first officers might be promoted to become complacent captains. Qantas thought the best 747 captains were those that had streamed through multiple aircraft types on their path to command.

110

I had been kneecapped. I had delayed taking a command on minor aircraft so I could simply move from the right-hand seat to the left-hand seat and retain knowledge for the wonderful 747 and long-haul operations. But now I had to move to another aircraft to get my command – which one?

Airbus was the new boy in the aviation industry – the maverick. Its heritage started with the Concorde (the first commercial aircraft to have fly-by-wire flight controls and digital computers), through the A300, A320 and the A330. The company intrigued me, not just as an aviator but also as a software developer. Airbuses were crammed with computers – they ran the plane – and I was curious how the software was designed and how it worked. Qantas had traditionally been an all-Boeing company, but in a surprising shift Qantas ordered ten Airbus A330s and twenty A380s. The A330 would arrive in 2002.

I started reading up on the A330 and getting really enthused. But I was also very sceptical of Airbus; I'd heard all the stories of the unfortunate accidents that had beset the manufacturer, and if I were to be comfortable flying Airbus aircraft I'd have to drill down into the reasons for these accidents and know how I would prevent similar mishaps. The more I read, the more excited I became. The A330 is a remarkably advanced aircraft. My scepticism evaporated; here was my route to a Qantas command.

Gaining my command on the A330 would not be easy. I would be changing from long haul to short haul, from Boeing to Airbus, from first officer to captain – and all at once. I'd be dumping the Boeing philosophies I'd learned over the preceding eighteen years and replacing them with Airbus's entirely new philosophy, almost tantamount to learning how to fly again. I would be flying sectors in regions and to airports I'd never visited before. It would be particularly hard making the Airbus conversion as well as stepping up to commanding the plane. I asked Murray Crockett, the management pilot in charge of the A330, if I could make life easier for myself and Qantas if I converted to the A330 as a first officer for the first six months to get used to the aircraft, then undertook my command course. Murray said no – there was no protocol in the training department for this process. I was the first to undertake conversion and promotion courses at the same time.

So it was A330 command or nothing. My colleagues called me crazy, and I thought perhaps I was a little bit crazy, but the thrill, challenge and the rewards of commanding the world's most advanced aircraft were too good to knock back. I saw Airbus as the future of aviation. So, I thought, why not?

CHAPTER 11

'Embrace'

I was the tenth first officer to convert to the A330. The two courses took me a gruelling five months to complete: three months for the conversion followed by two months for the command course. I almost gave up on the command course. It was only with the help of the training and fleet managers that I gained my captain's rank.

When you convert to a new aircraft you are taught the basic systems architecture, the location of switches and push-buttons, and what happens when they are selected. You also have to learn what can go wrong with the aircraft, and what to do about it. On the Airbus conversion it was considered enough to show pilots the basics of flying the aircraft and managing the checklists. But my brain worked differently.

I have more difficulty converting to new aircraft than most other pilots. I have to learn the machine from the ground up, not from the buttons and checklists down. I don't like controlling machinery I don't fully understand, a habit formed when pulling apart motorbikes and cars as a teenager. I need to understand the philosophy of how the machine is designed and assembled so I can understand the limits and standard operating procedures. I have to know the purpose for every checklist, rather than just relying on what the computer displays. When I converted from the Boeing 747 to the Airbus A330, I had to replace all my knowledge of Boeing philosophies and methodologies with the Airbus equivalents, not a trivial task because Airbus and Boeing aircraft were built and operated very differently. There was a lot to learn; I went through all the manuals, and I phoned engineers and I questioned designers and talked to test pilots until I fully understood what I was about to take control of. My brain was spent by the time I'd finished the A330 conversion course, and I hadn't even started the command course.

The first simulator flight on the command course was from Tokyo to Fukuoka. I had spent days studying countries and airports I'd never flown into, in a plane I'd never flown and with new checklists. The session got difficult when the cockpit filled with smoke, reducing our visibility to just 30 centimetres in the flight deck, the electrics were degraded to 5 per cent, and many of our navigation and radio systems were degraded. The weather at all the Japanese airports was appalling and the first officer was withholding proper support.

I was exhausted and drowning. I talked to a friend about my concerns. He said, 'Just push through and finish it!' I didn't agree. I had reached my limit and I needed a break.

I told one of the executives in the training section, 'I'm hating this – I feel so uncomfortable, I'm failing.' He said, 'You're not failing – you're testing yourself and seeing where your weaknesses are.' I wasn't convinced. I knew I was a good pilot and that I could fly, but I was angry and embarrassed that I was having trouble. He told me he was going to work with me and that he'd get me through.

I was so exhausted I couldn't stand the thought of more sectors in the simulator. So I went to the fleet manager, Murray Crockett, and asked for a week off the program to study. Murray knew me well from time we had spent together on the 747–400s. He looked at me and said, 'I'll give you three weeks off, but only if you don't look at a book for the first two weeks.'

I went away with Coral and returned happy and refreshed, and I was able to finish the simulator sessions. I then completed the final command check where you fly five sectors in the A330 with a senior check pilot. If the check pilot has to say anything, you fail. I flew my five sectors, and when I finally shut down the engines at Sydney I looked down and saw the captain's epaulets waiting for me on the centre console.

My peers didn't know how I did it – I had taken on too much at once and, luckily, I was given some R&R when I really needed it. That's what good management is: knowing when to ease off the pressure and how to get the best out of people. And that's what good pilots do: they know their limits.

*

It's important to understand the difference between Boeing and Airbus aircraft.

All aircraft perform within the physical laws of gravity, lift and propulsion. They have essentially the same types of moveable flight control surfaces: ailerons, flaps, slats, elevators, spoilers and rudders. These surfaces move, enabling the aircraft to do the seemingly impossible: take off and land on short runways, and cruise fast at high altitude where the air is so thin that, in the case of a decompression, the crew and passengers would start becoming unconscious within nine seconds.

While all aircraft use the same controls, each kind is constructed differently. In the lead up to the Second World War there were many different aircraft makers, each with idiosyncratic designs. The governments ordered so many aircraft for the war effort that flight controls and cockpits became largely standardised. When the war finished, and commercial aviation boomed, the Western world had a standard for flight controls and cockpits: instruments, gauges, rudder pedals, joysticks, yokes and throttles.

At the end of the 1970s there were three major manufacturers of large jet airliners: Boeing, Lockheed and McDonnell-Douglas. All three were American and their designs used the same flying philosophy, in which a pilot manipulated the plane with two rudder pedals in front of the seat, and a yoke (mounted on top of a control column that moved forward and back between the pilot's knees). The elevators on the tail plane moved when the yoke column was pulled or pushed. The wing-tip ailerons moved when the yoke was rotated. Long metal cables connected the cockpit controls to the flight control surfaces.

The new jet aircraft were bigger and heavier than their ancestors, and the flight control systems were becoming inadequate. Hydraulic assistance was introduced in the Boeing 307 Stratoliner to reduce the pilots' control forces (like a car's power steering), but this was only an evolutionary change. There was a need for a revolutionary change.

Airbus Industrie was created in 1970 by a European political initiative to counter the United States' domination of aircraft manufacturing. Airbus was a consortium of British (British Aerospace), French (Aerospatiale), German and later Spanish (CASA) aircraft builders who agreed to collaborate to build passenger jet aircraft. Airbus knew it faced enormous risks when it entered the civil aviation industry; they were competing against the Americans who were the undisputed leaders in aviation, with the most knowledge and experience.

Airbus took a conservative path for their first aircraft. The A300 would be a 300-seater aircraft with conventional flight controls. (It was called A300 because it was designed to carry 300 passengers.) The A300 entered service in 1974 and was a success.

With a successful aircraft on the market, Airbus now swung their interests to make a 100-seater passenger aircraft with computer-controlled fly-by-wire flight controls. Fly-by-wire simply means the flight controls are controlled electrically rather than mechanically, with the cables and rods connecting the pilots' controls to the aircraft's flight controls replaced with electrical wires. Fly-by-wire was developed by Aerospatiale and BAC for the Concorde in the 1960s. There was a reason Concorde had to have fly-by-wire, and that was the extraordinary fact that during its cruise phase, when it broke the sound barrier and went faster than Mach 2.0, Concorde heated up (some parts up to 200 degrees Celsius), and the airframe stretched by 30 centimetres. Subsequently, conventional cables and rods could not be used in the flight control systems and electrical wires were used instead.

NASA also introduced fly-by-wire on their unstable Apollo Command and Lunar modules that first launched in December 1968.

Fly-by-wire provided the Airbus designers with many benefits. Their aircraft would be lighter, and would cost less to build, maintain and operate than conventional aircraft. It would also enable the planes to take off and land at heavier weights and on shorter runways, and be easier to fly. From my own research I concluded they are much safer than conventional aircraft.

Fly-by-wire also includes 'thrust-by-wire', which is computer-controlled engine power, and 'brake-by-wire', or computer-controlled braking.

Airbus delivered its first A320 fly-by-wire aircraft in 1988. By the end of 2011, Airbus had delivered 7000 aircraft, with all but 816 being fly-by-wire.

The United States also used fly-by-wire – first in the space race and then in the US military (F-16 and F-18). Boeing's first fly-by-wire aircraft was the 777, launched in 1994. The 787 Dreamliner that launched in 2011 is also fly-by-wire.

Boeing and Airbus also use different cockpit pilot controls. All Boeing pilots have a control column and yoke between their knees, but Airbus took an innovative step. All Airbus aircraft (with the exception of the non-fly-by-wire A300 and A310) have a sidestick, a small 10 centimetre–long stick that protrudes up from the aircraft's side console (to the left of the captain's hand and to the right of the first officer's hand). If you let go of the sidestick (termed 'stick-free') while you're climbing in an Airbus, the aircraft will maintain the G of your climb and will keep you climbing. It also controls roll, and it won't let the aircraft roll until you tell it to.

When I first became a Qantas captain on A330s, it was 2004 and there were very few Australian pilots with a good word to say about an aircraft controlled by computers. There were not many Airbus aircraft in Australia then, so a lot of rumours went unchallenged. Some critics believed Airbus aircraft computers were not much more reliable than Windows, and that they could be 'hacked' from the ground, fused by high-power radio transmissions from nearby radio stations, afflicted by a virus or beset by the 'blue screen of death'.

On the A380 the flight control computers (FCCs) are designed so there's always at least one of the seven computers in control. The aircraft's network is also impressive. Hundreds of computers monitor 250,000 sensors throughout the plane.

For me, having left my beloved Boeing 747–400 after almost two decades on the flight deck, I was expecting to suffer a few of these negative feelings, but it didn't happen. I really loved the Airbus A330. My routes included fantastic ports in Japan, India, Singapore, Australia and China, and I was instantly impressed with how well the aircraft responded and performed.

I understood the fundamentals of the A330's flight control systems and computers, and recognised its advantages and detractions. Airbus had thought through what aircraft need to achieve and had programmed the systems to do it with little pilot input. If you take the time to learn the basics, then it takes little effort to achieve great results. Airbus pilots are systems operators as much as they are aviators.

And for all of the nay-saying about fly-by-wire being the end of real flying and real pilots, I found the fly-by-wire and automation made for a safer and more enjoyable experience. I can also now fly incredibly accurately.

Airbus's fly-by-wire is also the pilot's best friend in the case of an engine failure. An engine failure after take-off can be a daunting experience. Pilots have to ensure the aircraft clears obstacles, but their control is compromised as the aircraft yaws and rolls as the engine thrust decays. Control of the aircraft can be lost at this point if the pilot fails to react quickly enough. At least, that's the case on a conventional aircraft. If an A380 engine fails after getting airborne, and the pilots keep their hands off the sidesticks, the FCCs automatically introduce rudders to balance the aircraft, and ailerons to stop it rolling, and the aircraft flies away beautifully with a small 5-degree roll and a bit of a drift. The FCCs could have been programmed to fly the aircraft through the failure without yaw or a heading change, but in this case the pilot might not even recognise the engine failure and might have trouble identifying the failed engine.

Fly-by-wire has saved lives. A remarkable incident occurred on 17 January 2008 when both engines on a Boeing 777 failed to respond during the approach to land at Heathrow Airport in the United Kingdom. In Captain Peter Burkill's book *Thirty Seconds to IMPACT*, Peter documents the last 30 seconds of the flight. Peter's crew and passengers survived this unprecedented and 'un-survivable' accident because the 777's fly-by-wire flight control systems helped the flight crew to stretch the maximum glide during those last 500 feet after the flaps were partially retracted, enabling the crew to hold the wings near their maximum angle of attack.

In any aircraft, there are what we call 'non-normal checklists' – procedures for the actions taken by the flight crew when there is an emergency such as fire, engine failure, avionics failure or malfunction with the control surfaces. Most aircraft manufacturers produce their checklists in the form of a manual, known as a quick reference handbook (QRH). The Boeing 747 QRH consists of 270 pages detailing more than 240 checklists. When a problem presents itself on a large jet, one of the flight crew, usually the pilot who is not flying, reads the checklist aloud then does the prescribed action, and then moves to the next command. The pilot who is flying the aircraft oversees the checklist.

All of the Airbus checklists are held in a computer interface called the Electronic Centralised Aircraft Monitoring (ECAM), which is displayed on a screen on the flight deck. When there's an emergency, the ECAM throws up checklists until the problem is resolved.

While I was comfortable with this technology when I converted to the Airbus A330, many pilots were not and I can appreciate why they experienced problems. The ECAM system only ever gives the flight crew a simplified or 'veiled' version of what is actually going on in the aircraft.

Over the years I have spent a lot of time with Airbus test pilots and engineers, and I recall one engineer telling me there are so many computers, sensors and processors on board an Airbus that there is enough information to overwhelm most pilots. So the flight warning computer sifts through the flood of information, filtering out the extraneous, and presents only the summary information the pilots need to know. An engineer told me the Airbus computers only ever allow the pilots see 15 per cent of the information.

This is not a happy situation for most pilots. We are a controlling profession: if lawyers are cautious and firefighters are brave, pilots are controlling. Our employers and passengers like us that way. The best way to be a pilot is to get to the point where the airframe feels like an exoskeleton, like an extension of your body and mind. So when Airbus pilots become aware that they only get to see what they need to know, they can get annoyed and under-confident.

I counted myself lucky in that I loved the feel of the aircraft – I was, after all, a motorcyclist who felt comfortable throwing machinery around to see what it would do. But I was also a computer geek, and the challenge of new computer systems intrigued me. Still, I needed to go deeper than the Airbus system would allow me. I started talking to Airbus engineers and test pilots, reading all the manuals I could get my hands on and looking at as much testing data as Airbus would release to me.

I don't want to give the idea that Airbus is complicated and hard to learn. Many of the improvements Airbus made when it built the A300 – and subsequent models – have been huge leaps forward for the aviation industry. I am an inquisitive and technical person so I love Airbus designs and the challenges of aviation. After three years on type, I 'wore the aircraft around my body much like a glove around the hand' and I still got a thrill after every take-off from how the aircraft flies so smoothly and accurately. When we have delays on the ground, I tell the passengers interesting facts about engines or performance. They're interested (or feign interest!) when I explain to them how the flight controls steady the aircraft in the cruise and why it's such a delight to fly. It's hard work but fantastic fun.

No analysis of Airbus aircraft is complete without a discussion of what I think is the most remarkable flight this century. On 15 January 2009, US Airways flight 1549 flew through a flock of Canada Geese (big birds, Coral calls them flying wombats) after take-off from New York's LaGuardia Airport. The subsequent ingestion of birds caused both engines to lose thrust. What happened next became a remarkable display of airmanship, decision-making and flying skills.

Captain Chesley 'Sully' Sullenberger, assisted by First Officer Jeffrey Skiles, flew his disabled Airbus A320 to a safe emergency landing on the Hudson River, saving the 155 lives of those on board. The air traffic controller offered alternative airports that Sully considered but decided were outside his workable range. Sully's clear-headed decision to select the Hudson over 'stretched glides' to other airports shows his overarching priority to fly the aircraft and secure the passengers' safety over everything else. He made many rapid and excellent decisions that day, which reinforce the need for all pilots to be knowledgeable, well-trained and experienced. Sully's inspirational flight is a landmark survival case study for the aviation industry. Sully and his team rightly deserve their place in the annals of aviation.

CHAPTER 12

A380

In 2000, Qantas announced it would be one of the first customers for Airbus's new 'super jumbo', the A380. The double-decked, four-engine aircraft could carry 853 passengers in maximised format, compared to the 747–400's passenger load of 412.

Although the A380 is almost as long as the 747–400, it is noticeably heavier (569 tonnes versus 413) and has a much longer wingspan of 79.75 metres (261 feet) against the Boeing's 64.9 metres (213 feet).

Airlines were impressed by a plane that could operate over longer routes with 40 per cent more capacity per flight, but with environmental performance becoming a big issue for airlines and airports, the A380's noise ratings could also not be ignored: the A380 had half the noise footprint of the 747–400, produced half the noise-energy and had less than half the cabin noise recorded on the 747–400. It even flew 4000 feet higher at cruise, overflying congested air routes below. And with greater efficiency, greater payloads and less noise, there was very little compromise in terms of performance: the A380 was one third greater in size than the 747–400, but it could take off and land using less distance. This performance discrepancy was in large part due to the fly-by-wire computer system and superior wing shape of the A380. Each A380 wing is as long as a fifteen-storey building is high, and from tip to tip they measure just under 80 metres. It has a distinctive gull shape to lower the wing tip, keeping it underneath the runway's obstacle-free zone. And every square centimetre of the wing surfaces are designed by computers to optimise the airflow and performance. The A380's gull wing provides extraordinary efficiencies and it looks like a piece of art. But the A380 also owes a lot to the latest Rolls-Royce engine, the RB211 Trent 900.

For Qantas, with fully booked routes across the Pacific and to London, the A380 could not be ignored. The airline ordered twenty of the aircraft which had a market value of about A$420 million each (though Qantas negotiated a considerably lower price).

I put my hand up to fly the A380, of course. It was a big, new plane – the biggest commercial airliner ever – and I wanted to be a part of that. In March 2008 I trained on simulators in

Sydney and became fully licensed by Qantas for the A380, even though the first plane didn't make it to Sydney until September of that year.

Qantas sent the first few crews to Toulouse in France to do the eight take-offs and landings and the ten hours of flying CASA required on Airbus test aircraft. We were assigned to the A380 Manufacturer Serial Number (MSN) 4, the fourth A380 Airbus had produced. MSN 4 was a test aircraft, set up with 20 tonnes of special sensors, wiring and computer equipment for engineers and test pilots. Airbus used MSN 4 to certify the new Rolls-Royce Trent 900 engine and conduct heavy take-offs and landings.

The engines were hammered. Commercial airlines limit take-off thrust settings to the minimum of what is required to prolong the engine life and to reduce costs, but on MSN 4 the test pilots routinely thrashed the engines at take-off, meaning we got a great sense of how powerful those engines really were, and we could push the aircraft and 'see what she'd do'.

Behind MSN 4's cockpit spread an un-partitioned $30 million cabin configured for fifteen test engineers and scientists. The engineers sat at work stations in front of 8 foot–high racks crammed with computers, all joined by tonnes of bundled orange wires linking to Airbus's 'Mission Control' in Toulouse. Spread evenly around the cabin were hundreds of water ballast tanks used to simulate passenger weight for performance testing. Thousands of additional sensors sent a constant feed of data to the engineer's stations. It was IT nirvana for a computer nerd like me.

On our flights there were only six of us on board: three flying and three in reserve down the back. It was a delight being on the plane as we flew around Europe with two Qantas pilots and Pascal Verneau, the Airbus test engineer. Pascal oversaw MSN 4 from construction through to testing, and now through Qantas's proving flights. He sat behind and between the pilots and, in a very unusual situation for an airline pilot like me, Pascal had authority to call for the pilot to reject a take-off. While many pilots would be annoyed about being under the watch of a design engineer, I loved the experience: for five days I had total access to one of the most senior people behind the construction of this aircraft and he encouraged me to ask any questions I could think of, which I did.

I flew my sectors in the morning, and the other Qantas pilot with me, Mark Penklis, flew his sectors in the afternoon. On the first afternoon, Mark had an engine failure.

My first impressions of this aircraft were entirely positive. It was huge but it was quick; incredibly powerful, yet very quiet; it had a massive wingspan yet it was responsive. It felt just like the A330 – amazing given it was twice the size. Imagine if you took a car or a boat and doubled its size; you would expect the handling to be very different. But the A380's fly-by-wire was the same as the A330's, and the cockpit and controls were also the same. The control surfaces were larger, more numerous and improved, and the engineering of the larger aircraft was so superb that it was as agile as an Airbus A320 (which was one seventh the weight). One of the enhancements on the A380 over the A330 was the number of ailerons. On the A330 there are two ailerons on each wing while on the A380 there are three, giving it added agility and stability at cruise, and resilience to damage, which would be vindicated later. Ailerons roll the aircraft. If you are fortunate enough to fly in an A380, sit at a window above the wing and observe the ailerons during take-off or landing. If there's turbulence, watch the ailerons perform what is poetically called the 'Dance of the Ailerons'. The three ailerons (and two rudders) move independently to stop the wings flapping, the engines nodding, the fuselage jerking and the tail shaking like a dog that has just come out of the water. It is a majestic dance, it's the reason the A380 is famously smooth in flight, and it happens without anyone on the flight deck even touching a button.

As we flew south towards the French Riviera, along the Spanish border, then up the Atlantic coast towards Norway and back down over the Ruhr Valley, I didn't once have a feeling of flying a huge machine: it felt tidy, responsive and predictable. It did things with little drama. For instance, anyone who's flown in a Boeing 747 will know about the roar of the engines and slight shake of the airframe as the aircraft lifts off the tarmac and heads for the sky. The A380 used so little effort to take off and climb that all I could hear was a small whine from the engines at my first take-off: no shake, no roar and no drama. It banked and turned like a small plane, it landed superbly and, thanks to the three ailerons on each wing and the fly-by-wire stability systems, its cruise performance was the most stable and predictable I had ever flown.

*

Toulouse was quite seductive, and the town changed character at night when the streets turned into plazas with sidewalk bars and restaurants. We stayed in the old section of Toulouse and Coral came over for a week. We went driving with her sister Neralie through the south and then up to Normandy to see the de Crespigny ancestral home just up from Omaha Beach at Vierville-sur-Mer.

*

We returned to Sydney in June 2008, but the first Qantas A380 hadn't arrived. Qantas didn't want us going backwards by flying A330s again, so we cooled our heels and waited for the new plane and our new rosters.

I used this time to go through the A380 manuals – which were all electronic – and reverse-engineer the plane so I knew how everything worked and what the checklists would really mean if they ever came up on the ECAM.

On 19 September 2008, Qantas took delivery of the fourteenth A380 produced by Airbus and the sixth commercially available A380 (Singapore Airlines had taken the first five). Our aircraft was registered 'VH-OQA', and I remember seeing it fly into Sydney because I was running the half-marathon that day. It was huge and graceful, fast and quiet as it swept over Sydney Harbour.

Qantas named MSN 14 *Nancy-Bird Walton* in honour of the first woman to earn a commercial aviation licence in Australia. As it happened, she died on 13 January 2009, aged 93, but not before she attended the naming ceremony for that plane.

I was the second Qantas line pilot trained on A380s, but because the first pilot was assigned directly to training other pilots, I became the first A380 line pilot to fly a Qantas A380 when I flew Sydney–Los Angeles with Dave Evans in October 2008.

It was a most delightful and uneventful flight.

*

The arrival of the A380 on the international aviation scene was not a foregone conclusion. Its size and dimensions were such that even today – five years after Singapore Airlines put its first A380 into service – there are many airports that cannot comfortably accommodate the giant Airbus.

The A380 is called a 'Code F' aircraft in the international airport definitions. There are no aircraft bigger than Code F, and the only other Code F aircraft is the new Boeing 747–8. Other large planes, such as the earlier Boeing 747, 777, 787 and Airbus A330, 340 and 350, are all 'Code E', and even today there are many international airports that cannot accept Code E planes.

The coding is assigned to planes based on the wingspan and track of the landing gear. The coding is also assigned to airports: in order to accept Code E planes, an airport must have a certain width of runway, a certain width of taxiways and a minimum runway–taxiway separation so planes can pass one another without infringing each other's obstacle-free space.

Code E runways, for instance, must be at least 45 metres wide, but Code F runways must be 60 metres wide. The problem is that only the newer airports (i.e. Bangkok) fully support Code F standards, so the older Code E airports, such as Sydney, Changi, Los Angeles, London-Heathrow and Paris, have to restrict operations for A380 and 747–8 aircraft.

One of the anomalies is that the A380 can physically land at a Code E airport, but it can't always take off. This is because its landing gear track is so wide and the fuselage so long that it requires a 55 metre–wide turning area at the end of a runway in which to complete a U-turn so it can power-up and take off. This is not an issue when the runway ends are accessed by a taxiway, but when the taxiway connects midway along the runway and the turning circle at the end is smaller than 55 metres, the A380 can't make the 180-degree turn.

A few years ago, a Qantas A380 was diverted to Noumea, and when it tried to turn at the end of the runway to make its take-off it got halfway around the turning circle and couldn't make it. The airport sent out a tug to push the A380 back, but it didn't have enough power to move it. So they brought over another bigger tug and spent four hours pushing and pulling the A380 around the turning circle before it could straighten up for the runway. That scenario was made worse by the fact that the French airport markings (the traffic signals painted on the tarmac) are different to most other nation's airport markings and the Qantas pilot had tried to turn the wrong way, which would have been the right way at 99 per cent of all other airports.

Even the big airports have problems with the dimensions of the A380. At Los Angeles, the four runways are designated '24' and '25', of which there are 'Left' and 'Right' designations for both. The two 24 runways are to the north of the airfield, the two 25 runways to the south. Los Angeles controllers love us if we use 24L or 24R. The A380 is the only heavy aircraft with the performance to take off from the north runways so we can keep our operations to the north of the airport, have short taxi times and keep out of everyone else's way. It's not so pretty for the 25 runways. If we use runway 25R, the A380's wingspan infringes on the main southern taxiway and complicates movements in that area. The 747–8 will probably experience similar problems.

The A380 is here to stay and will become a mainstay of international long-haul hub-to-hub aviation. It's worth remembering that more than 80 per cent of all 747 movements occurred out of just 37 airports and a large percentage of these were in Asia. The A380 is perfect for this region, where most airports are 'slot-limited'; that is, they have take-off and landing times to limit congestion. Airlines can only make money flying through slot-limited airports if they carry the largest number of passengers per flight.

With the advent of the A380, the equation becomes more compelling for airlines wanting to fly through the increasingly popular and capacity-constrained Asia-Pacific hubs of Sydney, Singapore, Kuala Lumpur, Los Angeles, Bangkok, Shanghai and Hong Kong.

Qantas began their A380s with a four-class configuration that carried 450 passengers, but some of these aircraft are being changed to carry 484 passengers.

The absolute maximum number of passengers you can carry on an Airbus A380 is 853. This isn't the number you can physically accommodate within the fuselage – it's the number of passengers that Airbus demonstrated could be evacuated through half of the doors and down the emergency slides within 90 seconds. This is the certification test applied to all commercial aircraft.

More important to the people who run airlines is the length of sectors and the fuel usage: the longest Qantas sector is 16 hours 10 minutes (Dallas–Brisbane, 7900 nautical miles (14,630 kilometres)), and the Kangaroo Route to London is two sectors totalling 20 hours 12 minutes (Sydney–Singapore–London, 9633 nautical miles). Because of the long flight times, fuel efficiency and the cost per passenger-mile is crucial to making profits. The efficiency of the A380's wing, control surfaces and engines means this aircraft has an assured place in aviation's future.

While we're considering fuel efficiency, here are a few points to remember. Every drop of fuel and every knot of groundspeed counts on the long flights. So when we fly out of Sydney or Melbourne for Los Angeles, we bias our route to stay south so we catch the westerly winds, then dart across the equator in a northerly direction (where there's no wind), before turning right and picking up the Northern Hemisphere's prevailing westerly winds again into Los Angeles. On the way back to Australia

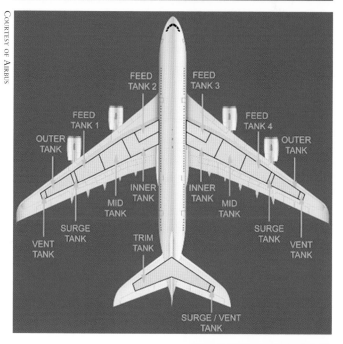

The A380 flight controls.

The A380 fuel tanks. Three of eleven were useable.

The pilots' seats on QF32.

My mother, Judith Patricia 'Patti' Champion de Crespigny (4 August 1930– 22 May 1974).

My family at Lorne, Victoria, in 1968. *Back*: Me, Michael and Simon. *Front*: Dad, Chris and Mum.

My brother Simon's Ariel Red Hunter (with the clutch intact).

Burning off testosterone at 'The Ponderosa' in 1974.

Wings Parade, 1979.

Graduating pilots of the RAAF 107 Pilots' Course, Pearce Air Force Base, Western Australia, December 1979. I am second row down, fourth from the right.

RAAF 107 Pilots'
Course, 1979
(Macchi jet).

On the wing of a refuelling Caribou, 1980.

Government House, Yarralumla, Canberra, 1982. *From left*: James Goldrick (Navy ADC), Brent Espeland (Comptroller), Sir Ninian Stephen, me, Rick Brine (Army ADC).

From left: Lady Stephen, the butler, me, a Federal policeman and Sir Ninian on board the BAC 1-11, 1982.

Governor-General Sir Zelman Cowen and me after a hit of tennis at Government House, Yarralumla, Canberra, 1982.

Helicopter submersion training at East Sale, 1983.

Me and my Iroquois helicopter, Tasmania, 1983.

Me in the Sinai Desert, 1984.

Coral in the Sinai Desert while visiting me at the Multi National Force and Observers base at El Gorah in December 1984.

Coral and me in Trysil, Norway, in March 1985.

77 Squadron – Fleet Support, 1985. I am to the left of the three white shirts in the third row.

'I do': 16 May 1987, St Mark's Church, Darling Point, Sydney.

Yikes! Sophia, Alexander and Coral, Whistler, Canada, 1993.

From left: Alexander, Coral, Sophia and me on a skiing holiday in Aspen, Colorado, in January 2010.

From left: Me, Coral, Dad, Mariea and two of my brothers, Michael and Christopher, in Alta, Utah, in February 2011.

Three generations in the cockpit of a Gulfstream V at
Avalon Airshow in 2009. Alexander, Dad and me.

From left: Me, Coral, Alexander, Sophia, Neil Armstrong and Dad on
board the *Lady Hopetoun* on Sydney Harbour, August 2011.

Coral: the wind beneath my wings.

Rolls-Royce presented Coral and me with the most extraordinary achievement in engineering – a Trent 900 High Pressure Turbine blade.

Sophia raising lion cubs at Inkwenkwezi Game Reserve, South Africa, 2009.

From left: Coral, Sophia, Alexander and me at Tembe Elephant Park, South Africa, in December 2009.

Coral and me on Sydney Harbour in our family fun boat in March 2012.

Mariea – my wonderful (wicked) stepmother and me.

Alex returning with empty tanks after a F/A-18 Hornet supersonic flight to heaven and back, RAAF Base, Williamtown, 2011.

Alex and Randy Neville, Boeing's 787 Chief Pilot in the 787 simulator in Seattle in January 2012.

from Los Angeles, we bias our route to spend more time flying west at the windless equatorial latitudes.

You might think this unbelievable, but some of the basic navigation techniques we used in the Caribous in the 1980s still come in handy on the A380. Although there are many radar systems that can predict whether the aircraft will travel over and clear the tops of a thunderstorm, pilots don't fully trust any of them, and the Earth's curvature and cloud distorts your view, making it hard to know if you will overfly the cloud that lies ahead. In the Caribou, we held a glass of water in front of our eyes and skimmed our eyesight over the top of the water's surface. This was a simple technique to find a level but it worked, and this trick is still used in the A380 – although a large 2-litre plastic water bottle delivers a much more reliable horizon!

As much as I loved the A380, and as incredible as it was to be the first line pilot on the new super-jumbo, my roster on the plane quickly dried up. Seven crews are required to keep one aircraft operating around the clock, and so we needed to train 84 crews for our twelve aircraft. The Toulouse gangs set up to fly the new aircraft found themselves edged out of the rosters with the flying going to the training department and the trainee A380 pilots.

Qantas is undergoing a shift in its fleet, from an ageing Boeing-intensive fleet to one where most of the long-haul flying will be done by Airbus A380s. So they're retiring old 747–400s and converting the senior pilots to A380s, which means there are too many A380 pilots as they wait for the new deliveries.

Someone has to miss out, and it is hard doing your regular simulator time and route checks when you are not spending time on the flight deck. When you fly a lot, you develop 'muscle memory' for the cockpit and the controls; your hands 'know' when and where to move at the right time. When you've flown an aircraft a lot and become used to it, the pilots say 'the aircraft fits like a glove'. It's a wonderful feeling when it happens, and uncomfortable when it doesn't. So you have to work twice as hard to stay current when you're not getting rosters. In order to stay current, we do time in the simulators and study manuals and updates. I normally spend about two hours studying every day just to keep current. While I stay active when not flying, I have only been flying 235 hours per year since converting to A380s and I think pilots should be doing at least 500 hours per year to perform at their peak.

This is not really a criticism. All airlines find it hard to match personnel exactly with their fleets. For instance, Qantas is currently phasing out its older 747s, 767s and 737s, not only because it's too expensive to keep these old airframes flying, but also because their systems are too old: the 767s and older 737s – believe it or not – have no GPS on board. The old fleets are also being retired in preparation for the arrival of the Boeing 787 *Dreamliner*, of which Qantas and Jetstar have ordered 50 between them. So the airline is starting to think about converting a whole lot of pilots to that new aircraft and, when it does, it will have the same frustration training pilots in time for those new aircraft as we had training pilots for the A380.

Anyway, I found myself in one of those periods where there were too many pilots and not enough planes. I focused on other plans including assembling data for my *Big Jets* book – a technical book for commercial pilots in large aircraft. I was fortunate to visit Airbus for a four-day period in July 2009, interviewing the test pilots, test engineers, design engineers and marketing staff. In 2010 I spent three days with Frank Ogilvie, who headed up the A380 aerodynamics team, and I visited the Rolls-Royce assembly plant in Derby, United Kingdom, where I was shown around the production line for the Trent 900 and met specialist Rolls-Royce engineers.

The knowledge I gained from these visits helped me understand the Airbus systems and gave me confidence when flying – something I was about to need on QF32.

CHAPTER 13

Pre-flight

The training and checking regime for Qantas international pilots is that they must pass four simulator tests per year as well as an annual safety procedures and route check. By November 2010, I'd done more checks in the A380 simulator at Sydney than landings in the aircraft. But there is little point in Qantas having an A380 captain just to let him become redundant, so the airline ensures they keep people like me 'current'.

And so it was that I passengered up to Singapore on the afternoon of 2 November 2010 with the task of bringing QF32 back to Sydney from Singapore. Harry Wubben would be the pilot checking me. However, in an unusual twist, Harry was training to become a check captain, so David Evans would be the check captain training and checking Harry to check me. As David Evans would later recount: 'It would be hard to find a more A380 experienced crew on the planet.'

On arrival in Singapore I checked into the hotel Qantas pilots always use – the Fairmont Hotel – read through my notes, called Coral and had an early night.

On the morning of the flight I ate breakfast in the hotel's restaurant and read Qantas's routine fax. It gave me a breakdown of the passenger numbers, the crew names, the meal numbers and requests, and the medical notifications. The passenger load was 319 and the meals booked were 310 (some people fall asleep and do not eat). The initial passengers were also broken into classes: FCL (first), JCL (business), PE (premium economy) and YCL (economy). I worked my way down the fax, noting the person flying for the first time, the elderly passengers (aged over 85) and those who spoke no English. Three passengers would arrive in wheelchairs. Last, I noted that Andrew Eccles, a Qantas A380 Second Officer, was passengering home in first class.

The night before, I'd phoned my flight crew – Matt Hicks (first officer) and Mark Johnson (second officer) – and said I looked forward to meeting them in the lobby of the hotel at 8.30 am. I'm not a stickler for hierarchy, but since captains fly with so many different crews it's important to the team dynamics that the captain be proactive. I like to set a happy and relaxed tone when we meet for the first time *before* we travel to the airport or take our places in the cockpit. This is not about ego; it's about organising people who hold great responsibility on their shoulders to quickly get focused into their roles within the team. I was forming the QF32 team and the crew needed clear instructions on what to expect. I also believe it is crucial for the flight crew to be as tight as a drum when they have other crew on the flight deck – in this case Harry and Dave. The two inspecting pilots would only observe the flight, playing no part in the operation of the aircraft, but there would still be five pilots on the flight deck where there would usually be three. I wanted to ensure we were a tight and effective crew.

Under Australia's Civil Aviation Regulations the person designated 'pilot-in-command' takes full responsibility for the aircraft and the people in it, and therefore has the ultimate authority. Once the pilot-in-command has signed for the aircraft, which they do before the doors are armed and the pushback starts, the aircraft is 'theirs'. The flight deck is not like a committee. Everything that happens between signing for the aircraft and handing over the aircraft after landing is the responsibility of the 'pilot-in-command'. Hundreds of lives are at stake and so, just like in the military, the position requires a disciplined person with knowledge, training, experience and credibility who can pay attention to detail, make and commit to decisions and lead effective teams. It's an awesome responsibility, and with it comes absolute authority.

I knew Matt because I'd flown on A330s with him in the past, but I had never met Mark before. We introduced ourselves, then Dave and Harry arrived. I'd flown once with

Dave Evans in the past and I knew Harry well. The conversation was relaxed despite the fact that either Dave or Harry could end my career that day with a 'fail' on the route check.

During the twenty-minute drive to the airport I told Matt and Mark I was undergoing a route check and to tell me if I stuffed up, though they might like to prioritise when to tell me. I emphasised the fact we were a team and there was no room for ego, and told them not to worry about Dave and Harry. I always mention prioritising comments and checking your ego at the airport door because I like my crew to be focused, helpful and timely for the team, not trying to prove something.

When we arrived at Changi, I sat down with Matt and Mark in the airline serviced offices. At Changi these have computer work stations, faxes and telexes, and cubicles where aviation professionals can meet and receive and send their correspondences, usually to a head office on the other side of the world.

The dispatch officer passed me a satchel containing 100 A4-sized pages. The captain has to know everything in that briefing document, and we give ourselves ten to fifteen minutes to read it, decide what we will do and order the fuel to be loaded onto the aircraft. I doled out the nine pages of critical (operational one) and 41 pages of non-critical (operational two) notices to Matt and Mark respectively. I studied the weather forecasts, flight plan and engineering notices. The three of us speed-read the 100 pages in five minutes, calling out any issues that would affect the operation. Our documents included a warning about a volcano eruption on Java that had created an ash cloud up to 60,000 feet – it was a code red, meaning it was dangerous.

Along with the turbulence warnings, we had pages of weather briefs for airports we might have to divert to: Adelaide, Darwin, Perth, Brisbane, Cairns, Jakarta and Denpasar.

Mark looked through operational two, which had the updates on runway conditions, radio frequencies and the state of the instrument landing systems (ILS) at relevant airports, which included all the airports an aircraft might have to land at if something were to go wrong en route.

I called the Qantas meteorologist in Sydney who told me the ash cloud was at 35,000 feet and heading west, so we planned a route that took us north of the ash cloud. I saw that Harry had taken a seat near our briefing table but was not involving himself. This was normal for a route check.

We were also given a published route for 'A576' (the standard Qantas route Singapore–Sydney) showing the 23 waypoints and the location of the volcanic ash cloud. The waypoints on our routes were loaded into the flight computer but we still had to know them in case we lost the flight computers and had to revert to standard navigation. We also had a weather plot of all the winds coming from Africa to New Zealand, the wind speeds and temperatures at various altitudes and any weather warnings.

The pre-flight briefing always contains the safety heights on the route: so flying out of Changi our 'safety height' was 5000 feet and over Bali it was 15,800 feet. These are minimum altitudes we cannot fly below on the designated air route.

Last and most important was the weight and fuel calculation. Even with all the computers and fly-by-wire systems, the captain still has to sign off on the fuel order, the take-off weight, the fuel burn off and the landing weight.

Head office in Sydney had allocated me 103.7 tonnes of aviation fuel, which would leave us with 14.4 tonnes of fuel when we landed at Sydney. But, having heard about the volcanic ash cloud and the new route to get around it, I ordered an extra 2 tonnes of fuel. That would give us about twelve minutes' extra flying time.

I asked Matt and Mark to call out points of interest and I took notes. Then, having assembled the full picture of our route, I asked for them to appraise the situation. It was through this process that I got the best picture of how much fuel I needed and which route I should take to get around the ash cloud.

Having committed to a fuel loading and faxed Qantas HQ in Sydney with the revised fuel amount and the new route, we left the offices and moved through the security gates and the departure lounge. At the gate I was handed the 'load sheet'. The load sheet is a legal document that states the name of the plane, the route, the weights for the passengers and crew, the fuel loaded and the take-off weight. It also designates the pilot-in-command.

We moved into the cockpit and took our seats, and I checked the load sheet. It listed five technical crew (pilots) and 24 cabin crew, along with fourteen First Class, 62 Business Class, 32 Premium Economy and 332 Economy passengers. There wasn't a spare seat in economy.

There were no dangerous goods on board and we had a take-off weight of 465,803 kilograms (aircraft, passengers, crew, catering, fuel, oil, water), which made us a very full plane. Weight is a major obsession with the aviation industry: weight doesn't just translate to safety at take-off and during flying, but also to profits. Your fuel efficiency becomes greater with less weight to carry around and so you have some airlines getting rid of shutters on the windows and head protectors; and all airlines are very careful about loading too much food or fuel. On a plane the size of the Airbus A380, the paint job alone weighs 1000 kilograms. Of course, some airlines go the other way: on the Emirates version of the A380 there's a bar and showers, which adds a lot of weight to their load equation.

I then opened and perused the 'technical log' – an engineering booklet in which faults and problems with the plane are documented. One of the comments on the technical log, from the London–Singapore leg, was a note about a possible bird strike to the nose or tail area. So I sent Mark out to make a careful examination for damage and tell me what he saw.

I don't wear a watch – I don't want to feel time pressures and I don't want to push them onto my crews, and I don't mind if I delay the plane for safety reasons. While Mark was walking around the plane, I read the 'load sheet' and Matt initialised the controls and started up the systems. I leaned towards Matt and told him there was no rush. I always say this to my crews. It sets the tone of our working environment, ensuring we all put the safety of the operation before the schedule. After the aircraft engineers, airport and catering staff have prepared the aircraft, the pilots are the last line of defence to protect the passengers and crew; we're the final safety check.

I signed at the top of the load sheet. This load sheet stays with the first officer at all times – if I ever have to make an unscheduled landing in an unexpected country, or if there's an accident, the first thing the police and airport authorities ask for is the load sheet.

Mark returned and said there was no evidence of a bird strike.

Next, the engineer responsible for the fuel loading delivered the refuelling log to me, and Matt, Mark and I read it and cross-checked the sheet with our own onboard systems.

The airport manager's representative then delivered a passenger manifest to me that contained the final count of who actually boarded the plane and what their seat number was.

By now we had a load sheet, an engineer's report, the re-fueller's report and the passenger manifest.

In the process of receiving these pieces of paperwork I had worked out the take-off performance: the runway condition, the wind, air pressure, temperature and weight that we put together to find the optimum thrust and flaps configuration for take-off.

I spent about five minutes briefing Matt and Mark of threats, aircraft status, route, special notices, take-off performance and weather, and then addressed important contingencies. An engine failure is the primary threat we always face for a take-off, so I outlined what I would do in that scenario.

I finished my brief and asked if anyone had any questions or comments.

Matt immediately replied, 'Nah, just don't crash!'

Then the cabin services manager, Michael von Reth, asked if he could instruct his crew to close all the aircraft doors.

Up until this point the airport manager had authority over the plane and passengers. If he had wanted to board a passenger that others thought was drunk, for instance, technically he had the authority to do so. But now the doors were closed and Australian law passed the responsibility for the safety of the 468 passengers and crew to me. I would be responsible for everything that happened until the end of the flight and the doors opened in Sydney. (If the airport manager had loaded the drunken passenger on my flight, now I would have the authority to re-open a door and eject the drunk.)

We were ready . . . almost.

I had something else to take care of. There was a potentially strange situation on the flight deck of QF32. I was the captain and the pilot-in-command of the aircraft, yet there were two senior pilots checking me. Even so, I was the pilot-in-command and I didn't like where Harry was sitting. The A380 cockpit is designed so the captain sits at the front left and the first officer (Matt) sits at the front right. Normally the second officer (Mark) sits in an 'observer seat' that is between Matt and me, but behind and elevated. This is a good configuration because the second officer plays a meaningful backup role to the captain and the first officer – they see all of the controls and are in a position to assist the other pilots. More important, the middle seat has its own radio panel with frequency selectors, transmit buttons and volume controls.

Harry had taken this middle chair, pushing Mark to the left rear observer's seat, one without a radio panel. I was very concerned. I had gone to great effort to 'form' my team as we'd travelled to the airport, but Harry was now interfering.

I released the lock to my seat, slid it backwards and turned sideways to Harry with my arms folded and asked where he was intending to sit.

Harry said, 'In this seat between you and Matt.'

'I've got a problem with that, Harry – you're inhibiting my crew.'

Harry didn't seem too fazed, and asked what I wanted him to do.

'I want Mark in that seat, thanks Harry,' I said.

Harry was now shocked and said incredulously: 'But Rich, I can't see you if I sit in Mark's seat. How can I check you?'

'That's your problem,' I said. 'I want my crew together and I want Mark in your seat!'

The air chilled as Dave Evans said, 'Richard, you're being unreasonable. Harry has to check you, he has to sit there.'

'He's right,' Harry said. 'I have to check you, Richard.'

'That's your problem, Harry. I have a flight to command and I want my crew operating properly.'

I think Harry could see my point. He had overseen the pre-flight checks and finals; he'd checked for what he had to check for and he should have vacated that seat.

There are five stages of team-building: forming, norming, storming, performing and adjourning. I had formed the team in the bus, normed at the airport and in the flight deck (with SOPs, briefings and checks), and now I was storming (dealing with fractures and disagreements).

Harry could see the stalemate. He came to the rescue: 'Look, Richard, if it helps, I promise I'll be the second officer if I have to be.'

'Fantastic, thank you, Harry,' I said, trying to defuse the situation.

I now had two second officers supporting me; I had my team back together, and so I was happy. Win-win!

'Let's go,' I told Matt.

I asked Matt for a pushback clearance. He pressed the transmit switch on his sidestick: 'Singapore Clearance, Good Morning. Qantas 32 Super for Sydney, Bay Charlie 23, 469 Persons on Board – ready for start and push.'

The controller replied ten seconds later with our clearance: 'Good Morning. Qantas 32 cleared for pushback and start, face north for Runway Two-Zero Centre.'

On most Qantas international flights there is a three-minute wait between when the last door is closed and the pushback really begins. This period allows for Qantas Load Control to finalise our A380's weight, fuel distribution and balance, and confirm the aircraft is within the centre–of-gravity limits to take off. When Load Control is happy, they send us a coded message with vital performance statistics that we send to our flight management and flight control computers.

To get this final loading, operations in Sydney runs the weights through sophisticated software and calculates where the plane is carrying most of its weight, and how, therefore, to trim the plane for take-off. Mostly this involves operations telling us how to trim, or 'set', the horizontal stabiliser, which is the wing that sits at the base of the A380's massive tail. The entire wing pivots on a horizontal axle and it has elevators on its rear edge. This crucial configuration is designed to ensure the aircraft is trimmed to maintain the initial climb-out speed. Pre-trimming the aircraft this way provides the pilots with a consistent 'feel' and response for every take-off regardless of the weight and position of the centre of gravity, and makes it easier to maintain a consistent take-off at any weight and thrust, and on any runway.

It's a truly remarkable experience being in control of an A380 that is taking off. There is no other experience like it. While you accelerate along the runway, hundreds of computers measure and monitor the 250,000 sensors in the engines, hydraulics, flight controls and the rest of the four million parts. The take-off is critical; most of the warnings are filtered out so that the pilots are not distracted by trivia. For every second we spend charging down the runway, we have two seconds less time to reject the landing and stop if something goes wrong. It's a tug of war: we have to accelerate to take off, but we have to be able to stop if something goes critically wrong and the aircraft cannot fly. We end up catering for the likely failures like an engine failure, but hoping that the catastrophic failures like two engine failures don't happen until we are safely flying away. This might sound frightening but it's not. For a take-off to be dangerous in a commercial jet, we'd have to lose two engines on one side before reaching a safe height. One jet aircraft takes off every second around the world, and on average an engine fails only once in every 300,000 engine hours. I'm not aware of two engines ever failing at the same critical time on take-off. So it's safe – very safe! Take-off is an absolutely remarkable achievement for propulsion, engineering and safety.

We pushed back and taxied out, and had a slight delay in the taxi: Changi Airport has a runway which can impinge on military airspace, so there are two altitude constraints on commercial traffic: SUDPO 2000, which is a requirement to get to 2000 feet by a certain waypoint; followed by SUSIN 4000, which means you have to be at 4000 feet by the second waypoint.

The A380 and most 747s can't make SUDPO 2000, and so they have to warn Air Traffic Control and request to have the SUDPO restriction removed. Before I could ask Matt to make the call to Air Traffic Control, Harry leaned over and reminded Matt to call ATC for a waiver on SUDPO 2000.

This meant Harry was indeed being an active second officer.

We had programmed the engine to provide 72 per cent of full thrust, and selected 'FLAPS 2' for take-off, which gives a good trade-off between gaining speed quickly and maximum lift. If I'd selected 'FLAPS 1' it would have given us the highest performance after take-off, but it requires more thrust to gain the higher take-off speed. Airlines are particular about thrust: using the top thrust settings burns a lot of fuel and shortens the maintenance cycle of the jet engines.

Singapore tower: 'Qantas 32 – Clear for take-off, Runway Two-Zero Centre.'

Every A380 take-off is a technological marvel, and the beginning of a process where every bit of knowledge, training, experience and teamwork might be put to the ultimate test. So like all pilots, we had prepared for the worst and since it was my annual route check, I was hoping for the best, a smooth ride and a faultless sector.

'Take-off!'

With a firm wide grip I pushed the four large thrust levers from their idle position, forward through about a 50-degree angle to the take-off setting. The engines, flight instruments and aircraft systems responded. As the aircraft's fuel flow increased to 14 litres of fuel per second, each engine's bleed valves closed to engage the 113,000 horsepower turbochargers. It took about twenty seconds for the engines' giant 2.95 metre-diameter fans to slowly rev up to the take-off setting where the fan tips are travelling well in excess of the speed of sound. At full thrust, each engine provided 72,000 pounds of thrust with each of its 24 fan blades sucking in 1.2 tonnes of air per second. To put this into perspective, for every eight seconds at full thrust, all four engines suck in all the air a person would breathe in a 100-year life.

Nancy-Bird Walton responded. She surged forward down the runway, 465 tonnes of the most advanced machinery accelerating faster than almost every road car. Yet it's so smooth and quiet inside that the passengers barely lower their newspapers to notice that they are in a 'rocket sled', beginning what will become the ride of their life.

During the take-off, only operational topics may be discussed. This state is called a 'sterile cockpit'. My job was to make sure we were on the runway and Matt's job as the first officer was to peruse the engine gauges and confirm the engines were working normally. He called, 'Thrust set,' and then, '100 knots.'

A few seconds after accelerating through 100 knots the flight warning computers call 'V1'. V1 is the speed that provides enough control to continue the take-off if an engine fails, but normally too much speed to be able to reject the take-off and stop on the remaining runway. So when I hear 'V1' I know the option to reject the take-off has passed. This important change in take-off strategy is displayed physically by the captain moving his hands away from the throttles. And that's what I did. My left hand was now holding the sidestick, and my right hand was on my knee. Whatever happened, we were getting airborne!

Next Matt called, 'Rotate,' and I pulled back on the sidestick, lifting the nose into the air. When the aircraft pitch reached 12.5 degrees nose up, I released my pull on the stick. The sidestick returned to the neutral position. With the sidestick 'stick-free', the fly-by-wire software now commanded a constant 'G', which in effect keeps the attitude constant. The aircraft locks on to the pitch and airspeed, and everything is stable – magic!

It was 9.57 am.

Now, the aircraft that everyone thinks 'is too heavy to fly' launches into the sky. It's an orchestra with 250,000 musicians – put together at a cost of €12 billion (US$16 billion), proving 110 years of aviation research and development. And the best part is I'm the conductor.

CHAPTER 14

Boom! . . . BOOM!

We took off that day into the southwest and lifted off with plenty of spare runway remaining. I raised the nose, aiming for the next waypoint, SUSIN at 4000 feet, engaged the auto-thrust, then called, 'Flap 1.' Matt retracted the flaps one step, which reduced the drag and increased the climb angle. For the pilots, this change in performance is dramatic as the thrust increases 15 per cent to 87 per cent full thrust; for the passengers, it's barely noticeable other than a slight increase in sound and a more pronounced push in the back as we climbed and accelerated away.

From a performance perspective, the take-off and climb from Singapore is very comfortable. The four Rolls-Royce RB211 Trent 900 engines are so powerful and the A380 wing is so well designed that not much thrust is required to make the plane meet its performance requirements.

I couldn't miss crossing the next waypoint or I'd fail my route check, so I made sure we crossed SUSIN at precisely 4000 feet. I was pleased; most of the difficult work was behind us. At this point we continued to climb, banked left following our route towards the southeast, then selected 'FLAPS 0' to retract the flaps and leading edge slats, and accelerated to 250 knots, our intermediate climb speed. For a normal aircraft, the changing thrust, flap settings and speed would all cause the aircraft to pitch up and down – changes that have to be countered by the pilot – but on the A380 it's seamless. The flight control computers automatically trim the horizontal stabiliser to minimise drag and optimise performance.

We were tracking the few remaining legs from Singapore that would align us with our route to Sydney, which would take us through 23 waypoints that include locations such as Bali, Curtin, Alice Springs and Parkes.

After the flaps were retracted, I called, 'After take-off checklist.' This is a command to Matt to call up the ECAM (Electronic Centralised Aircraft Monitoring) checklist that checks the aircraft has been 'cleaned up' after the take-off phase and is now in the right configuration to accelerate and climb towards our cruising altitude. If something is not right with the plane, or if we'd forgotten to action something, we would usually get our first hint of it in this post take-off check. The ECAM 'After take-off' checklist senses that the landing gear, flaps and slats are already retracted, the APU is shut down and other items are satisfied, so the checklist displays all these items in a greyed font – which means that there are no additional items to action. It's that simple.

Matt looked at ECAM. There was nothing to report.

During this time it was still a 'sterile cockpit' – no one talked unless required. Everyone was intensely focused on what they were doing and they didn't want distractions. ECAM also supported this sterile cockpit. During take-off the ECAM – which collects inputs from 250,000 sensors around the plane – dynamically filters the information provided on screen to what is important during that phase. All ECAM warnings were inhibited during the take-off above 80 knots except those warnings that would have recommended I abort the take-off. Once we climbed through 1500 feet, with the runway well behind us and the risks subsiding, most of ECAM's 1225 messages and checklists now became enabled.

We were now climbing at 2000 feet per minute up to 10,000 feet, and while we were starting to relax there would be no idle chatter until we climbed through 20,000 feet. We were picking up speed, it was a beautiful day, and I was looking at the radar screen for a hint about the weather that lay ahead. The cabin crew wanted to start serving and I had to ensure we were clear of clouds, thunderstorms and turbulence before I could turn off the 'seatbelts' sign. The weather radar was clear and, as we passed through 7400 feet, I was sure the passengers would be thinking just how true the stories they had heard about the luxurious A380 were. The cabin was spacious, with comfortable seats and a fantastic video screen showing the aircraft with the ground streaking past below. And it was so quiet.

At 10.01 am I was about to turn off the seatbelt signs when . . .

BOOM.

I looked to my right to see if Matt had heard it too.

BOOM! This one was louder than the first and the airframe shuddered.

'Bing-bing-bing-bing-bing . . .' The master warning system was set off.

The first sound was like a backfiring car, and could easily have been the noise resulting from an engine surge we get from time to time on the big jets. A surge occurs when the high-pressure air travels from the combustion chamber backwards through the compressors and out through the engine intake. Jet engines can recover from a surge condition and the flight might even be able to continue to destination.

But the second boom was like nothing I'd experienced before. Two booms one second apart. Was it the first engine having more grief or had I lost another engine? There was no time to think . . .

'Bing-bing-bing-bing-bing . . .'

There were two master warning lights: one in front of Matt's eyes and one in front of mine. Big red lights to grab our attention in only the worst emergencies. They were both lit up in brilliant red.

My mind raced, my senses of sight, sound and touch were in overdrive. Then the benefits of my hours spent training for engine failures in the simulator kicked in.

My first reaction to the booming sounds and the master warning was instinctive – I hit the 'altitude hold' button, which told the autopilot to lower the nose and level the aircraft at the current altitude.

Matt hit the 'master warning' pushbutton to cancel the red light and the 'bing-bing' alert. He then instinctively started the aircraft's stopwatch – if this was a standard engine problem we would have it secured within 30 seconds.

I knew our safety height was 2100 feet, so I knew we could stop the climb and still remain safely above nearby mountains. By hitting the altitude hold and dropping the nose the auto-thrust should immediately reduce engine thrust to maintain our selected speed of 250 knots, an action that would reduce stress on the engines and airframe.

I learned this technique from a fellow Qantas pilot and ex-US Navy F-14 top-gun pilot. I was a passenger in his B767 aircraft travelling from Melbourne to Sydney in 2001. We were climbing through about 15,000 feet – about ten minutes after taking off from Melbourne – and I remember turning to another passenger-pilot beside me and remarking that the engine beside us sounded very loud. In fact it reminded me of a lawnmower– and the last time I'd said that about an engine, it blew up!

Ten seconds later . . . *KABOOM!*

The engine exploded! A massive fan blade had separated from its hub at the front of the engine, punctured the engine nacelle immediately in line with me before screaming sideways and narrowly missing the fuselage. The entire aircraft rocked and vibrated violently. My first thoughts were that either a bomb had exploded or a passenger door had been blown out of the aircraft. I was sitting only 4 metres from the engine. I was lucky the blade didn't penetrate the cabin.

After a few moments I heard the engine's revolutions winding down and the aircraft's violent shaking gave way to a quick rocking – the seats, overhead lockers, everything was rocking to and fro quickly, but not violently.

The pilot had reduced the stress in the airframe and inside the cabin dramatically. We got back to the ground in one piece with everyone on board shaken but uninjured. It was an amazing piece of flying, to get the violent rocking under control so quickly, and I caught up with the pilot after the incident and asked how he'd shut down the thrust so fast. 'I didn't,' he said. 'I just hit the altitude hold button.' It was a classic example of airmanship at its best.

So as the second 'BOOM' on QF32 shook the cockpit, I hit the altitude hold. The nose dropped but I didn't hear the engines come back to idle. The speed was increasing. Something was wrong! At this point I knew we were dealing with a serious problem. The airframe was still shaking from the second explosion and there was no engine reaction to the 'altitude hold' – not in terms of sounds or the controls. So I instinctively pulled back on the thrust levers, taking thrust from 95 per cent down to idle to de-stress the situation. After a few seconds I realised the auto-thrust system had failed. It was a very bad sign – the auto-thrust is at the heart of the fly-by-wire philosophy. It should not fail – but, if it does, then something is seriously wrong.

I was trying to stabilise the aircraft. I had locked it to a constant altitude, locked the thrust to maintain a constant 250 knots airspeed, and I'd locked the heading, all of it manually. I was confident I had control. We were flying and we were safe for now.

I had to keep the plane in the air so I just sat there and watched the displays for a few seconds – until I was confident everything was stable and I could include other scans into my field of view. We were still a 'sterile cockpit' – I was the only person who spoke, reading out the 'flight mode annunciator' status from the display in front of me. It showed that our altitude and heading were holding steady and autopilot 1 was engaged. There was shock around me as the other pilots waited for me to speak. With the aircraft flying straight and level, and at a constant speed, I now focused on the engine and warning display, the top display in the middle of the instrument panel. Engine 2 looked very sick. All of the sensors for thrust, temperature and pressures were replaced with crosses telling us there was no data to display. It appeared that all the sensors had been blown off that engine. This was a catastrophic failure.

But I felt confident the plane wanted to stay in the air for now and I knew we had a serious problem with Engine 2. So I broke the silence.

'ECAM actions,' I said, and Matt charged into action.

*

ECAM (Electronic Centralised Aircraft Monitoring) is a computer program that tells you what is wrong with the plane and makes suggestions about how to resolve it.

In the Airbus, the ECAM not only tells you what is wrong and gives you the 'fix', it also intelligently prioritises the problem, so you deal with fire, for instance, before an overheated engine, or a data link error. ECAM's instructions evolve as the damage is detected and fixed, so you're always fixing problems in the order Airbus intended.

The first ECAM warning checklist that morning was 'ENGINE 2 TURBINE OVERHEAT'. The checklist's first instruction was to move the number 2 thrust lever to idle. Matt called the action and I moved the lever (only the flying pilot touches the thrust levers). The second item was to move the 'Engine 2 master switch to off' – this shuts off high-pressure fuel flow inside the engine and closes down the engine. I was guarded about that because when you shut an engine down you might lose the ability to restart it later.

Then the threat changed. Matt suddenly found himself at the top of a new checklist – 'ENGINE 2 FIRE'. The ECAM had detected indications of a fire in Engine 2 and so prioritised that procedure to the top. The fire checklist appeared and then disappeared so quickly that I don't remember seeing it. I was busy flying the aircraft and keeping a broad assessment of the whole situation, so I was not preoccupied with the ECAM checklists.

Fire on a plane is something to be feared, and the explosion followed by the frenetic and confusing alerts had put us in a flurry of activity, but Matt and I kept our focus on our assigned tasks. The ECAM line instructed 'Fire bottle – push in 30 seconds', then began counting down the time delay before we would action the checklist item. This pause gave me the ideal opportunity to notify air traffic control of our problem and to make a PAN call. PAN is a message to air traffic control indicating a situation that requires priority. I pressed the transmit button on my sidestick and calmly transmitted: 'PAN PAN PAN, Qantas 32, engine failure, maintaining 7400, and current heading.'

The Singapore Approach controller replied: 'Qantas 32 copied.'

Air traffic control could now monitor our predicted track, vector other aircraft clear of us and keep us above any obstacles.

Shortly after that I made another call: 'QF32, Engine 2 appears failed. Heading 150, maintaining 7400 feet, we'll keep you informed and will get back to you in five minutes.'

This call made it clear that we were now giving the instructions, not asking for them, and that, when it suited us, we would make other demands. The intent of this succinct radio call was to impress on ATC that we were focusing on the problem and didn't want distracting radio calls from them. It worked a treat. ATC left us alone, but monitored us and notified other airport and rescue services that we had declared an emergency. In just ten seconds we had sorted out ATC and taken control.

Aviate, navigate, communicate. With these three golden rules now satisfied, my attention was then directed back to ECAM.

The ECAM checklists started with engines, hydraulics, flight controls, then fuel, each of them with a series of fixes we had to perform to see if we could get the problem under control. The explosions had obviously started a fire and disabled an engine, which we'd shut down, hopefully containing or extinguishing the fire. But the fix for the fire in Engine 2 was only the beginning of it: Engines 1, 3 and 4 were degraded in different forms, the fuel system was in a total mess, the hydraulics and electrics and pneumatics were plundered, and even our flight controls were compromised.

Any of these problems alone could disable an aircraft – having the hydraulics and electrics on the blink is a potentially catastrophic situation when you consider all the control surfaces in an Airbus run on hydraulics and electrics. Yet, unknown to us, we had a bigger headache.

We knew one fuel pump had failed, but after a few minutes we realised five more had also failed. This, along with other failures, prevented us shifting fuel around the aircraft to ensure the engines could keep firing.

We were barely seven minutes into this nightmare, still heading southeast with severe engine problems, and now moving on to process the hydraulic checklists. The main ECAM page was bad enough – so many serious checklists. There was a sea of red lights above us on the overhead panel, and pages of red synoptic displays spewed up failed systems from all over the plane. The problems with the fuel tanks and hydraulics, in particular, were growing. The ECAM system was becoming overwhelming.

Matt suddenly looked up from the screen. I looked over and I could see it in his eyes: he was worried. In fact he was now thinking that we could end up in the water. Matt suggested we turn back for Changi. Matt is absolutely one of the best FOs in Qantas; I had flown with him before and he had my complete respect. I had thought of turning back to Singapore at about the same time, but I did not want to stop Matt and distract him from these critical ECAM checklists while I made the ATC request. The aircraft was flying, and at that time we were safe above the hills. But I think Matt had reached his critical point and he wanted to head towards lower terrain and the security of Singapore.

CHAPTER 15

The Armstrong Spiral (HAC)

By this stage to any observer, the cockpit would have appeared to be in utter chaos. We had to deal with continual alarms sounding, a sea of red lights and seemingly never-ending ECAM checklists. We were all in a state of disbelief that this could actually be happening.

When they recruit pilots, the Air Force and commercial airlines look for confident personality types that tend not to panic. As pilots, we learn to control our stress and minimise the adrenaline rush in panic situations and keep our reasoning going.

We were worried, but our training kicked in. We knew every part of the A380. I had been flying for 35 years and had over

15,000 hours of flying experience, plus at least a thousand hours in simulators experiencing stressful scenarios. The aircraft was flying and, although our heartbeats were elevated, we knew we needed to stay calm and in control.

There were five pilots on the QF32 flight deck, but we operated the aircraft exactly as per Airbus SOPs – as a two-pilot aircraft. We had three extra pilots behind us as a resource – for delegated duties, monitoring and to offer assistance. In a flight deck team, you never have all pilots focusing on the same functions: you have task sharing, which means each pilot is responsible for their activity, and together they support each other. Matt's job was to read out and action the ECAMs, and that was occupying 100 per cent of his time. My job was to fly the aircraft, maintain a global situational awareness, monitor Matt's actions and make the radio calls to ATC. There was no confusion. The other three pilots monitored and assisted us.

There is a real danger in flight decks where there are surplus pilots. It would be easy for everyone to be distracted into looking at one area, meanwhile the aircraft flies into a hill or runs out of fuel. In an infamous accident, an aircraft did just this: the pilots were preoccupied running through a long checklist and failed to share tasks and monitor the fuel on board, so they ran out of fuel, and crashed.

It is even more common for 'group think' syndrome to take hold, where individuals who detect faults fail to expose them because they believe the group is more intelligent and more correct. The 'group think' problem is remarkably prevalent in crews augmented with management and checking captains, because junior pilots feel intimidated.

I had been clear on the drive to the airport and in the discussion about Harry's seat just before pushback of what the team responsibilities were and how the team would function. It was going to plan. I remember telling Mark when he was standing behind me: 'If we are all looking down, then you look up. If we are all looking up, then you look down.' Harry and Dave were watching us, Mark was supporting us, and we were working together.

I thought about Matt's request. Returning to Singapore had to be a safer option than continuing south-eastwards and trying to fix the plane. The checklists were still coming – they didn't stop. It was like taking a plate from the top of a plate dispenser in a cafeteria – it would simply be replaced with another. We did one checklist after another, and they kept coming – serious checklists, ugly checklists. I was getting concerned at just how much of our aircraft had failed and what we'd be left with. There was no way to know if the problems could be resolved or if one of those problems would suddenly be the reason we could no longer fly the plane.

I pressed the transmit switch for VHF radio 1 to our air traffic controllers: 'Singapore, Qantas 32, we require a left turn back towards Singapore to hold while we fix our problems.'

I breathed deeply to control my stress and proceeded to bank that huge, crippled aircraft as gently as I could. I had no idea what such a manoeuvre would do to our chances of staying in the air. The aircraft was flying smoothly, but the extent of our problems with hydraulics and electrics was so great I couldn't determine how much it would affect our flying performance. Something as basic as a turn might cause something else to break. As we turned northward, I asked Dave to make a PA to the passengers assuring them they were safe. Dave's initial PA was brilliant, textbook perfect and broadcast calmly. It did a great deal early on to inform and calm both the passengers and crew. But besides telling the passengers that we were in control of the plane and were dealing with technical issues before landing, I saw no advantage in going into too much detail.

I think it was the longest banking turn ever completed in an A380, and when we were finally heading north, and everyone had stopped holding their breath, we got back to work.

The fuel system had so many failures and was leaking from so many points it was hard to know where to start. Looking at the fuel synoptic page, I thought we had leaks in the feed tanks for Engine 1 and Engine 2 as well as the transfer tank that sits in the left wing and fills the feed tanks. We had a fuel jettison valve failed open, slashed fuel transfer galleries, we had failed main and standby fuel pumps in feed tank 2, and we had failed transfer pumps for the left inner fuel tank.

We had very hot pneumatic bleed-air leaking from slashed ducts in the left wing. And a low reservoir air pressure over the hydraulic oil that prevents the hydraulic pumps cavitating, meaning degraded hydraulics. Some of our fire extinguishing systems had failed and, as we worked the lists, our control surfaces came up damaged too: aileron actuator faults, outer ailerons damaged, mid ailerons damaged, backup emergency electric aileron actuators failed. It was an extraordinary amount of damage – more than I'd ever seen or imagined before, and more damage than an Airbus aircraft had ever experienced in the air.

It was now about twelve minutes since the engine had exploded. I didn't like the rate of fuel loss or the lack of ability to pump fuel to our engine feed tanks. So I made another decision shortly after we'd made the turn for Changi.

'Qantas 32, request climb to 10,000 feet and keep us within 30 miles of the airport.'

I wanted enough altitude so we could glide back to Changi should we need to. Emergency glide and forced landings were part of the standard syllabus in the Air Force. In one of my early RAAF Macchi jet flights over the Indian Ocean more than 30 years earlier, our Macchi's engine developed a vibration which got progressively worse. My instructor asked me what I wanted to do, and I said I didn't like the sound of the engine or the way it was shaking the airframe. So I took the aircraft to altitude in preparation for an emergency glide and forced landing, should our only engine fail. Now, in the A380, I had the same instinct.

Singapore Approach replied: 'Qantas 32 roger. Climb to 10,000 feet.'

The atmosphere in the cockpit suddenly changed. Harry and Dave, and then Matt and Mark, all said 'No!' The thought of trying to climb with such a damaged aircraft seemed crazy to them – they thought I was talking about a maximum-thrust climb. They thought we were lucky enough to be in one piece and still airborne, and they didn't want to be in the air when another engine failed or the fuel leaks increased, which a sudden change in attitude might trigger. I had the call and I had also dialled 10,000 feet into the altitude selector without discussion. But the other four pilots were adamant: they wanted to get the plane lower, not higher.

I think Dave took particular exception to my plan. From what he could see on the ECAM, he initially thought we might actually be flying on only one engine: Engine 2 had failed and showed 'XX' (no data). Engine 3 had been switched into an alternate mode and the thrust was degraded by 4 per cent. And although Engines 1 and 4 were notionally operating, they showed 'XX' in their thrust indicators – no data. Dave was technically right: it was possible we were flying on one normal engine, and trying to coax more thrust out of it to climb to 10,000 feet might have been a bridge too far. It might have forced a further incident in an already heavily compromised aircraft.

The other pilots perhaps wanted to make a sprint for Changi, but I was prepared to be slower arriving at Changi in order to have an ace up our sleeves: what I called the 'Armstrong Spiral'.

Neil Armstrong, before he went to the moon with NASA, was a NACA test pilot who used to fly rocket-powered planes out of the Earth's atmosphere. Once they'd spent their fuel breaking through the atmosphere, the pilots used small impulse rockets to lower the nose and steer their planes to re-enter the atmosphere and then glide back to the airfield. They performed a descending glide-spiral approach that used a reducing radius (as the speed reduced with altitude) around their air base. Neil Armstrong's spiral glide descent was widely acknowledged as the best glide descent and was subsequently used to design the Space Shuttles' descent approach (also called the Heading Alignment Cone).

I wanted to be in a position to glide into Changi in an Armstrong Spiral should the engines give up.

The aircraft was so injured, and so many of the 250,000 sensors were complaining, that I had reached the limit of my ability to absorb them all. The ECAM threw up so many failures, degradations and checklists – especially in the fuel system – that I could not evaluate all the interactions and consequences of the cascading failures. I just wasn't confident how much of the aircraft we had left. So I wanted to be ready for the worst possible contingency – a no-engine landing.

But, for the others in the flight deck, my desire to climb set off alarm bells: the systems were so degraded we may have unknowingly been carrying a small fire, just waiting for fuel to explode all over the plane if we asked for too much thrust. A glide strategy would also have been, for them, the psychological point of defeat, the aviation equivalent of telling the crew and passengers to man the life rafts.

I was shocked the others didn't agree with me, but I didn't have time to discuss it. So I silently decided to accept their wishes and told myself that if the situation deteriorated further, I'd stop the ECAM checklists, head for overhead Changi, discuss my thoughts, and then climb to 10,000 feet, preparing for an Armstrong Spiral.

In the meantime I backed down and radioed Changi: 'Qantas 32, disregard the climb to 10,000 feet. We will maintain 7400 feet.'

We went back to focusing on the central ECAM checklists – we were at that stage in the middle of a complicated fuel checklist and it was making us all feel stressed. It looked like we had hardly any fuel – and no access to the fuel we did have because the transfer tanks had failed. We were all wondering how much flying time we had left before we ran out of fuel – would it be enough to fix or land the plane?

CHAPTER 16

QF32 Down!

While we were busy in the cockpit dealing with the never-ending ECAM checklists and the vast array of failures, people on the ground were also coming to grips with the situation.

At the Qantas 24-hour Operations Centre in Mascot, Sydney, there is an Integrated Operations Centre (IOC), which is sort of like the Houston command centre depicted in movies about NASA. From this centre, aviation engineers can use a program called Airman to monitor any Airbus aircraft's systems, and pilots can call the IOC from their cockpit using their satellite phones.

At 1.01 pm Sydney time on 4 November, the screen in front of the engineer on duty erupted with a rapidly scrolling list of messages from VH-OQA (QF32) – at a rate he had never seen before. His job was to monitor all 160 Qantas Boeing and Airbus aircraft, and so when one aircraft appears to be in distress he needs specialist advice. The volume and severity of messages streaming from VH-OQA was unprecedented in Airbus's history. It seemed unbelievable. So the IOC engineer, thinking the Airman systems had malfunctioned, threw back his chair and made his way to the maintenance watch desk for the A380.

A380 Maintenance Watch provides 24-hour support to Qantas A380 aircraft worldwide, tracking the aircraft state, unserviceabilities and planned maintenance (overseas or at home in Sydney), and answering satellite phone calls from pilots. The engineers also have priority phone lines to Airbus and Rolls–Royce's 24-hour support engineers.

The IOC engineer and the A380 maintenance watch engineer watched more than 130 gruesome red (warning) and yellow (caution) messages scroll down the screen. They couldn't believe they were true – it meant the plane was in catastrophic trouble. The idea was confusing and terrifying.

Meanwhile, Peter Wilson, the Qantas chief pilot, who happened to be in a meeting just 30 metres away from the engineers' desk, first found out about QF32 when he received an SMS message from his son, which said, 'Have you lost an aeroplane?' Peter quickly called Lyell Strambi, the group executive manager for Qantas operations, who was also unaware of our predicament.

Unbeknown to us, the exploding turbine disc from our Engine 2 had fractured into at least four pieces. When Airbus designed the A380, they assumed that in the event of a turbine disc failure the parts of the disc would have infinite energy – wherever the pieces were going, nothing would stop them. This was a wise assumption. In our case the chunks of the disc exited the engine core, cleaving the back of the engine's nacelle from the strut. Chunks opened up the wing like a sardine can, creating a wall of shrapnel that peppered the fuselage. The engine's rear cowling landed in a residential area of Batam, an Indonesian island just south of Singapore. The locals heard a loud explosion and, looking up at the sky, thought they saw a Qantas plane on fire. Turbine blades screamed like fizzing fireworks as they rained down to earth. A large 70-kilogram chunk of the engine's intermediate pressure turbine disc smashed through the roof and wall of a home in Batam's suburbs, and smaller pieces into a primary school classroom. Luckily no one was injured. With debris strewn across the landscape, locals in Batam started tweeting that a Qantas aircraft had crashed. The tweets were immediately picked up by Reuters, Fox News and CNN, who quickly reported the news. All the tweets were wrong, but it didn't stop the information ringing the world within minutes. The chief executive of Airbus, Tom Enders, received an email at 8.41 am German time from a Batam resident, containing a photo of an airframe part that had fallen from the aircraft, narrowly missing his wife and daughter, along with a close-up of the serial number on the wreckage. The resident's message was clear: 'How could this happen today?' and 'Please ensure this does not happen again.'

At 10.14 am Singapore time, thirteen minutes after the explosion, the Qantas share price started collapsing.

After receiving the SMS from his son, Peter Wilson hurried across the floor to the A380 maintenance watch desk to see what was going on. There was now a crowd huddled around the screens, astonished at the number and the seriousness of the alerts being broadcast out of our flight deck.

At about the same time, Roz Wheatley, manager of the Qantas emergency response, looked up at her TV screen to see CNN's breaking news about possible crash of a Qantas aircraft in Indonesia. Without pause, Roz called the duty manager who is on 24-hour standby to activate the Crisis Management Centre. A room quickly filled with twenty experts from every corner of Qantas: operations, legal, political, HR, safety, engineering and financial. Captain Peter Probert was there representing the A380 fleet manager. Alan Rowland-son, the A380 fleet support manager, raced up to the centre as soon as he received his SMS. The crisis plan included booking hotels, notifying airport managers and consulates, perhaps even warning hospitals and requesting ambulances and fire crews. Unfortunately, with 469 people aboard a severely damaged aircraft, the operations people were also combing the passenger manifest and preparing contact lists for the crews and passengers' next of kin, should the situation end in tragedy.

*

All of that was happening on the ground unbeknownst to us. We were very busy on the flight deck. We were still actioning serious checklists. We had normal communications with Changi ATC. When we requested for them to keep us in a holding pattern for 30 minutes, they had asked, 'What's the problem, Qantas? Which engine is giving trouble?' They couldn't understand why we wanted to hold so long for an engine failure.

I replied, 'Qantas 32, Engine 2 has failed and there's a hole in the side of the engine. The other engines are okay but the wing is damaged and we have extensive checklists to complete. We need at least another half an hour in the hold before returning to Singapore.'

At 10.29 am, 28 minutes after the explosion, Singapore ATC advised us that debris had been found on the ground in Batam.

Technically, we were alone on the flight deck of QF32, alone and in a bubble. The explosions had taken out both of our satellite telephone systems. Maintenance watch did send us a data-link message, asking incredulously, 'Confirm operations normal?' We sent back an adequate reply – 'No!' We could not talk to Qantas even if we wanted to, and Singapore ATC would not be able to help with A380 specifics. But I never thought we needed external help in the air. ECAM was doing a brilliant job prioritising then listing the faults, and then helping us either fix the system or mitigate its failure. Matt was racing through the ECAMS as fast as he could, with all of us monitoring him. Indeed, I think that any contact with Qantas via sat phone would have only slowed us down.

We weren't even speaking to our cabin crew. The main intercom system ringtone that was blaring was impossible to hear among the cacophony of warning alerts. We had a secondary system called the 'EMERgency Intercom' that connected us to the cabin crew, but all of the emergency systems were beeping, and the flashing 'EMER CALL' light on the overhead panel was lost in a sea of red failure lights. Quite simply, none of us saw the intercom light or could hear the buzzer for all the other rings and buzzes emitted by the flight warning computers.

*

Back in the cabin, the passengers had been aware of the explosions too. There had been worried chatter, but luckily no one had started a panic. The cabin crew on airlines are trained to identify people prone to panic and to neutralise them quickly. As any experienced cabin services manager will tell you, the trick is to not allow the first panicked person to get out of the box. Because, if you let that ringleader start charging around the plane preaching doom and panic and demanding to have the windows opened, some of the other nervous passengers will follow suit, simply because they are also scared. And once you have 440 passengers in a state of anxiety, panic and anger – refusing to sit down, demanding action, arguing among themselves – you lose control of the plane and it is much harder to deal with the initial crisis.

On QF32 we were lucky to have Michael von Reth as the cabin services manager (CSM) in the cabin. A veteran of this work, and an expert in identifying personality types and acting quickly on them, Michael had felt the explosion at his seat at 'main door 2 left'. He would later tell me the second explosion was followed by what sounded like 'a thousand marbles being thrown onto a corrugated iron roof'. This was the shrapnel exploding out of the engine, through the wing and against the fuselage.

Michael tried the intercom to the cockpit, but no one answered. He then pressed the 'PRIO' and 'CAPT' buttons to select the emergency channel to the flight deck, but no one answered. The airframe had stopped shaking and Michael realised that, for whatever reason, he would have to manage the passengers without information or instruction from me.

From his seat at the door nearest Engine 2, Michael noticed the passengers were starting a loud hubbub of worry. Grabbing a handset, Michael announced to the passengers: 'Ladies and gentlemen, the plane is safe. Please take your seats; the captain will speak to you soon.' He visited the cabin crew stations and warned them that the next minutes were a crucial time to assert their authority and enforce calmness. In particular, the seatbelts-fastened sign was still on and there had just been an explosion, so he wanted the cabin crew to keep everyone in their seats.

Having briefed the crew, he started his walk down the aisles of the plane, searching for the ringleader, whom he found at the start of the Economy section: a man in his forties who had left his seat and gone to one of the fuselage doors.

The ringleader didn't want to move from the door, so Michael raised his voice, pointed at the man and repeated his announcement in a very strong tone. The ringleader backed down and returned to his seat, where Michael joined him and had a quick chat about the situation.

Michael von Reth later told me he saw that armwrestle with the ringleader as the watershed moment in the crisis. 'If we'd lost him, we may have lost the rest of the passengers,' he told me.

Michael continued to look for ringleaders and disarm them before they could build momentum.

*

I knew nothing of this in the cockpit. What I realised, after we'd turned north for Singapore, was that we couldn't speak with the cabin crew, which meant we couldn't get a triangulated view of the damage to the plane. We knew what parts of the plane had been damaged, degraded and taken out altogether. And we had two cameras that gave us footage of the exterior of the plane. One of those cameras is mounted on the tail and looks forward down the roof of the fuselage, and the other camera is mounted beside the main landing gear bay and looks forward towards the nose wheel. But with these camera angles we couldn't get a proper view of the engines or the underside of the wing. The tail camera allowed us to see a big hole in the top of the left wing, but not much else. As pilots we wanted to assess the condition of the plane externally before making decisions.

Once we had a north heading at a safe altitude, and we had Changi ATC ready to receive us at the airport, I tried to sit back and take a more broad view of the situation. We had completed a number of significant engine checklists and I had a freer mind space to gather an overall view of the crisis. So I asked Mark, who had been standing behind us monitoring everything, to go back into the cabin and have a look at the wing.

CHAPTER 17

ECAM Armageddon

There were fourteen people in First Class and they stared back at Second Officer Mark Johnson as he emerged from the cockpit. One passenger asked him what was going on, and he told them the plane was safe and to stay in their seats. Mark recognised Andrew Eccles, a Qantas second officer passengering back to Sydney, who showed Mark the SkyCam screen, part of the inflight entertainment system. Andrew pointed to the view of the aircraft taken from the camera mounted high up the tail fin. Mark then realised that everyone on the aircraft also had the SkyCam displayed on their inflight entertainment screens, so could see a clear view of the fuselage, including the holes in the left wing and a stream of fuel flooding from the rear of the wing. What interesting inflight entertainment!

Crossing to the left side of the cabin, Mark looked out through the small window in the middle of the door and observed the left wing. Engine 2 was destroyed, and the rear cowling that sported the red Qantas logo was gone, exposing the naked waist and inner workings of the Rolls-Royce turbine and exhaust sections.

The wing was peppered with holes and fuel was gushing out. There were also several holes in the top of the wing; one, a large jagged hole about 1 metre across and a metre back from Engine 2's pylon mount, was big enough for a man to fit through. Another hole was further back along the wing, about half a metre long and 10 centimetres wide. There were many other smaller holes. A wide fan of fuel, about 2 metres wide, streamed out through two of the holes on the upper wing. This was complemented by another larger stream that appeared from underneath the trailing edge of the wing. Together they formed a chilling sight.

As Mark moved through the cabin, passengers grabbed his arm and said, 'Look at that!' He was shown many other holes on the wing's top surface – one that penetrated through the leading edge slats. The implications were obvious: the engine explosion had produced shrapnel with enough force to pass up *through* the 2-metre thick wing and exit on the top side, slicing through two 15 millimetre–thick aluminium plates like a knife through butter.

The hoard of fuel system alerts we'd received from ECAM now made sense as 90 per cent of the fuel is held in the wings. There are eleven fuel tanks on the A380, ten of them in the wings. Mark later told me, 'I put on my best poker face in front of the passengers and tried not to look too alarmed, and to tell everyone it was okay. But shit, it really wasn't.'

Mark sought out Michael von Reth, who was at the Business Class crew station issuing orders and making frequent announcements. Identifying and calming the ringleaders was one component of Michael's strategy, the other part was to make regular communication with the passengers, who were all confined to their seats. Once Mark had established everyone was okay, he and Michael swapped information. Michael needed insights that he could share with the passengers, and we needed to know what was happening around the entire aircraft.

Coming back into the cockpit, Mark explained what he'd seen and been told, and so we built a more complete picture of what was going on with the plane, based on what the ECAM said, what Mark Johnson had seen and what Michael von Reth and Andrew Eccles could tell us.

We knew at that point that we had one failed engine, two degraded engines and one engine registering revs but no thrust. We also had holes in the wing, holes in the hydraulics, holes in the pneumatics, degraded electrics, degraded communications, degraded computer systems, leaking fuel, failed fuel pumps, degraded flight controls, a few imbalances and a whole bunch of other stuff.

All of the power to the left wing had been shut down and half our normal electrical generators depowered, but we had curtailed the possibility of starting an electrical fire inside the left wing, which was loaded with 45 tonnes of fuel. We had additional power available. The auxiliary power unit (APU), located in the tail section, drives two generators large enough to power a small town. We started the APU but it refused to distribute power to the plane. In the worst case, that of a total electrical failure in flight, the ram air turbine (RAT) was also available. The RAT is a small windmill that drops into the airflow behind Engine 2 and turns an emergency generator to supply power for essential services.

The A380 uses a lot of power and we were down to about 40 per cent generation capacity. This was powering the cabin, flight deck and emergency electric flight controls. Michael von Reth reported that the cabin environment was very disconcerting – the normal and emergency lighting was flashing on/off throughout the aircraft, accompanied by persistent alert and warning sounds.

The engine had exploded like a cluster bomb. Shrapnel had torn through anything in its path, including QF32's wing, fuselage and systems. The fuel pumps and ailerons on the A380 are powered through dedicated wires that run through the leading edge of the wing with redundant wires routed through the belly of the aircraft. All these wires were cut. We'd also lost half of our spoilers (for turning and braking); the leading edge slats (which help us slow to land) on the left wing failed; and our brakes were reduced down to 28 per cent on the left and right wing. I was amazed: of the 22 systems on QF32, 21 were damaged. Only the oxygen system was (luckily) unaffected. I don't think an Airbus aircraft had ever been damaged so severely, but there was good news – we were still flying.

Yet we were lucky: none of the exploding engine parts hit a passenger, even though a lot of the shrapnel hit the fuselage. One of the massive chunks that travelled through the wing and punctured the inner fuel tank, then continued up and over the top of the fuselage, missed the top by just 2 centimetres. The engines on A380s are staggered in their placement so that shrapnel from an exploding engine does not fly directly sideways and frag (wreck) the neighbouring engine. This stagger saved Engine 1 from destruction. They are also set forward from the wing to limit catastrophic damage to the wing, fuel, flight controls, electrical and hydraulic systems in the case of a turbine disc failure. These offsets did not work so well given the amount of damage to the wing. Still, there is only so much you can do to protect the airframe from an engine explosion, short of encasing it in concrete.

*

We were now in an oblong holding pattern over a patch of water where the Singapore Strait meets the South China Sea.

From this holding pattern to the east of Singapore, we flew and plotted, flew and plotted as we stabilised damaged systems, all the time assessing how much fuel remained and whether we had the luxury to be able to continue actioning the never-ending checklists, or whether the aircraft was a ticking time bomb with limited flying time left and we should just get onto the ground immediately with whatever systems support we could muster.

Another thought cycled in the back of my mind that chilled my senses. Was the wing on fire? If the wing was on fire, fed by our many fuel leaks, then I'd be forced to make a quick decision, a decision so dreadful I'd always hoped I'd never have to make it. If the wing was on fire, we would have insufficient time to make the runway and I'd have to ditch the aircraft in the ocean. I had not seen the 'ENG FIRE' checklist flash up on the ECAM and there were no reports of fire, but it was in my thoughts.

I keyed the radio after we'd entered our holding pattern and updated Changi ATC with a few details of our failures, in part to explain why I anticipated we would need to remain in the holding pattern. I didn't know how many ECAM check-lists were queued up. I assumed the checklist we were working on was the final checklist and, once we'd completed that, we would need an additional 30 minutes to prepare the aircraft, cabin, crew and passengers for landing.

But the checklists kept coming and coming.

The biggest job at our end was to work out how to get the 440-tonne aircraft on to the ground with everyone intact. We started with the fuel. If we couldn't keep it flowing into the engines, we wouldn't stay aloft and we wouldn't have time to work up a plan for landing. The displays showed we'd taken off with a total fuel load of 105 tonnes but after twenty minutes of flight we were already down to 93 tonnes remaining. Nine tonnes of fuel had leaked from the wings. There are eleven fuel tanks on an A380: one feed tank over each engine, three transfer tanks in each wing, and the trim tank located in the horizontal stabiliser at the tail. We had leaks that couldn't be plugged: five leaks in the forward wing spar, at least two holes in the bottom of the wing, and a minimum of two on the wing's top surface. Both of our fuel quantity management system computers failed, and there were multiple problems in the left wing where six fuel pumps failed, transfer galleries (pipes) and vent pipes had been severed, and the transfer and jettison systems were failed. The system to transfer the 13.5 tonnes from the trim tank in the tail to the wing transfer tanks had failed. Losing the two fuel transfer systems meant we couldn't shift fuel from the transfer tanks in the wing to the feed tanks located above and feeding each engine.

It was getting very hard to resolve all these failures. The fuel quantities in the eleven tanks didn't make sense. Engine 2 had failed, but it appeared there was a bigger hole in the feed tank to Engine 1 than there was in the feed tank to Engine 2.

Each engine was burning about 3 tonnes of fuel every hour. So, leaks notwithstanding, it was easy to calculate we had about two and a half hours of flying before the number 1 engine ran out of fuel and then we'd be flying on the two engines on the right-wing only.

Not only were we losing fuel in an uncontrolled way but we could not voluntarily dump fuel either. The jettison system was a mess. In fact the jettison valve was jammed open, which might have allowed us to lose fuel, but the transfer galleries were severed and many fuel pumps had failed, so the computers inhibited the jettison system. We also had many fuel transfers that failed to initiate, and so the fuel distribution became non-standard and the aircraft became out of balance.

ECAM detected these problems and gave us a solution. The 'FUEL: WINGS NOT BALANCED' checklist instructed us to transfer fuel from the heavier right wing into the feed tanks in the lighter left wing.

Matt was doing a fantastic job actioning the ECAM. He wasn't rushing, but he couldn't go slowly because, on many occasions, he'd be in the middle of a checklist when another higher priority checklist would flash up and interrupt his flow. It was very distracting. So Matt did his best to apply the check-list fixes before another alert and action leaped onto the screen. The 'FUEL: WINGS NOT BALANCED' checklist appeared and Matt was reaching up to open the fuel cross-feed valves when I suddenly called out 'STOP!'

It seemed instinctively wrong to me, and I stared at the ECAM and the fuel synoptic display, then back to the ECAM.

'Should we be transferring fuel out of the good right wing into the leaking left wing?' I asked.

'No!' Mark, Harry and Dave all said loudly.

I didn't have to say anything more. They all knew the case of Air Transat TS236, an A330 flight from Toronto to Lisbon in 2001. During that flight an extremely rapid fuel leak devel-oped in one wing. The crew followed the checklist procedures and transferred all the fuel from the good wing to the bad.

But the fuel that transferred was lost overboard and both engines flamed out. The aircraft then conducted a superb glide landing at the Azores and luckily everyone escaped without injury. This was a remarkable incident and it provided a valuable lesson.

I wasn't going to let us fall into the same trap of transferring fuel away from the engines that were working. So we agreed to ignore the checklist.

Matt had commenced actioning the next checklist, 'FUEL: NORM+ALTN XFR FAULT'. It was a checklist I never ever expected to see in any aircraft and a sign of how grim things were. The A380's fuel system is so impressive – with so many redundant pumps, valves and galleries – that I never thought both the normal and the alternate fuel transfer systems could fail at once. But here it was, and Matt was reading out the checklist when Mark interrupted and said, 'I think we missed something when looking at the fuel synoptic page during the previous checklist. Can we revisit it sometime please?'

I told Matt to stop the checklist and display the fuel synoptic. It showed a sea of red failures for our left wing. It was hard to see past the red and identify the white components that were working normally.

'I think we have another lateral imbalance,' Mark said. 'When we actioned the engine failure checklist, the checklist called for us to do an emergency transfer of fuel from the outer transfer tanks into the feed tanks. The right outer tank has transferred, the left has not!'

Mark was the first to identify this. I had missed this added imbalance. This was not a good result as far as control of the aircraft was concerned. Our confusion was continuing to rise and our confidence started to wane. We began to think about an emergency landing with increasing urgency.

CHAPTER 18

Apollo 13

The fuel imbalance was a major issue. One of the problems with modern fly-by-wire aircraft is that the distribution of the fuel critically affects the safe loading and balance of the aircraft for take-off, cruise and landing. We needed to get the plane balanced if we were going to land safely. Even small imbalances can potentially be fatal.

Matt had tried to transfer fuel in the outer tanks to the feed tanks. The imbalance across the outer tanks was now 300 per cent outside the flight manual's published limit. It made for an uncomfortable atmosphere in the flight deck. What would happen on an Airbus when the outer fuel tanks are not balanced? How well can you turn? How do you land? None of us knew the answers.

No pilot ever wants to operate or land an aircraft out of its published limits, because either the aircraft has failed certification requirements or it has never been tested. You don't know which of these two cases applies, so you just avoid operating outside the limits. But sometimes you don't have a choice. On QF32 we had a badly compromised aircraft in which the centre of gravity wasn't perfectly located in the middle of the fuselage between the wings, but instead somewhere to the right, between the fuselage and Engine 3. None of us knew how an out-of-balance A380 would perform at landing at the best of times, but in the shape that *Nancy-Bird* was in, it was causing us great concern.

Our suspicions about the fuel system were about to be made worse because ECAM was not helping us. Matt was actioning a fuel ECAM and he called out the message: 'CG OUT OF LIMITS FOR LANDING'. This was understandable. There were 13.5 tonnes of fuel stuck in the trim tank in the tail plane that would push our centre of gravity way back. The next message read: 'TRANSFER TRIM TK FUEL'. This was also understandable. The computers would always transfer this trim tank fuel forward 74 minutes prior to landing to help balance the plane. But our thoughts were stopped by the next messages: 'TRIM TK NOT USEABLE'. And 'TRANSFER SYS INOP'.

Was this a joke? Why did the ECAM tell us to transfer the trim tank fuel if the transfer system was inoperative? It wasn't logical. Clearly the ECAM was not programmed to cater for this many concurrent failures. I felt like I was on a TV game show where you are given a challenge and have to think your way out of the problem. The game host was the ECAM; the problem was our shredded fuel system.

I stopped for a second and thought about it. It didn't make sense. We were in longitudinal balance when we took off 25 minutes earlier with the same amount of fuel in the trim tank down the back, so how could we be so far out of longitudinal balance now? I started to have doubts about ECAM.

There must be another way out of this quandary. I remembered a graph deep in the manuals that showed the 'CG envelope' for all phases of flight. That graph flashed in front of my mind. I grabbed the A380's laptop and thrust it back into Mark's hands. 'Mark, would you find the graph for the CG envelope in the Flight Crew Operating Manual and tell me what you find.'

Mark, like all of the second officers on the A380, is a true professional pilot; in fact, he had flown F-111s and Hercules aircraft in the Royal Australian Air Force. He knew the manuals better than I did. It didn't take him long to find the graph, and his conclusion was clear. 'Rich, we are currently over our maximum landing weight, and our current CG is greater than the ideal, but we are within an acceptable CG range. We're okay!'

We all looked at the graph before I said, 'I agree with Mark, I think we are okay and that we can ignore these ECAM CG messages.' Everyone agreed – and that problem was quickly resolved.

What wasn't okay was the other two imbalances in the weight distribution of the aircraft. How would we get everyone on board safely to ground with so many problems? The ECAM kept warning us that the wings were not balanced, and we knew there were some big holes in the fuel system which meant the imbalance was growing, but we couldn't work out whether the fuel leaks were in the engine or in the wing. If the fuel leak was in the engine, then shutting down that engine might stop the fuel leak. But we had so many other problems. Did I really want to take a bad situation and make it worse by shutting down an engine to try and isolate a fuel leak – NO!

By this time we had developed a routine of dealing with all the external stresses – the master warning horn continued to sound frequently, but would be quickly cancelled by Matt or myself. The ECAMs kept coming, one after another, each one still serious. When would this stop and what aircraft would I be left with? I knew I was coming to the end of my tether. We were chasing a computer program around when perhaps we should have been flying the plane and just landing.

Then both fuel quantity management computers became so confused they failed. The fuel synoptic displays showed only red double crosses 'XX' – no data.

I slumped lower in my chair. I felt like a pole being driven into the ground by a pile-driver. Both fuel systems had failed. What was next? Whatever I was doing, I was not climbing back on top of the situation. I knew the fuel imbalances would challenge our controllability for a landing, but so many other systems were failing I was losing the ability to track all the failures and work out their dependencies and consequences.

I knew I was now *overloaded*. I said nothing.

Think . . . Think . . .

Matt soldiered on brilliantly. He followed the ECAM instructions to reset both fuel quantity management computers and, bit by bit, the fuel synoptic displays flashed back into life. It looked like the scene from *Apollo 13* when the astronauts powered up the command module before entering the Earth's orbit. That frozen dark capsule fired up into a sea of lights, dials and buttons. There was silence in the cockpit except for the continued buzz and ring of the alerts from the flight warning computers.

I looked at the fuel synoptic page and I said loud and clear to all: 'I'm looking at this fuel synoptic page and I don't understand it. Does anyone understand this fuel display?' I wasn't trying to be smart: I didn't know the answer and I was asking for ideas. I was asking for help.

The rest of the pilots shook their heads. There was silence.

My confidence in ECAM was waning. It was just a computer program, it was just a checklist. It wasn't good enough to tell us where the leaks were, it couldn't adapt for multiple failures in one system and it couldn't help us fix the leaks even if it could identify them. There weren't enough sensors – there'd never be enough sensors. And, even if there were enough sensors, we lacked crucial pumps to shift fuel, we lacked intact galleries that connected the tanks, and there were holes all over the place.

*

And then I had my epiphany. My mind switched.

I inverted the logic. I remembered what Gene Kranz, NASA's Flight Director, said during the Apollo 13 mission: 'Hold it, gentlemen, hold it! I don't care about what went wrong. I need to know what is still working on that space craft.'

We went back to the basics and it became easy: 'All right, let's keep this simple. We can't transfer fuel, we can't jettison it. The trim tank fuel is stuck in the tail and the transfer tanks are useless. The only useable fuel is the fuel in the three feed tanks sitting on top of each engine. I don't care which fuel pumps have failed because we are below our fuel gravity ceiling, so fuel will drip into each engine. So forget the pumps, forget the other eight tanks, forget the total fuel quantity gauge, and instead let's concentrate only on the fuel in the feed tanks above each engine. We're burning 3 tonnes of fuel per engine per hour, and I see 8 tonnes of fuel in feed tank 1 and 11 tonnes of fuel in feed tanks 3 and 4. So we have two and a half hours of fuel in Engine 1, although it's leaking fuel very fast, and we have three and a half hours of fuel in Engines 3 and 4.

'I say we forget analysing the fuel system any more. We concentrate only on feed tanks 1, 3 and 4. We have up to two and a half hours of flight time before we lose Engine 1. We'll monitor the feed tank fuel and our endurance every five minutes. I'm happy. Do any of you have any thoughts?'

'No,' came the reply from everyone.

I said, 'I'm happy for Matt to continue actioning the next ECAMs. Any thoughts?'

'No,' they all replied.

'Okay, if anyone is worried about the aircraft and wants to ditch the ECAM checklists and just get the aircraft onto the ground ASAP, then mention it and we'll discuss it, otherwise I'll review our situation again in ten minutes.'

In the moments directly after the explosion I'd felt I had basic control over the aircraft: I could hold at an altitude and I managed a banking turn to the north, and was now managing repeated banks as we flew our holding pattern. But I was not overconfident of our control when we would slow and commence our approach. The errant weight distribution in the wings and tail posed a significant risk to our controllability, so I turned my attentions to the control surfaces, which, if set incorrectly, might put us into an unusual and dangerous flying attitude.

The basic flight controls – flaps, elevators, rudders and ailerons – seemed to be working even if our displays showed severe degradation. Without control surfaces, you can't fly. And even if you can fly in the cruise, landing may be impossible if control surfaces such as flaps and slats are damaged. The big concerns when it came to control surfaces were the failed slats along the leading edge of both wings and the failed ailerons.

The A380 is the first aircraft built with three ailerons on each wing. The very large outer ailerons are only used at slow speeds such as during take-off, approach and landing. The small inner aileron moves hundreds of times per minute to provide finesse in roll control, but are too small to control the aircraft during approach. The mid aileron is the star performer in the A380's patented 'dance of the ailerons', a unique and complex movement that stops the wings, engines and airframe oscillating and gives the A380 its trademark rock-solid ride. These mid ailerons were also designed to provide additional roll control in the case of severe failures, such as the situation we were now experiencing.

On the A380 each of the four engines turn two hydraulic pumps to pressurise two independent hydraulic systems. The hydraulic systems are called Green and Yellow, each holding 550 litres of oil that is pressurised to 5000 pounds per square inch (psi). The A380's Green system is driven by Engines 1 and 2, and the Yellow system is driven by Engines 3 and 4. There are also lightweight electrical backup hydraulic actuators located at selected flight control surfaces that are powered by two independent electrical circuits.

Eleven computer systems combine with the two hydraulics and two electrical-hydraulic systems to control all the slats, flaps, ailerons, rudders and elevators, and the horizontal stabiliser.

We switched the synoptics display from fuel to hydraulics. We had already switched off four hydraulic pumps, or lost 50 per cent of our hydraulics before we got into our holding pattern east of Changi. The Green hydraulics had failed. Now we had more problems looming.

The ECAM told us the yellow hydraulic system pressure was low and commanded us to turn off hydraulic pumps 5 and 6 in Engine 4. It's a one-way switch – once the pump is disconnected it can't be restored. The switch is guarded by a metal cage to prevent inadvertent activation.

Matt's fingers went up and lifted the metal guard that protected the switch. He paused, waiting for my confirmation to press the button . . .

'STOP!' I called. 'Can we all please think about this for ten seconds?'

I wasn't happy. We'd all become overwhelmed with the sheer number and layered complexity of ECAM alerts, and the 'logical' way ECAM was trying to check and fix the aircraft. The alerts had already perplexed me with the instruction to pump fuel out of a good wing and into a damaged one. We'd already shut down 50 per cent of our hydraulic pumps and now the ECAM wanted us to shut down a further 25 per cent of our pumps – oil pumps that enabled our ailerons and slats, the control surfaces we needed to safely fly the aircraft. I didn't want to be left with two hydraulic pumps out of eight. We had only one small operational aileron on the left wing and two small ailerons on the right. Our ability to roll the aircraft was already reduced to 35 per cent, so I didn't want to degrade the few remaining ailerons further – I wanted them strong, responsive and filled with as much hydraulic pressure as we could generate.

Yet the ECAM was insistent we shut down pumps 5 and 6. Why was it demanding this? I could understand shutting down all the hydraulic pumps for the Green system on the left wing, as both engines one and two had been damaged. But Engine 4 was mounted to our extreme right. The fuselage separated Engine 4 from Engines 1 and 2. So how could shrapnel pass over or under the fuselage, then travel all that way and damage Engine 4? It didn't make sense.

I didn't verbalise any of this to the other pilots. I wanted to know what they thought first. I started by asking Mark what he thought. Mark said he could not see how the damage we had could have spread to Engine 4. I looked to Harry, but he was unsure. We looked at the synoptic display – pressure and quantity were all normal. The hydraulic actuators looked normal. I made my way up the chain to Dave, who said much the same but added that, even if we lost all the hydraulics, we still had the electrical backup actuators, so we could shut down the pumps. Matt agreed.

It was now my turn. I reasoned that perhaps a metal chip detector in the hydraulic system had detected iron filings in Engine 4's pumps; that in this case Engine 4 might take out Engine 3's hydraulics, and so I suggested we turn off pumps 5 and 6 to preserve pumps 7 and 8. Everyone quickly gave a thumbs-up.

So, with trepidation, I told Matt to shut down hydraulic pumps 5 and 6 on Engine 4. Our hydraulics were now down to 25 per cent depending on pumps 7 and 8 on Engine 3.

We were cautious of ECAM, so we had queried this checklist, investigated it, and then decided to complete it as shown. We had now turned off 75 per cent of our hydraulic pumps and were down to one hydraulic system. If we were on any other similarly savaged aircraft, we'd be declaring a mayday and seriously considering landing immediately. But we were in an A380, with remarkably eighteen of the 21 electrically powered flight controls still functioning, so we still had control.

My overriding philosophy was still to focus on what was working. The fuel was okay – we had as many as two and a half hours on Engine 1. Hydraulics were okay – we had two pumps powering one system, plus reserves. Flight controls were okay – we had control in all axes, for the moment.

There was good and bad news. The bad news was ECAM was still pile-driving us into the ground with high-priority failures, so I knew there would be more ECAMs to come. The imbalances coupled with limited flight controls could be a real problem. It was not the shape you want to be in when you also have one wing heavier than the other. But the good news was we were building our basic plane from the ground up. We were not sure how to fly the approach, land and stop it yet – that would come later – but so far it looked like being an acceptable machine.

Time for a 'gross check'. We were facing ECAM Armageddon. We were actioning the worst type and most number of checklists we could ever have imagined and the workload was extreme, but we were under control. I selected the Fuel Synoptic page. Engine 1 still had the least fuel; sufficient for about two and a half hours before it would flame out; we were generally within gliding range of Singapore – in the slot for an Armstrong Spiral. We were safe for now.

I was concerned about the passengers and cabin crew. I knew if it were me in their situation, I would want to hear comforting and reassuring words from the flight deck. I wanted to give them more information, but my attention was focused on stabilising the aircraft. My announcement would have to wait.

The aircraft was flying in control, banking smoothly into the turns with no buffet or vibrations. The passengers were aware of the damage to the wing and engine and probably thought, because of David's address, that we were dumping fuel from the left wing, so nothing new had occurred. However, they weren't aware of the barrage of checks and problems we were facing in the flight desk. The passengers could wait a little longer before my first public address.

'Is everyone happy to continue actioning more ECAMs?'

Everyone replied, 'Yes'.

CHAPTER 19

If You Can't Trim, You Can't Fly

Our problems were mounting against a background that not many Airbus pilots will ever have to deal with: the aircraft was no longer being managed by the normal fly-by-wire program.

Within a few seconds after Engine 2 exploded, the flight control computers detected damage to the airframe. Some damage can be tolerated, some cannot. In our case the computers detected the slats on the left wings had failed, so locked the slat-brakes to inhibit the slats on both wings, then redirected the active control of the aircraft to a different and simpler software program, or flight control 'law'. All three primary flight control computers swapped to the alternate law program.

The Airbus fly-by-wire flight control system comprises seven flight control computers – three primary, three secondary and one back-up. If all the primaries failed – which would probably only occur in the event of an extraordinary software error – then any one of the three secondary flight control computers (SECs) would kick in to control the aircraft. A backup control module kicks in if all six computers fail.

The A380's fly-by-wire flight laws are impressive, resilient and extraordinarily reliable. The pilots' two sidesticks feed directly into seven computers functioning in one of three modes: normal law, alternate law or direct law. The aircraft is expected to be flown in normal law, which is programmed to be capable of retaining control when a single system or flight control surface fails. When multiple sensors or flight control surfaces fail, the flight control computers swap to one of the six alternate laws that have been specially crafted to cater for the particular failures. In extreme failure cases, advanced direct laws are enacted.

In normal law, the fly-by-wire system controls the engines (auto-thrust) and flight controls surfaces, responding to inputs from the pilot/autopilot and six protection systems that prevent the aircraft exceeding operating limitations. For instance, 'barrel rolls' and inverted flight are impossible in normal law. And just so all travellers can relax, the A380, in normal law, won't let you pull into a loop.

When the plane is traumatised to the extent that the flight controls or sensors are damaged or inoperable, the computers switch to alternate law. The flight computers recognise that the aircraft is degraded, so inhibit most of the protections of normal law either because the protection sensors have malfunctioned or to prevent the protection systems harming the aircraft. There is a good chance the autopilot still functions in alternate law.

Airbus provides six different versions of alternate law, depending on what's damaged and/or inoperable. Since under alternate law most of the protections provided by normal law are lost, an aberrant pilot could attempt a barrel roll or loop, but this would be unwise because in alternate law there's no protection against stalling. This is a basic tenant that every Airbus pilot learns early in their conversion – if you pull back hard enough and long enough, you will surely go outside the aircraft's safe performance envelope and stall. Add a bit of rudder and you might even enter a spin. As dangerous as this appears, alternate law is really very good and pilot friendly. The flight warning computers will warn you of an approach to the stall – flashing a red light while a stressed voice announces 'STALL, STALL' – warning you that you're about to fall out of the sky.

If more of the aircraft and computer systems fail, then the flight control computers switch from the alternate law program to the direct law program, which cuts out the autopilot and gives the pilot direct control over the control surfaces and the engines, with no protections, just like a Cessna. You also have to manually trim the aircraft.

Direct law is potentially dangerous. Direct law would engage in the event of severe failures, perhaps multiple flight control computer failures. Chances are that if you are in direct law, you might also be distracted with the aircraft being distressed mechanically or even upside down.

On the QF32, the master primary computer that was controlling the aircraft detected the damaged slats on the left wing and switched to alternate law. When the ECAM presented the alternate law warning, I called out to the pilots: 'We're in alternate law – we've lost most of our protections but we still have a stall warning.' At that time I didn't realise just how useful that awareness would be.

The autopilot still functioned, but the auto-thrust failed because three engines were degraded. I manually set the thrust to maintain 235 knots, which was our minimum fuel consumption speed. I engaged the autopilot, and the aircraft behaved and flew well. However, 75 per cent of our roll control had been lost, but I didn't realise this and the system didn't care – it just moved the remaining functioning ailerons as much as required to do what was required.

Our engines, flight controls and flight law were degraded, and most of our protections were lost. There were some actions in particular I would have liked the fly-by-wire to take care of (especially thrust and a bit of feedback about how stressed the flight controls really were given the three imbalances and failures across the airframe), but I was comforted knowing I had absolute control and every input into the aircraft would be mine – there would be no sudden and confusing inputs or corrections by the flight control computers respond-ing to damaged sensors. In essence, I was piloting a very basic Cessna aircraft that I understood and felt comfortable flying.

I remember discussing overweight landings with a very senior test pilot at Airbus in 2009. I asked: 'My manual recommends that if you must land at a weight greater than your maximum landing weight, you should use the autopilot because it'll do a better job than the pilot. What do you think?'

His answer still resonates in my mind: 'The auto-land system is just a simple computer program, catering for the simplest failure cases. You are the pilot, you are in command, and you should never be afraid of your aircraft. Fly the aircraft!'

Some of the people who complain about Airbus fly-by-wire will tell you Airbus pilots are no longer flying their aircraft like the old pilots did – that the new breed are losing or perhaps have even lost their physical flying skills. Aircraft are now so reliable, they say, that 'soon we'll see a monkey flying a big jet across the Pacific'. Perhaps aircraft might even be as reliable as cars, but we don't see monkeys driving cars yet. The crucial difference is that when a modern car breaks down, we can generally pull over to the side of a road and call for help. No such luxury exists in the air. We are alone, in our case very alone, with 469 souls in a cluster bombed aircraft. So I'm old school in this respect: on board I believe the pilot's job is exactly as written in the federal laws; pilots are 'responsible for the safety of the passengers and crew' regardless of what stands between them and disaster. Whether it's a fly-by-wire computer or a few cables connected to your rudder pedals, your job is to know your plane, be unafraid of the plane and to *fly the plane*.

CHAPTER 20

Housekeeping

The alerts kept sounding and ECAM continued presenting checklists. At least the checklists were prioritised: engine checklists first, then hydraulics, then flight controls, fuel, electrics, brakes, pneumatics, landing gear, airconditioning and, finally, auto-flight. Matt and I had both settled into our respective tasks. We were not scared, but we were busy. We were not relaxed, but no one was panicking. Air traffic control were vectoring us around our holding pattern, keeping us within 30 nautical miles of Changi, exactly as I had requested so we had the necessary proximity should our aircraft be reduced to a glider. I held the Armstrong Spiral 'ace of spades' card consciously up my sleeve.

However Singapore wasn't a security blanket: it was a constant reminder that we had to do something. Changi ATC was calling us every fifteen minutes, asking 'What's really wrong up there, Qantas 32?' They wanted to know whether we had control of the plane, what we needed and when we would be making an approach. Changi ATC were professional and helpful, and it was a comfort to have them at the other end of the transmit button.

We didn't have any real answers for ATC because we had so many factors to deal with and they seemed to pile up on each other as we dealt with one problem after another. We had asked initially for 30 minutes' holding. We then updated our holding requirements another six times to enable finishing the checklists and preparing the aircraft and cabin for an approach. Before attempting a landing, I wanted to get through as many of the critical checklists as I could. The Airbus ECAM is predicated on a system called 'threat and error management' – essentially, when faced with a problem, you try to fix the error, and if you can't then you try to reduce the risks and recover a safe operation.

By the time we'd been in the air for an hour, the ECAM had identified about 100 significant errors and checklists and given us actions to try and fix them. ECAM then helped us secure systems that we could not reset or fix: Engine 2 was shut down, hydraulic pumps were turned off and pneumatic leaks were isolated. ECAM presented lots of errors in the fuel system but no remedies.

By inverting our logic and looking at what was working, we were able to build our basic Cessna aircraft from the ground up with sufficient bits to build a basic fuel system, flight controls, brakes, landing gear and electrical supplies. This process took over an hour, but I am convinced it was time well spent.

Alerts kept appearing on the ECAM, but we'd been through the biggest items and attempted fixes.

Some non-critical problems could not be fixed. One of the two cooling systems for the racks of computers underneath the flight deck had failed. If we had lost the backup cooling system, then I would have expected most of our computer systems to fail. The landing gear was also degraded and we'd lost one of the two landing gear systems. If we lost both, we'd still be able to lower the landing gear by gravity, but we would have had no sensors to confirm the gear was down and locked.

Some critical problems could not be fixed. The fuel leaks and compromised flight controls and brakes posed a serious threat to safety. We flew on regardless, aware that we'd have to find methods later to mitigate these failures.

We shut down systems to prevent them overheating, and then we couldn't get some redundant systems restarted. The auto-thrust had failed early and we'd never get that back. We'd lost both channels of our ground proximity warning system (GPWS) – an essential warning, when flying in cloud or at night, that will prevent you from flying into the ground. We'd also lost one of our three air data and inertial reference units (ADIRU), which would probably confuse many aircraft systems and stop the APU generator connecting to the aircraft. Both satellite phones were failed because the left wing was unpowered, so our radio connection to Qantas in Sydney was lost and was never recovered. The cabin was a mess; with cabin lights flickering continually, alarms sounding and the control panels blanking.

Network cables, generator feed lines and critical wires were not just cut, they had probably shorted, which must have confused the associated systems. The generator feed cables were isolated quickly, but they might have arced with other wires and parts of the wing, which would have posed a risk of fire.

Rethinking the state of the plane to establish what worked came down to the two most basic requirements: fuel and control surfaces. Did we have sufficient fuel to keep us in the air? Did we have enough control surfaces working to control the aircraft and land in one piece? I didn't want to express it like that when we were all holding our nerves, so I didn't say it to Changi. I have seen a transcript of my radio calls to Singapore ATC and their responses. It was a revelation because both parties sounded quite calm but deliberate. We were very busy, and so I told ATC only what they needed to know and no more. I didn't want to tell an 'outsider' how bad it was and engender panic when we had not even completed the five phases of our ECAM checklists. If I started listing the problems and telling them we'd be coming in heavy, I would be articulating what everyone on the flight deck was thinking – that we were in serious trouble – and I didn't think it was time for that. It was time to keep fighting, to have full control of the plane and to stay positive, and for this reason I kept my responses simple and vague to Changi ATC, just telling them: 'Qantas 32. We have one engine failed, fuel and hydraulic fluid leaking from the wing and extensive checklists. We need another 30 minutes in the hold. Please advise fire services that we'll be stopping at the end of the runway.'

We ended up holding for about one hour and ten minutes.

I declared a PAN, not a MAYDAY. A PAN implies an emergency where immediate assistance is not required. A MAYDAY call means there is grave and imminent danger, and immediate assistance is required. I was happy to retain the PAN, and the crew agreed with me. Losing an engine is not a critical problem on a four-engine aircraft and doesn't necessarily warrant a MAYDAY. We practise engine failures of the worst kind every three months in the simulator, and aircraft performance is always calculated on being able to lose an engine during take-off or at any stage of flight and being able to safely land at an acceptable airport. This would also be my fourth real engine failure. I was not ready to elevate the emergency to a MAYDAY based upon the other failures either. ECAM identified many failures, but also gave us the processes to fix the errors or to mitigate the resulting threats. I didn't know the true state of the aircraft or our options until the five ECAM phases and our threat and error management were completed. When these processes were finished, I was happy that the aircraft we had built 'from the ground up' in my mind was sound and acceptable.

I also didn't declare a MAYDAY because I didn't think I was going to die. I hadn't stopped to think of my wife Coral and my children Alexander and Sophia. I felt confident we would get *Nancy-Bird* safely on the ground.

Little did we know that Changi ATC's repeated calls and requests for information were triggered by what they were hearing from CNN and Reuters, due to the Batam Island debris.

Afterwards I would find out that at this time, Alan Milne, the Qantas head of maintenance operations, was in the Integrated Operations Centre with three colleagues, standing around a TV screen watching CNN showing pictures of the engine nacelle taken by residents of Batam Island. Alan recalls it as being a quiet time, thinking the worst but hoping for the best, until that 'Oh shit' moment when the camera revealed an image of the turbine disk. At least Alan could see from the Qantas 'AirCom' computer displays that we were holding at 7400 feet.

We were flying at a steady altitude, so he figured we had control of the aircraft, but he knew little else. Then Alan's mind fast-forwarded to thinking about our eventual arrival. His mind froze when he thought of us on the ground and making the life-and-death decision whether to evacuate the passengers down the slides onto the runway or to keep them on board. Alan remembered an A330 Qantas captain who was in the same situation in Osaka only a few years earlier who made the decision to evacuate the passengers and crew. The captain made the correct decision for those circumstances, but a few passengers were injured during the evacuation, with one passenger breaking his hip. Alan didn't want us to be faced with the same decision and evacuate unnecessarily, so he put his immediate attention to ensuring stairs and buses would be in position for our arrival.

While the situation was critical and the flight deck was tense, we were still not panicking. I don't think it's fair to expect passengers to be calm and cooperative only to discover later that the pilots were beside themselves with fear. It wasn't that way for us; we didn't have the luxury of time to reflect and panic. We remained 100 per cent focused on what lay in front of us and what we had to do. Every word uttered was definite, measured, almost robotic. We were following SOPs and, although the checklists didn't stop coming, we crosschecked and verified the bad news ECAM was reporting with what we could deduce from the synoptic displays before we actioned any checklist. The ECAM was making sense and guiding us through the mechanical Armageddon, and we felt in control. It was an eerie flight deck, with the continual warning 'beeps' every time the flight warning computers registered the next incoming failure, sometimes interrupting with a new higher priority procedure. The system displays and the overhead panel were a sea of red as Matt read the latest alerts and paced his way through the checklists.

Months later, when I presented the QF32 story, I would play the soundtrack of the cockpit aural warnings to illustrate to the audience what happens when the ECAM starts issuing piercing alerts and won't shut up. I haven't seen an audience yet that can handle the noise for more than 30 seconds before people screw up their faces and demand that someone switch the sound off. We endured it for much longer – it was like being in a military stress experiment.

We wanted to continue through the checklists, but I was very conscious of our fuel situation and how long we could remain safely airborne. We had a maximum of two and a half hours in the air before Engine 1 failed, and that became our mantra: *we have two and half hours, we have options! We have time to run the checklists, we have time to stabilise this plane, understand it, then configure and get it into shape. We have time to plan a landing. We have time, we have time . . .* but that was two and a half hours *maximum*. Fuel was pouring out of the left wing at an unknown rate so this time could be slashed. If Engine 1 ran out of fuel we'd have to reconfigure for a slightly more complex two-engine-out approach and landing.

I was growing tired of being reactive to the ECAM and I wanted something positive to focus on. There were too many alerts, too many things broken and not much to be achieved by dwelling on them. If you lose half your ailerons, you can't just sulk that it's not perfect. I remembered back to my brother's Arial Red Hunter bike in the Victorian bush; I was too small to both start the huge motorbike and keep it upright, so I'd start it on the rear wheel stand and rock it until it rolled off the stand, and I'd be off. My goal was to ride the bike – not to complain about what didn't work.

It was 50 minutes into our flight. We'd attended constantly to the ECAM and attempted to make the fixes on the alerts for failed and degraded systems. I considered that process to be ECAM phase 1 – fixing the broken items or shutting them down, and stabilising the aircraft to remain safely in flight. But we had to move on from chasing the ECAM; we had to move on to phase 2.

ECAM's phase 2 is all about 'what'. What is the state of the affected systems after the checklists have been run? ECAM now displays the diagnostic displays for the degraded systems. For a simple engine failure ECAM would only show a few displays: the hydraulics, electrics and pneumatics. However, in our case the failures had bridged so many systems that ECAM presented almost every system synoptic display. As Matt pressed the 'tick' pushbutton we were taken on a tour of all the failed systems. The aircraft was making sense to us and it was at this stage I was able to gain confidence in my inverted logic. Fuel: it was a mess, but we had more than two hours before Engine 1 would fail. Hydraulics: two out of eight hydraulic pumps working – fine. Electrics: the left wing was electrically dead, but the right wing was fine, and we had started the APU to provide two more generators when needed. Wheels: the brakes were a mess and hydraulics were shot, the auto-brakes had failed, some anti-skid modules were inoperative and brake-control systems had degraded to the emergency brake mode . . . *forget that!* But if I put my foot on the brakes, they would work. Flight control: the enormous outer ailerons had failed, and they were slipstreaming in the air, both sitting at about 70 per cent up. We must have been losing a lot of lift. *Stop that!* We have two small high-speed ailerons and one medium-sized aileron – not much so I'd better do a control-check and be smooth on the approach. We knew the aircraft pretty well at this 50-minute mark, but it was a relief to have ECAM get us to the point where it had done all it could be expected to do, and all that was left was for it to say, 'I'm done, handing over – now it's your turn!'

ECAM phase 3 could be described as housekeeping. Phase 3 is identical for every ECAM checklist, containing procedural checks that might provide a remedy. We pondered whether any of our failed systems could be reset. We have about 60 reset switches located on the overhead panel, their purpose being to reboot computers – much like <CTRL+ALT+DELETE> on a PC. I asked if anyone wanted to investigate resetting any systems. There was a long pause; resets take a long time, they would probably not work, the aircraft was extensively damaged, and we wanted to get on the ground.

Next, I asked Matt to run the abnormal checklist for over-weight landing as we would be landing 40 tonnes over our maximum landing weight. This checklist would change some of our procedures to mitigate the threats.

The combination of a fuel imbalance and a reduced roll capability was a definite concern. Along with the issue of fuel generally was the problem of how it was distributed in the fuel tanks and the effect an imbalance would have on the centre of gravity. The large outer ailerons on the left and right wings, and the mid aileron on the left wing, were failed, reducing our roll authority, particularly in strong crosswinds or turbulent conditions. Together, these two failures combined to reduce our lateral control of the aircraft.

We were also inhibited by our control of the engines. Engine 2 was failed, Engines 1 and 4 degraded, and Engine 3 was also degraded but not quite as severely. Having failures in all three remaining engines did not spell disaster in itself, but at a time when we had centre-of-gravity imbalances and only 35 per cent of our roll control surfaces working, it was a complication we didn't need. It wasn't that we lacked the skills on QF32, it was more that since we had one failed and three degraded engines we didn't have large margins of error. If we set our thrust incorrectly we might cause a yaw motion that induced a roll motion that absorbed more of our limited roll control – not ideal. During a go-around, if we moved the thrust too far forward we thought we might over-temp and blow up another two engines, and then we'd be left trying to fly over-weight and on only one remaining engine – impossible!

We had multiple failures affecting control of the aircraft, so I configured the plane for cruising as best as I could. None of the engines was operating normally, the auto-thrust was failed and we had limited roll capability. Losing auto-thrust meant I had to control the thrust manually, and this task would be made harder every time I added thrust to enter a turn in the holding pattern. Any thrust imbalance would yaw the aircraft and consequently cause it to roll. So I set Engines 1 and 4 to a mid-thrust level, then took my hands off those thrust levers and controlled the speed by varying the thrust on inboard Engine 3. This worked well, the speed was easy to control accurately and I could shift more attention to managing other issues.

My method wasn't perfect and you certainly wouldn't want to fly for twelve hours across the Pacific with the aircraft in this trim state. But it was a safe fix needing little brain space and monitoring while we worked out how we were going to get *Nancy-Bird* and her passengers safely to ground.

CHAPTER 21

It Won't Do It!

With ECAM phases 1, 2 and 3 completed, we'd come to a point where we had tried everything to fix the aircraft. Now it was time to take stock of what was remaining and seriously look at what we could do about landing.

In phase 4, ECAM transitions from trying to fix the errors to accepting the failures and providing advice to mediate the threats. Normally ECAM would display a maximum of two or three INFO (information and guidance) items in the case of an engine failure. On our flight, Matt read out an eye-watering two pages, each page displaying fourteen INFO items. It must be an Airbus record.

In the second part of phase 4, ECAM displays a list of redundant systems that have failed. (Redundant systems by definition have backup systems, so they should be resilient to simple failures.)

In the four years I'd been flying the A380, I don't think I'd ever seen more than two or three failed systems in this list. On QF32 we had an unprecedented large number of failed systems. Matt started reading through the list of failed systems, one item after another. I mentally tracked each failure before acknowledging it – a sign for Matt to announce the next item. Then Matt started reading page 2 – *page 2!* I'd never seen two pages of faults, and it was taking Matt a long time to read through the list. As I heard each failure announced only to be followed by another, I felt that pile-driver again pushing me deeper into my seat. I was trying to fly the aircraft, monitor our environment and, at the same time, listen to Matt's calls, but I was becoming fatigued. I'd seen the failures before in earlier parts of the ECAM and I had already decided it was better to think of what was working rather than what had failed. Then Matt called, 'Press "More" for the next more page.' I thought, *What? Another MORE page?*

Matt's voice was hoarse, he was tired and, like me, he had also inverted his logic. Finally, as he called out more inoperative systems on page 3, his voice broke and he added, 'Whatever.'

We had a list of failures of redundant systems that spanned three pages, each page containing two columns – another Airbus record that will hopefully never be challenged. I agreed with Matt: the list of what was not working for our landing was well established. We'd just spent the last 55 minutes trying to fix all these systems. We created a new term in the Airbus lexicon that day: 'ECAM fatigue'. Mark could sense the stress and mental exhaustion in Matt's eyes, so passed him a fresh bottle of water.

We progressed to the next stage of the landing prep: phase 5, and the LDPA. The LDPA is an acronym for LanDing Performance Application; a Java program that runs on our two laptops. These laptops are stored either side of the two pilots and are connected to the aircraft's networks by a 2 metre–long umbilical cord.

The pilot enters the airport, runway, weather conditions and aircraft status, then the LDPA calculates the landing performance. It sounds simple, but it's a very complex calculation. Luckily ECAM was designed to support the LDPA. ECAM presented a list entitled 'ALERTS IMPACTING LDG PERF'. This list contains the names of the failures that affect our landing performance that must be entered into the LDPA. For a normal engine failure that we practise in the simulator, we might see one item in this list. But we were in for another shock that day. I'm sure I must have sighed and sunk yet lower in my seat as I viewed the list in front of us. It wasn't just a few items, the list once again extended over two pages!

We needed a break. Matt was exhausted, I was eager to talk to ATC and the passengers, and ECAM phase 5 was now a ten-minute computer exercise. I asked Dave and Harry – two expert A380 pilots to calculate our LDPA performance.

While Dave and Harry went to work on the laptops, I handed the flying of the aircraft over to Matt. He needed to rest his voice, and flying the aircraft would be the ideal way to relax. I explained that controlling the thrust and speed would be easy if he just varied the thrust on Engine 3. I then asked Mark to monitor Matt and the aircraft.

I spoke to ATC again. I told them we would need more orbits in the holding pattern before we could start our approach, that we were still leaking fuel and possibly hydraulic oil from the left wing, that we would need a long 20-mile final for a stable approach to Runway Two-Zero Centre, and that we would need fire services to meet us at the end of the runway.

After updating ATC, I was contemplating our position, fuel and options when Dave looked up from the laptop screen and shrugged.

'What's wrong?' I asked.

Dave said, 'Richard, I've run an LDPA calculation and it won't work. It won't calculate our landing performance.'

'Dave,' I called, 'take out all the crap and leave only the critical failures.'

'I have!' Dave said.

'Well . . . keep trying.'

We had built ourselves an aircraft that was flying well, and we had fuel, which gave us time and options. We were safe. I needed to wait until Dave and Harry came up with a performance solution for our landing, and that would clearly take time, so I now had an opportunity to brief the passengers.

I again asked Mark to monitor Matt and the aircraft. I had to be careful. I told the pilots that everything we said from now on would be on YouTube within 30 minutes of our landing.

My caution was well founded as Ulf Waschbusch (seat 55A) was recording the 'sights and sounds' in the cabin. I thought for a while before I keyed the cabin announcement system and commenced a long briefing to the passengers. I had to be calm and empathetic. I'd just spent the last hour overseeing a very technical response to a systems crisis on the world's largest and most technologically advanced passenger aircraft, and I didn't know what our landing was going to be like. But we had one of the most experienced A380 crews on the planet on board that day, we were working as an exceptional team, and I was very confident we would eventually solve the problems in front of us and get everyone off the aircraft alive. I took a few long, deep breaths, then keyed the PA.

I spoke to the passengers for about ten minutes, explaining only what they already knew: that an engine had failed, there was a hole in the wing and there were fuel leaks. I spoke in general terms about the engine because I wasn't aware of why it had exploded. 'Don't be worried about the engine failure – Qantas pilots train for this type of failure every three months in the simulator, and we come out sweating, so this is just another engine failure.' I explained how we had spent the last hour reconfiguring the aircraft, that we were flying safely, we were in control of the aircraft and that we'd need another 45 minutes to set up for our approach before we landed. Foremost in my mind was to give the passengers the confidence that I felt – that we would be okay.

'The A380 is the newest and most advanced aircraft in the world,' I said, 'and although there has been some damage, we have reconfigured the systems and the aircraft is safe – you are safe. Don't worry when you see fire engines surround us after landing,' I said. 'And back in Australia, 100 people have assembled in the Qantas Crisis Centre to look at our flight and monitor us, and they are looking at your personal details now. They will look after you, so don't worry about missing any connections.'

Privately I knew the Crisis Centre would not be worrying about passenger connections – they would be focused only on whether we would be able to land. And, of course, I didn't have a clue what Qantas actually knew about us. Both of our satellite phones had failed, and our only contact with the outside world was via Singapore ATC.

However, I think it was comforting to tell the passengers about the Qantas Crisis Centre. In fact I had toured the centre two weeks prior to this flight, and had met and quizzed the centre's manager, Roz Wheatley.

In closing off my very long public address, I concluded: 'Don't worry, you are safe. We've practised these procedures many times in the simulator, and so now it's time to run the procedure. Klaus, the cabin supervisor, will take care of you now, and I'll see you on the ground.'

My PA was technical and direct, but I'm not so sure it was empathetic. Michael von Reth sensed the atmosphere was too tense; my PA had not relaxed people sufficiently. He grabbed the PA and said, 'Actually, folks, it's good the captain has spoken to you, but I would like to correct two points he just made. First, my name is not Klaus, it's Michael, and, secondly, I am not the supervisor, I am THE MANAGER!' The cabin filled with raucous laughter. I'd mistakenly called Michael 'Klaus' because 'Klaus' was his official name on the crew list (General Declaration). Because he's so good at his job, Michael saw a chance to make some fun out of my mistake and lighten an otherwise grim mood. He took people's fear and converted it into humour. Good people like Michael are priceless.

I turned off the PA – and turned back to the flight crew. I was so fortunate to have additional pilots the calibre of Matt, Mark, Harry and Dave in the flight deck. The whole time I had been speaking to the passengers, Matt and Mark had been calmly flying the aircraft and operating the radios while Harry and Dave worked the complex performance calculations.

However, we were not sure what our performance was and how we would land the aircraft. I was worried our fuel and centre of gravity imbalances were getting worse, fuel was still leaking and the fuel feeding Engine 1 was getting lower. Now it was time for the real work to begin – it was time to land.

I rejoined the crew just as performance information for our landing was coming forward from Dave and Harry. I heard Matt being asked to enter the approach speed of 145 knots in the flight management system (FMS).

With his left hand, Matt started keying buttons, then he stopped and thought. His eyes rose up to the left looking through me in a daze, and then he said: 'It can't be 145 knots – it's far too slow!'

Matt was right. At 145 knots and with our weight and configuration, we wouldn't stay in the air, we would stall. The speed Matt had been given was the base approach speed for an aircraft with functioning slats. We had no slats. It was a simple mistake, but it would have had interesting consequences if not picked up before our approach. Heads went down again in the back.

Matt was 100 per cent on the ball. After a long hour of actioning ECAM checklists, and with a hoarse voice and a tired mind, he still had enough mental space, thought and common sense to catch what the rest of us had missed. Pilots make mistakes and they cannot process data as fast as a computer. But pilots have *judgement*. It was a brilliant moment from Matt.

A short time later a call came from the back with the blessing: 'Richard, we have performance – we have 100 metres!'

We had a stop margin of just 100 metres. Changi's longest runway is 4000 metres. An A380 at maximum landing weight requires 1800 metres on a wet runway. We would need 3900 metres to stop. If we came in 3 knots faster than 168 knots, the LDPA predicted we would overrun the runway. Clearly, maintaining an accurate speed would be critical. I think flying Iroquois helicopters had preconditioned me to flying in limiting conditions. The small speed margin on this approach would be just another limit. I was not worried; the margins were thin, but achievable.

There were many failures that pushed our usual 1800-metre stopping distance up to 3900 metres. We had a dangerous combination of being 41 tonnes over our maximum landing weight and 23 knots faster than our normal approach speed. We would be touching down with 48 per cent more kinetic energy, but with dramatically less stopping power (64 per cent full brakes, applied late, and reduced spoilers, reduced aileron brakes and reduced reverse thrust).

I had the utmost faith and respect for Harry and Dave. They knew the performance applications better than I did, and if these two check captains independently thought we could land the aircraft within the constraints of the Singapore runway, and had crosschecked their data, then that was good enough for me.

Dave had made a few changes to get the calculation. First, he realised the software had defaulted to selecting the 'wet runway' setting, which adds an extra 15 per cent to our landing distance. If Singapore's Runway Two-Zero Centre had been wet then, according to the LDPA, we'd have flown off the end of the runway like a ski jumper in the Winter Olympics.

There were a number of issues we had to resolve and brief before we could start the approach: cabin preparation, fuel on board, fuel leakage, aircraft damage, aircraft weight, fuel imbalances, flight controls, control checks, emergency gravity extension of the landing gear, long stabilised approach, go-around potential (engines, partial gear retraction, fuel), landing speed, increased aircraft attitude, pitch up on touchdown, nose wheel touchdown, manual braking, runway length, taxiing potential, brake fires, fuel fire, fire engines and then the emergency evacuation.

*

When considering performance for landing, you have to assure yourself the balance of forces and energy are just right for the runway environment. Mass and velocity are not to be messed with, especially when you're landing an overweight aircraft at 166 knots (307 kilometres per hour) with half the brakes. These may sound like brutal components of a safe landing, but every pilot must grapple with these considerations, whether they are landing a space shuttle or Dad's single-engine Piper Arrow.

Our aircraft's rate of descent was a critical factor. It couldn't be so high that the landing gear collapses on touchdown. I knew that the landing gear would probably collapse if our descent rate on touchdown was more than 10 feet per second (41 tonnes overweight). But the increased weight on QF32 meant our approach speed had to be increased. Our actual rate of descent during the approach was 14 feet per second.

The approach speed was also critical. We only had a 4-knot margin in our speed during the approach. Speed was our conundrum. The speed that is your friend in the air, providing enough lift to stay airborne, becomes your enemy when you approach the tarmac and then want to stop on the preciously short runway. The runway overrun area at Changi was not bad: 300 metres of pasture, a road, then another 300 metres into the sea.

We couldn't make ourselves lighter by dumping fuel because the jettison valves and pumps had failed; and we couldn't burn off excess fuel by staying in the air for five hours because number one engine would run out of fuel in two hours, and fail.

We were stuck with a very high approach speed. The shrapnel damage to the leading edge of the left wing had destroyed both motors that drive the droop-nose and slats. The slats are panels at the front of the mid- and outboard wing sections, which are deployed at lower speeds to aggressively control the airflow and increase lift, and so enable the aircraft to approach at slower speeds and conduct safer landings. The airflow over the inboard sections of the A380's wing is more aerodynamically robust and reliable, so for these sections, the complicated slats are replaced by droop-nose sections. The slats are audible when you're a passenger: about three minutes before touching down you can hear them 'whirring'. However the slats and droop-nose surfaces were inoperative and locked tight. We were going to have to land without those crucial components.

We had another significant problem. The plane was over-weight with degraded aerodynamic and engine braking, and there was now more reliance on our degraded brakes – they would absorb 50 per cent more energy than they normally would. With the brakes working so hard to stop the aircraft, they would burn white-hot and provide a new hazard, given the amount of fuel pouring out of the wing. Fire.

Then there is the other factor that comes into play when discussing a tricky landing: stalling.

CHAPTER 22

Through the Looking Glass

Most people think that when you stall an aircraft you simply run out of speed, which means air is no longer flowing over the wing's surfaces fast enough to create the differential pressure effects that create 'lift'. In this case, the law of gravity takes over from the rules of aerodynamics and you crash. To be a bit more precise, an aircraft doesn't stall – the wing stalls. It's not a stall of the engine, but an aerodynamic stall where the wings do not have sufficient lift to support the aircraft, and an immediate increase in airspeed and a decrease in pitch attitude is needed to recover. Furthermore, the wing does not stall at a given speed, it stalls at a certain angle of attack (the angle at which the air impinges on the wing). Most commercial jet wings stall at an angle of attack of between 10 and 20 degrees.

Stalling training is a scary event for beginner pilots. Initially ignorance is bliss as you enjoy the pleasures and serenity of controlled flight, thinking 'this is easy'. But soon enough your overconfidence is shattered, interrupted by shaking, wild oscillations and partial loss of control. Your stall training might end up as spinning training – as I discovered on my first flight with Bill Evans!

Commercial aircraft should never be flown close to the stall. Our normal minimum speeds are selected to guarantee high margins – we can lift 20 per cent more weight in the cruise and 51 per cent more weight as we approach to land. This means the aircraft can encounter turbulence and wind shears yet still have sufficient margin to accommodate the flare. The flare is when we lift the plane's nose and consequently slow the rate of descent to touchdown. Then we present the landing gear to the tarmac and gently fly the wheels onto the runway, kissing the ground and giving that gentle landing that pilots and passengers like so much.

In the case where we do mishandle a degraded aircraft, the Airbus flight warning computers give us two types of warnings of an approaching stall. The first warning is a loud aural warning, 'SPEED, SPEED', that interrupts everything else. This warning tells you that you must add thrust immediately to speed up. If you ignore this warning and continue to slow, then a very loud 'STALL, STALL' deafens your senses when the angle of attack increases to within 2 degrees of the stalling angle of attack. During my 25 years of flying in Qantas, I had never heard any stall warnings except in the simulator.

Landing an A380 is a precision exercise. Pilots are trained to factor the many variables in the aircraft, runway and weather to execute a safe landing every time. The speed must be flown accurately – too slow and you might stall as you flare the aircraft to land – too fast and you might touch down on the nose wheel first and 'trip' the airframe over. The rate of descent is also critical. At the certified maximum landing weight of 391 tonnes, if it's higher than 12 feet per second the landing gear will probably collapse. Then you have to touch down in the landing zone – if your wheels touch down short of the runway, they might be ripped off as you mount the lip to the runway. If you flare too high or too slowly and float along the runway, then you risk overrunning the runway. Pilots aim for a smooth touchdown on dry runways, but a firm touchdown on wet runways to prevent aquaplaning on top of the water and overrunning the runway. Finally, the A380's long and wide airframe provides additional limitations for a safe landing. We have to ensure we touch down with the wings level and the nose not too high – otherwise we'll scrape one of the US$18.5 million engines, the wing tips or the tail. So pilots minimise the risks by calculating their actual landing distances then factoring this distance by another two thirds.

Most of our safety margins (and factors) are reduced in the event of emergencies. The LDPA Dave and Harry used to calculate our landing parameters reduced our approach speed to give a 19 per cent speed (41 per cent weight) margin to stall instead of the usual 23 per cent speed (51 per cent weight). Also, the landing distance would not be factored – we would have to land the aircraft more quickly but just as accurately as the Airbus test pilots when they certified the A380.

I was acutely aware of the compounding errors that would challenge every skill I had developed in my 35-year career. We were going to be coming in too fast and landing an aircraft that was way too heavy, out of balance, with damaged wings, little rolling capability and broken wheel brakes, speed brakes and an inoperative engine reverser. Perhaps all these failures would add up to be an impossible mix. Perhaps we would be unable to stop on the runway. Perhaps we were looking at an inevitable runway overrun.

Dave and Harry's calculations were a great relief. We had a 100-metre margin on the Changi runway. It wasn't much, but it was sufficient.

As we discussed the approach one of the pilots said, 'Rich, be careful – you can't afford any excess speed. You'll have a high nose attitude, and there's little or no flare.' Despite these concerns, my pragmatic conclusion was the same: we would ultimately have to land this aircraft, and there was a limit to how long we could remain airborne to look at other options. I thought we were safer orbiting Singapore than any other airport. There were no runways in Indonesia or Malaysia that were longer than Singapore's runways and that could provide us with extra safety margins.

The 'little or no flare' comment also triggered danger signals in my mind. I thought, What are we going to do? Come in at 166 knots (307 kph) and *not* flare? There was no way I would land this A380 without flaring. We didn't have slats and we couldn't use full flaps – both of which would let us approach at a slower speed. And we were 41 tonnes overweight. All these factors would cause our approach speed and our rate of descent to be increased, and we could easily buckle or break the aircraft at touchdown.

I didn't really resolve these concerns. We had full use of the elevators, which were the control surfaces used to pitch the aircraft up into the flare (or a stall if you overdid it) although our centre of gravity was close to our aft limit. We had lost 65 per cent of our aileron roll-control, so the fly-by-wire computers that lift the spoilers to initiate roll would probably work them more aggressively now. Spoilers spoil lift over the wing, and so increase the stall speed. Increasing the stall speed is not a problem when you approach to land at a speed 23 per cent faster than your stall speed, but nasty consequences were possible when our margin was reduced to 19 per cent or even lower. And I would discover later the landing performance application calculations and pilot airspeed displays were faulty.

I was initially happy to accept the computer-calculated approach speed of 166 knots, but I had this nagging thought at the back of my head: a computer using 250,000 sensors may be the greatest thing to happen to aviation, but it was still just a computer that was still subject to the rule: 'Garbage in – garbage out!' It couldn't and shouldn't override the common sense of an experienced pilot. My job was to fly the plane and apply a sense of reasonableness, not to just blindly follow commands from a computer program that had just failed to give us performance data. We had a very high approach speed, a broken aircraft, and only 100 metres of surplus runway.

I paused and looked away. With our weight, imbalances and complex failures I now had growing doubts the aircraft would be manageable at our approach speed of 166 knots. My primary concern was whether we would have sufficient roll and pitch control. Even though the flight control software had degraded to alternate law, which meant we had no stall protections, I was not worried about this at the time because I knew the A380 had an independent stall warning system that bypassed the flight control computers, and I had told the others as much.

I was not too worried about stalling the aircraft at that time, but I was not aware of all the damage to the wings and the flight controls.

I asked Matt to read through our status screen, starting with the landing gear. The normal landing gear extension system had failed but we could default to a standby gravity system. It would take a few extra minutes, but we had time on our side. So we could get the wheels down, but one of the landing gear computers had failed, so we would lose half our gear indications. Bottom line: emergency gravity extension, three extra minutes, half the sensors.

The brakes were a mess. We'd lost the auto-brakes and the anti-skid was failed on the wing brakes. Half the spoilers were failed. The brakes had reduced to the emergency system, reducing the wing brake pressure from 3000 psi to 1000 psi and we would have only six brake applications before we ran out of pressure. Bottom line: I could press hard on the brake pedals once and only after the nose wheel touches down.

Flight controls: three fuel imbalances, centre of gravity problems, half spoilers and 35 per cent roll control. Bottom line: use the autopilot for finesse. Lock thrust levers 1 and 4, then use only Engine 3 to control the speed. This should minimise yaw-roll and flight control (aileron and spoiler) demands.

Fuel: trashed. But we had at least two hours of fuel remaining on Engine 1 and more on Engines 3 and 4. Bottom line: sufficient fuel, but don't go around unless absolutely necessary.

Engines: three engines working – great. But unsure whether Engines 1 and 4 will overheat and blow up if we attempt a go-around. Bottom line: no problems, but don't go around unless absolutely necessary.

Flare: flare late to minimise float distance and runway stopping distance. Flare early to arrest rate of descent to less than 6 feet per second. Bottom line: don't crush the landing gear!

We were still left with the major headache of landing without stalling, breaking up or running off the end of the runway. Somehow we had to get our approach speed low enough to affect a safe landing, without flying so slow that we stalled and fell out of the sky.

There was only one thing we could do: we'd have to confirm the aircraft's performance before we landed. We'd have to perform a series of control checks to set our real minimum airspeed, as opposed to our theoretical performance as stated by the computers. With 469 people on board, we'd have to see how close we really were to a stall.

This decision to do control checks would be controversial to 90 per cent of commercial pilots. The control check involves actually inducing the aircraft to do what the controls are communicating or warning against. There is no reference in any Airbus manual for how to conduct control checks in fly-by-wire aircraft. Indeed it is a mark of the divisiveness of this issue that nowhere in Qantas literature, manuals or SOPs is there any mention of control checks. Neither is there any reference from Australia's Civil Aviation Safety Authority (CASA) – our federal aviation safety regulator.

Flight control checks are not spoken about. To people who don't fly for a living, conducting a flight control check might seem reckless and inviting disaster. Even to many who do fly for a living, the idea of knowingly pushing an aircraft to the point where you might get a stall warning in the cockpit is regarded as cowboy behaviour.

I was taught control checks in the RAAF; the idea is that if your aircraft has taken enemy fire or you've collided with a friendly plane while in formation, and you have a damaged airframe and/or flight controls, you have to be able to test how the aircraft performs when it approaches, slows and flares *before* you try to do it seven seconds and 50 feet above the tarmac. If you worry that your aircraft has damaged slats and holes in the wings, and you're not sure how it will perform, you typically do a control check as you change to each successive configuration, all the while circling your runway at a safe height so you can accelerate and recover if you start to lose control.

It may be, in our case, for instance, that your computers tell you that you'll stall at 160 knots on a 3-degree approach slope. So you don't want to fly the approach at 166 knots – you really want to do it with an extra 19 per cent margin – at 190 knots.

So you do flight control checks at a safe altitude to see if you can gently manoeuvre the aircraft in roll, pitch and yaw. If the aircraft departs normal flight, or if a stall warning siren is triggered at any stage, then this indicates significant wing and flight control damage and so the approach speed should be increased (by about 20 per cent) to remove the risk of losing control during the approach and landing manoeuvre. I have to stress that this is my own very basic procedure based upon standards test pilots use to certify aircraft stalling speeds.

Of course, the passengers might not have felt comfortable knowing we were about to do a control check, so that was one more announcement I kept to myself. A control check has a certain element of risk to it, sure. However, the greater risk is committing to a landing when you are not certain about the information or the integrity of the systems you are acting upon.

To me, the control check was a must and the best option.

CHAPTER 23

It's Now or Never

Iknew that Changi's 20 Centre runway was 4000 metres long and we should come to a halt in 3900 metres if the computers were right. But I had to know how the aircraft was going to flare. The landing distance for an Airbus A380 is calculated from the point where the landing gear is 50 feet above the runway to the point where the aircraft stops. Simplistically, the test pilots are expected to have the aircraft transition from 50 feet to touchdown within about seven seconds. If you take more than seven seconds to touch down, every additional second represents 85 metres less runway available for braking and stopping. We had only 100 metres of runway to spare, so every second saved in the air would be critical. My highest priority was to do a landing as good as or better than the Airbus test pilots on their certification flights.

As I was contemplating this challenge, my mind flashed back to 1980 when we were learning to conduct short take-off and landing (STOL) landings in the Caribous at night on grass strips only 300 metres long. All we had then were six lights and lots of adrenaline. As we descended, it was imperative to lock our eyes and our flight path to intercept the runway at an exact point, our aim point. As we transitioned through the last hundred feet of height above the runway, just as the ground expanded and exploded in your peripheral view, that was the time to lift the nose and flare the aircraft; at exactly the right height and rate. If the flare is done correctly, the rate of descent is arrested concurrent with the wheels kissing the ground. No floating, no being suspended 1 foot above the runway as precious stopping surface melts away behind you. Caribou STOL landings were precision procedures, learned through repetition until we got it right. The pressure was on. If I could eyeball land a Caribou in Tarpini, I could do the same with an A380. All I had to do was to have *Nancy-Bird* touch down within seven seconds from passing 50 feet. I would need to be smooth with the controls, accurate with the speed control and eagle-eye accurate with my aim and flare point.

Matt got on the radio to Changi Approach and asked them for a descent to intercept a '20 mile final at 4000 feet for Runway Two-Zero Centre'. A 'final' is your final approach, where your aircraft trajectory aligns with the runway centreline that has been extended out and up at a 3-degree angle. The final approach is a narrow cone that reduces your variable dimensions down to just one: speed. You are aiming to slow the aircraft and put it at a 50-foot wheel height above the runway on speed and configured to land.

Most pilots normally intercept the ILS final approach about 10 miles from the runway at 3000 feet altitude. From here they progressively slow the aircraft, while configuring the slats, flaps and landing gear. The aim is to be in the cone, configured, on speed, with the engine thrust stable at 1000 feet above the runway. But I wanted longer finals.

I knew we had to conduct multiple control checks as the configuration was changed. We had to lower the landing gear, then I had to do my final control check fully configured, gear down, with 'FLAPS 3' at 166 knots. This would be my final dress rehearsal of the landing. Once we were descending on finals, if I wanted to put on full thrust and go around I was not sure if our remaining engines would overheat, and I knew we would be unable to raise the landing gear. So in the back of my mind I was preconditioning my mindset that, once I commenced finals, I would continue to land and not go around. I thought it was best to get our landing 'dress rehearsal' out of the way at a safe altitude of 4000 before I committed to the approach and landing. All these thoughts flashed through my mind as we approached the finals.

Changi tower vectored us to the north to position for a U-turn then the 20-mile approach to Runway Two-Zero Centre. They cleared us to descend to 4000 feet.

Mark spoke up as we rounded the turn to finals: 'Rich, do we have a commit altitude?'

It was an excellent call from Mark, reminding me I had not sufficiently briefed the other pilots and cabin crew. I explained my reasoning and why I didn't really want to go around, including our worsening fuel and balance condition, and left it at that. The other pilots understood; we needed to land this aircraft now.

Finally I realised I had not warned the cabin crew that we were about to start the approach, so I sent Mark into the cabin for the last time to brief Michael von Reth on the state of the plane and the 'best' and 'worst' scenarios for what hazards the landing might produce. Those scenarios included a 'heavy' landing, collapse of landing gear, runway overrun, fuel fire and airframe break-up. It isn't pretty but this is what aviation crises come down to, and it's what we train for. Mark told Michael: 'We might not be able to stop on the runway and there might be a passenger evacuation.' Michael replied confidently, 'The cabin, passengers and crew are ready.'

The passengers knew we had circled for more than an hour before trying to land, and some were nervous, holding hands and praying, and they were being watched intently by Michael and his crew. Their interests were best served by maintaining a sense of calm and ensuring the cabin crew were prepared.

We were also tense on the flight deck: Matt went into the pre-landing routine, actioning our deferred checklists and then our approach and landing checklists. The flaps were now extended to the first position, 'FLAPS 1'.

I was cautious because I didn't trust the landing performance calculations and I had decided I was going to control-check the aircraft to satisfy myself the aircraft was controllable and we had a good margin to the stall speed. I anticipated at least one of the other four pilots might register their complaint because the discussion of control checks never arises in airline textbooks, particularly with passengers on board. I was conscious they might think I was a 'cowboy' and reckless.

We were being vectored in a long, sweeping left turn onto our final heading. As we headed into the south and straightened for our final, Matt called our altitude – 4500 feet – and I said: 'We need some control checks.'

I heard the sound of shifting weight behind me but neither of the check pilots spoke. I don't know if Harry and Dave wanted to stop me, but I had timed the announcement to catch them unawares. By the time they'd swapped their glances, it was too late.

With complete silence on the flight deck, I disconnected the autopilot and I pushed the sidestick left and right carefully, then forward and backwards vigorously to ascertain that I had control of the aircraft and that it was responding to my inputs. We watched the flight control synoptic displays as they showed what was happening on the wings. Both outer ailerons and one mid aileron were unpowered and slipstreaming in airflow – at about 80 per cent full up! In addition, at least one spoiler was also unpowered and raised into the airflow. I had read about this in the aircraft manuals, but I was not ready for the shock I felt when I saw this. The conclusion was obvious: if a wing spoiler and 65 per cent of our ailerons were floating up when they were failed, then we were losing a LOT of lift over the wing forward of these surfaces. As I rolled the aircraft through about 10 degrees of roll to the left, then to the right, we could see the remaining ailerons were moving through about 60 to 70 per cent of their full travel. As I jerked the stick forward and back, I waited to see if I could feel any buffeting over the tail plane that would indicate an approach to the stall. It felt good to me. Back in the cabin, however, Second Officer Andrew Eccles recognised I was doing a control check. He would later tell me it made him feel worried about the state of the plane; it was clearly worse than he had expected. He realised our risks and pulled his seatbelt tight.

We then extended the flaps to positions 2 and 3. I conducted a quick flight control check after each selection.

Then we turned our attention to the landing gear. The normal gear-extension systems had failed and we had to initiate the gravity-operated emergency extension. It can take up to two minutes for the gear to fall and lock into place. And once the emergency landing system is down, it can't be retracted. When Matt asked for confirmation, I called 'CONFIRMED!' Matt lifted the cover, then activated the emergency electrical switches to have the 18-tonne landing gear fall out under the influence only of gravity. What if the emergency modules were damaged by the explosion? What if our gear failed to lock down? It was a quiet time. The gear normally takes about 60 seconds to fall, and the over-centre locks fall into position before we know whether we have our 22 wheels down and locked.

Two minutes is a long time: Matt was thinking about his wife and kids.

We heard the 'clunk, clunk, clunk, clunk' as the main landing gear locked down into place. Eighty seconds had elapsed; but no nose wheel? Where's that fifth strut?

There was a long 20-second pause before 'clunk' as the final gear strut locked down. We only had half our indicators showing our landing gear positions, but we were expecting that, given that one of our landing gear control systems had failed.

It was now five minutes before we were aiming to land: 'QF32, Singapore Tower. G'day. The surface wind is 180 degrees at 5 knots. Runway Two-Zero Centre clear to land.'

It was time now for the final dress rehearsal of our landing. I disconnected the autopilot again and started the last control check. Because it's a fly-by-wire aircraft I wanted to check how much our controls had to be pushed in order to give us normal performance: would there be a lag between my sidestick and the control surfaces? Would the fly-by-wire try to protect degraded control surfaces by inhibiting my instructions to them? To test this I gave the sidestick 60 per cent of its available travel, which is a fairly dramatic movement. There was not much response from the plane's control surfaces or the aircraft itself. It wasn't a great result – we didn't have normal control, but we were flying.

If I had to narrow down any one part of the flight that I think was critical to our successful outcome, it was the flight control checks. We conducted a full dress rehearsal of the landing at 4000 feet and the aircraft performed admirably.

No matter what happened during the subsequent approach and landing, I felt I had confirmed the aircraft was safe to land.

I reconnected the autopilot as we made our final turn onto the ILS centreline. It was time to land. But then the auto-pilot tripped out for no apparent reason. 'Beep beep beep' the warning horn went off for about the hundredth time so I was not really surprised, but this time the ECAM didn't display 'AP OFF' (meaning auto-pilot off). Instead it displayed 'RAT OUT'.

I couldn't believe it. Would this ever stop?

The ram air turbine (RAT) is a last-ditch electrical generator that keeps the A380 on electrical 'life support'. With the RAT deployed the aircraft would automatically degrade to provide only the essential and emergency systems. We would lose four of our seven flight control computers, all autopilots, auto-trim, all flight directors, all engine reversers, all radio altimeters and normal brakes. Our flight controls would revert to direct law, we'd have only 28 per cent of maximum braking, and the fuel cross-feed valves would open and complicate our fuel leaks.

I couldn't recall all of these items when the 'RAT OUT' message appeared on the screen, but I knew we were due for even more trouble. That pile-driver was pummelling me into my seat again and I entered a cold sweat, waiting for another barrage of bells and alarms as the aircraft would again degrade and we'd have to tackle our next series of failures. But the bells didn't sound; the screens and radios didn't go blank. It took a few seconds to appreciate that the 'RAT OUT' message was in amber – not green. The amber colour meant the RAT was being commanded out, but it had failed to deploy – hallelujah! At last, a failure that actually helped us!

The APU was running and I thought we were saved from the total electrics failure – albeit for a little time!

A magical silence pervaded the flight deck. Total silence for a while. It was now one hour and 30 minutes since the explosions, and we all shared the same thoughts: had we completed all the required actions? Had we missed anything? We'd actioned about a hundred ECAM warnings and checklists. We'd stabilised the aircraft, built ourselves a Cessna replacement, and we'd briefed ourselves, the cabin crew, the passengers and air traffic control. Were we ready?

Yep, I thought, I'm happy. Now let's put this aircraft on the ground!

I had practised emergency landings in the simulator – now it was time to run those procedures. We had kept to our SOPs the entire flight, including all the task sharing, so we all knew what our responsibilities were, what we would say and when. Even though we were all working at 100 per cent, the cockpit was now very quiet.

I asked for one last look at the fuel page and told everyone to think about a possible evacuation, and then said, 'Let's do this.'

The nose lowered and we started our way down.

CHAPTER 24

Threading the Eye of a Needle

Harry called out loud and clear: 'Richard, you can't be fast!'

Harry was worried about our speed control. I was using only one inboard engine to control our speed. This non-standard technique enabled me to contain the speed within 165 to 168 knots during the final approach. On a digital aircraft, one knot can be the difference between safe flight and a speed warning. I still had set the two outside engines – 1 and 4 – to the same thrust and was controlling the throttle on Engine 3 to minimise the yaw and roll divergencies. Airbuses are terrible to fly with manual thrust; they are designed to be flown with fly-by-wire and auto-thrust, and so they don't have the manual thrust-balancing system that operates so well on a Boeing 747–400.

Balancing the thrust to prevent yaw and roll was a good idea, but not good enough. We had lost 75 per cent of our aileron roll authority on the left wing, and I would not find out until one year later that the spoilers on the right wing rose whenever I moved the sidestick to the right to command a roll to the right. Our stall speed would increase every time the spoilers lifted, and this would be the last thing we needed if we were already flying with less than our normal margin to the stall.

I was happy with my speed control, but the flight warning computers were not. We were locked in a silent tension, when even the slightest change felt like a harbinger of our worst fears. As it happened, I found Harry's concern worrying because I thought it was a sign that he probably didn't trust the landing performance data either.

My mind flashed back to the China Airlines 747 over-running Kai Tac airport exactly seventeen years earlier – this would not be my story! Passing about 2000 feet I looked up at the runway. It was a perfect surface with about 300 metres of overrun before a road and sand dune. If we ran off the runway, the 220-psi tyres would cut like a knife into the soft tropical soil just like my brother's Ariel Red Hunter motorcycle at the Ponderosa and that would probably help us stop. I looked to the left and right of the runway to see what side would be prefer-able to put a wheel into the dirt and slow us faster if an overrun was imminent. But Runway Two-Zero Centre at Changi is a perfect Code 'F' runway – 60 metres wide, easily accommodating our 14 metre–wide wheel track. I decided I'd wait until I had landed, to determine which side of the runway was closest.

*

I tried to maintain 166 knots exactly but it's difficult to read the speed as you're flying (a good argument for a head-up-display), and as we passed 1000 feet the speed dropped one knot to 165. Immediately the flight warning computer broke the silence in the cockpit with 'SPEED! SPEED!' The autopilot disconnected, handing back control to me. I felt everyone stiffen and I touched the thrust on Engine 3, advancing it a bit, lifting the airspeed back over 166 knots. I had no idea why the autopilot was failing. There wasn't time to diagnose, just to fly, so I ignored it and flew the aircraft manually for the remainder of the flight.

How on earth could we get a speed warning? I was flying at about 165 knots and our speed tape showed we were faster than the lowest speed that would guarantee a 19 per cent speed margin to the stall.

During my entire aviation career, the only time I ever heard the speed warning was in 2004 during a simulator exercise. I was shocked to hear it now.

At that moment I didn't really care why it had sounded. I knew the aircraft was safe to fly at 166 knots – the control check had proved it. But it was not safe to fly at 165 knots. All I knew was that I was safe if I kept exactly at 166 knots, not any more, and certainly now not any less. I had to thread the eye of a needle.

Silence befell the cockpit again and I could sense the two senior pilots sitting behind me were just as confused as I was and just wanted me to stop mucking around with the speed and get us on the ground. But I wasn't satisfied. Being two knots over 166 knots at landing would halve our surplus stopping distance, and being three knots over would take us off the end of the runway.

My attention was fully focused. My eyes rapidly flicked between the two most important variables: runway, speed, runway, speed, runway, speed.

'Confirm the fire services on standby,' Matt asked the control tower.

'Affirm, we have the emergency services on standby,' replied the tower controller.

'Thank you.'

'Welcome,' replied the tower. The tower controller seemed normal, even jovial, but it was anything but normal. Their attitude would soon change.

QF32 had now passed from the watch of the Singapore approach controller to Tony Tang, the tower controller located in the eagle's nest atop the 80 metre–high Singapore Tower. Tony later spoke of his curiosity after hearing relays of our calls requesting fire services to meet us at the end of the runway, and now he watched to see the plane come into view on its approach. And then the horrible reality appeared before him. The terrifying silhouette of our aircraft filled Tony's binoculars and the cold reality of what we faced set in: 'I could clearly see the QF32 on finals. Fuel was streaming from the wing. I have never seen that before in my twenty-six-year career.' We were approaching 500 feet. I was head down and busy, while Matt was free to assess our approach path and make the final assessment whether we were safe to land. He quickly asked the tower what the surface wind was (170 degrees at 5 knots) while he watched the rate of descent (800 feet per minute), speed (166 knots), flight path (in the cone) and thrust (stable). It was Matt's call that comprised the final decision. If he called 'STABLE', then I knew I had his blessing to continue and land. If he called 'NOT STABLE', the SOPs call for me to initiate a go around, I would have to – something I didn't want to do considering the state of the plane.

Matt was cool – taking it all in.

'STABLE!'

Phew!

This was followed almost immediately by 'SPEED! SPEED!' It was okay this time. My speed had dropped a knot, but a touch of thrust to Engine 3 fixed the problem. I almost felt fully in control. But if I slowed the aircraft too much more, the flight warning computers would escalate the speed warning to a stall warning.

We were on a knife edge as the runway loomed closer. Our weight and failures meant there was little we could do about our fast descent: 14 feet per second, well above the maximum certified 12 feet per second for the landing gear.

And even with such a high rate of descent, that huge bird was coming in with its nose held so high that it felt *slow*.

We were committed, and as we descended, Matt counted down the altitude to himself while I lined up and tried to find a perfect attitude for the stricken plane. The runway's painted landing zone – my 'aiming point' – loomed large. Matt called the wind velocity to me as we approached the airport perimeter. The flight warning computers cried 'One hundred' as the wheels passed 100 feet. The A380's flight control computers slowly morphed our flight laws into a flare law, inhibiting the trim, locking the static stability and changing the elevators to direct law. Any dynamic compensation the flight control computers had been making to account for an aft centre of gravity was locked now, and I was handed the tail-heavy aircraft in its most raw state.

At 14 feet per second, our rate of descent was too high not to flare. The paint of the runway markers filled our windscreen. As the computers called 'FIFTY', I pulled back slightly. 'FORTY'. I pulled back more. 'THIRTY', 'TWENTY' – the nose was coming up. But as we rotated, that metallic voice squawked out into the cockpit: 'STALL, STALL!'

CHAPTER 25

Round (Phase) 11

The stall warning filled all of us with disbelief. This was the first time I had ever heard a stall warning during a landing. I didn't want to hear it now. The last control check I'd performed had provided a full dress rehearsal of the landing conditions, so I had been confident we were never going to approach the stall speed. Why were we hearing it now? There was no time to think about our condition, only time to act as the runway continued to fill the windscreen.

I was powerless to prevent the plane from crashing in a stall. It was a case of 'Brace yourself, *Nancy*!'

Something was wrong with our performance – very wrong. But our flight control checks had proven our aircraft safe to fly and that was all that mattered. The speed and stall warnings were trying to tell us something that the performance and flight instruments could not, that we approached at a speed too slow to give us the regulatory margins to the stall. But if we had sped up three knots we probably would have run off the runway. The control checks saved the day.

The rapidly lifting nose during landing was creating another problem. The main landing gear trucks are mounted about 26 metres behind the pilots, well aft of the aircraft's centre of gravity. So, as the nose lifts, the landing gear at the other end of the 'see saw' is thrust downwards. Now I was getting very close to runway impact, at a high rate of descent, with the stall warning blaring in my ears, and the landing gear also descending as the aircraft pitched perilously close to the ground. It was not an ideal situation, and there was only one thing to do to rescue the landing – a radical manoeuvre that has to be timed very carefully.

At a fraction of a second before I sensed the landing gear crashing down onto the runway – I pushed the side-stick full forward. This is not a trained technique as the risks of damaging the aircraft generally outweigh the benefits of the manoeuvre. And it's not something I aim to do on any landing, but it's a fix that works if timed accurately. As the nose lowered, the wheels behind the centre of gravity rose, and the aircraft's rate of descent reduced as the plane settled onto a pillow of air trapped between it and the tarmac (a phenomenon pilots call Ground Effect). The fast descent rate washed off. *Nancy-Bird* cushioned onto the runway and we touched down at only two and a half feet per second. I was very pleased with the smooth touchdown made a short distance after passing the runway threshold.

Touchdown 11:46 am Singapore time.

It was a challenging landing, but I was pleased. I'd hit my aiming point, giving us the best chance of stopping short of the runway's southern boundary. The flight data recorder shows we only took five seconds from 50 feet to touchdown, a fast transition, but a smooth one with no 'float'. In fact we touched down two seconds earlier than the Airbus test pilots I was trying to mimic, so this gave us additional ground distance to stop.

The A380's brakes were degraded from the explosion. Just like the fuel system, there were too many failures affecting the brake systems for my mind to absorb. So I had inverted my logic and reduced the braking system complexity to that of a car. I thought to myself, 'After the main wheels touch down, I put the nose wheel down and then, and only then do I push hard on the brake pedals and leave them on until the aircraft stops. Not too early, only one application. That was understandable, that was easy!'

We only had half our thrust reversers to help us stop. The A380's reverse thrust is only installed on Engines 2 and 3, and we'd lost Engine 2. So I selected full reverse thrust on Engine 3 and heard it roar, while feeling no discernible slowing of the aircraft. Taking a plane from 166 knots to standstill in

3900 metres is not a problem when everything is working together. Doing it when 41 tonnes overweight with only 64 per cent of your brakes and 50 per cent of spoilers and ailerons (which act as speed brakes) and reverse thrust was not fun. We had too much energy and not enough brakes. To put *Nancy-Bird*'s energy into perspective, my daughter Sophia, who spent a year in South Africa, tells me *Nancy-Bird* had the equivalent energy of 3800 stampeding male African elephants!

We were now on the ground but our problems were far from over: if I pumped the brakes, then our emergency brake accumulators would run out of pressure and the wing brakes would fail; if I applied them too early I'd blow the wing tyres. And with only 64 per cent of our total braking capability remaining, our landing distance was increased. The plane slowed, but not dramatically. I never really felt the brakes kick in.

Harry jumped in: 'Max braking, Rich!'

Matt jumped in: 'Brakes! Brakes! Give it full brakes, Rich!'

I replied: 'I am!'

My feet were pushing the brake pedals hard flat against the floor. My back was being jammed back into the seat cushion. Matt didn't believe me – the aircraft wasn't slowing. There was just too much kinetic energy. Matt put his feet up on the brake pedals and discovered they were fully depressed hard to the floor. 'There was nothing left,' he would say later. There was lots of noise from the reverse thrust, but not much action. The first 1000 metres went past in a blur. I kept pushing the brake pedals hard against the floor.

Matt called out: 'Keep it in, Rich. Hammer them!'

At the 2000-metre runway marker the plane finally started to slow to about 120 knots and I felt better. We were going to make it.

As we went past the 3000-metre mark I could see the end of the runway followed by a paddock, then the perimeter road and 300 metres of sand dunes to the ocean and the Singapore Strait. The green expanse seemed to fill my vision. I didn't discover till later that I totally missed seeing a few fire trucks, to the left side, that we passed midway down the runway. They were positioned short in case we crashed and didn't make it that far, but as we passed they took chase down the runway following us to our stop point. But I also knew my fear of overrunning the runway was just the adrenaline playing tricks. I was now confident we'd pull up short of the paddock, and I was looking for a large area with lots of concrete around us where the fire trucks and emergency rescue services could assemble and protect us.

As I switched Engine 3 out of reverse a rush of relief swept through the cockpit when we all realised we would be able to stop.

'Beautiful,' said Matt.

'Fantastic,' said Harry.

*

Michael von Reth was also relieved. As we slowed he jumped on the PA and, in his typically cool and unflappable dulcet tone, addressed the passengers: 'Ladies and gentlemen, welcome to

Singapore. The local time is five minutes to midday on Thursday 4 November, and I think you'll agree that was one of the nicest landings we have experienced for a while.'

It wasn't an easy task for a man who'd spent the past half-hour briefing his crew on their responsibilities in case of an emergency landing and an evacuation. Michael was not relaxed, yet he projected a sense of calm, confidence and control that could only come from a long and distinguished career.

But our mutual self-gratification would be short-lived. As we slowed down through 80 knots the ECAM transitioned to flight phase 11, with the result that all the ECAM checklists that had been inhibited inflight now became enabled. The calm cockpit atmosphere was suddenly pierced again by the sounds of ever-more warnings bells and ECAM checklists.

'Bing . . . bing . . . bing . . . bing . . .' The emergency wasn't over yet. Far from it. It was like a bushfire; just when you think you have it under control, the wind shifts and it all changes direction.

As we came to a halt, I looked out to the runway markers: we'd pulled up just short of the 3900-metre mark. I switched the parking brake to 'ON', then keyed the public address push-button and called in a clear and deliberate voice: 'Attention! All passengers remain seated and await further instructions!'

I commanded Matt to focus on the ECAM checklists. We had to make sure the plane was safe before we let the passengers disembark. Then I contacted the tower controller: 'QF32, we have stopped now. Please advise fire services we have very hot brakes and fuel leaking from the left wing.'

My PA to the passengers may seem like a low-key announcement coming at the end of a harrowing journey, but it was just the beginning of yet another tense time for the 24 cabin crew. With those simple words, I was officially starting a formal 'alert phase', during which the cabin crew would prepare for a possible emergency evacuation down the escape slides.

Michael von Reth was worried. The holes in the wing that were above the fuel level in flight were now below the fuel level when the aircraft sat flat on its wheels. He looked outside to see fuel gushing even faster from about 70 holes in the wing. He knew there would be hot brakes and he knew the situation was extremely dangerous, and so he tried to contact me to tell me about these threats. He pulled out his interphone handset and pressed the 'PRIO' and 'CAPT' buttons to establish emergency communications with the flight deck. No one answered. Michael had lost communications with us again, but this time the situation outside the aircraft was dire.

Michael then turned his attention to keeping the passengers calm. Even though he couldn't reach me, he made a PA to the passengers, announcing I'd be speaking to them soon, aware that at any time he would hear the piercing screech of the evacuation siren that signals the beginning of a dangerous passenger evacuation, when the task sharing ends and every cabin attendant becomes their own leader with the sole responsibility to evacuate their passengers out through their door and down the slides as rapidly as possible. Tensions were high, but no one panicked.

Not everyone is up to this. A friend of mine, the solicitor Peter Reid, was a passenger in an aircraft that made an emergency landing on an ice-covered runway at Chicago O'Hare Airport about twenty years ago. The captain informed the passengers that the landing gear would not extend and for the purser to prepare the passengers and cabin for a belly landing. The purser cried, 'I don't want to die,' before breaking down and collapsing to the floor. Peter stood up, took the instruction sheet from the purser, then read the preparation checklist over the PA to the passengers.

It was now 11:49. We had been stopped for less than a minute actioning even more ECAM checklists. At the request of the tower controller, we shut down all the engines so the fire services could approach the aircraft. Matt dialled 128.5 into VHF radio 2 to make contact with the fire commander. It was unfortunate that we shut down the engines and contacted the fire controller at the same time.

Now it got really stressful.

When we moved the three remaining (1, 3 and 4) engine master switches to 'OFF', the high-pressure fuel valves in each engine should shut causing the engines to flame-out. As the engines wound down, the generators fell off-line, the bleed air valves closed off and, in yet another twist of the knife in our already wretched wounds, all the major power systems became unpowered. The cockpit went dark as all lights failed. This should not have happened! The aircraft was now pneumatically and electrically dead.

The cabin crew were confused. Bells and alarms sounded throughout the cabin. Cabin lighting was flashing as the cabin crew checked their emergency exits. The cabin crew 'evacuation' message was displayed on the cabin screens but there was no aural alarm. All of this was happening around them, but the crew did not panic.

We had started the auxiliary power unit (APU) over one hour previously to provide backup pneumatic and electric power, and expected the APU's two generators to take up the aircraft's electrical loads when we shut down the engines. Neither did.

So instead of having a fully-powered flight deck as we sat on the tarmac, our beleaguered *Nancy-Bird Walton*'s 910kVA electrical generation capability had collapsed, either shut down or failed. *Nancy-Bird*, now gasping for electrical power, switched itself across to its last remaining line of defence – the 'Electrical Emergency Configuration', which essentially uses two car-sized batteries to power a few emergency aircraft systems.

The A380's Emergency Supply Centre detected the generator failures, so shut down 99 per cent of the aircraft's electrical systems, leaving us with only the most critical of emergency systems functioning.

We had fuel leaking out near hot brakes, we had shut down our engines and we had now lost 99 per cent of our electrics, but our situation would get worse.

The aircraft was dark and confusing.

Matt again tried to contact the fire controller on VHF radio 2 – no answer. He tried three times – no answer. We opened our window and yelled at the firefighters – they couldn't hear us. We were out of luck: we were sitting in a lake of jet fuel and unable to talk to the fire crews we could see clearly outside.

We finally realised that VHF radio 2 had failed! We swapped the VHF radio 1 to the fire controller frequency and finally got communications with the firefighters.

That day threw up some enormous challenges: keeping the aircraft in the air was one and landing it in one piece was another. But lurking in the back of our minds was the major question of fire or, more accurately, what happens when tonnes of jet fuel meet white-hot carbon brakes and metal.

Aviation jet turbine fuel (avtur) is kerosene. It is highly refined and expensive. Jet fuel is based on kerosene because kerosene packs 10 per cent more energy by volume than gasoline and it has a very high flash point making it safer than gasoline around the super-heated environment of a gas-turbine jet engine.

However, jet fuel is not the 'safe' fuel that many people assume it as. Avtur has a flash point of plus 38 degrees Celsius and will auto-ignite if it reaches 220 degrees Celsius. On QF32 we were now carrying just over 72 tonnes of jet fuel and our overworked brakes would have already passed 500 degrees Celsius. So we had large fuel quantities and we had an ignition source that was not only greater than the 38-degree flash point, but might also be directly under the leaking fuel tanks.

We were riding a bomb, and many of the passengers knew it.

Dr Derwyn and Carolyn Jones, passengers behind the wing in seats 80A and 80B had seen the entire catastrophe. They had seen the explosion rip open the wing, the fuel gushing out and now that we were stopped on the runway, the situation had clearly not improved. Carolyn could see Engine 1 was still running and fuel pooling on the ground. 'It did not take any imagination at all to work out that one spark and we were cinders,' she said later. 'We both thought we've had a great life together, we've got a fantastic family and if this is how it's going to end, then so be it.'

I was relieved to see the Singapore Emergency Services accomplish everything exactly by the book. I had stopped the aircraft to leave adequate tarmac space for the fire services that would surround us. There were six fire trucks. One truck held slightly back. This was the master fire truck, front and centre, carrying the fire controller – the only fireman who wears a white helmet and who coordinates all fire defences. The area inside 30 metres was reserved exclusively for the active fire trucks. They had the job not of putting out an aircraft fire, but of protecting the passengers as they evacuated the aircraft. If a fire started, the master fire truck would protect the slides and clear an exit path for the passengers. Backup fire trucks were positioned slightly behind. Outside 100 metres I saw the police and ambulance triage take positions.

The alert call is the cue for the cabin crew to go to their emergency exits and check to see if there's any reason why their emergency exit and slide shouldn't be used, such as a fire or damage outside. Having ascertained if their door is useable for an evacuation, the cabin crew then monitor the passengers in their area and keep the calm. If an evacuation is commanded they will hear 'EVACUATE, EVACUATE, EVACUATE' over the PA, and then the evacuation alarm. These are the signs for the cabin crew to go into an autonomous mode.

A passenger evacuation is a very dangerous procedure. If it's safe to open the door and deploy their escape slide, then the cabin crew lift the doorhandle. Large motors power the door open, and when the exit is clear, compressed air turbines blast air into the slides, thrusting them out and inflating them within ten seconds. The cabin attendants scream as loudly as they can to the passengers, 'EVACUATE, EVACUATE, UNFASTEN SEATBELTS, HIGH HEELS OFF!' Their loud voices are meant to penetrate through the 'frozen' minds of those passengers paralysed with fear. When the slide has deployed, the attendants scream: 'COME THIS WAY, FORM TWO LINES, STAY TOGETHER, KEEP MOVING, JUMP AND SIT, GET OUT! HURRY! HURRY! JUMP! JUMP!'

All passengers are directed through their emergency exit as fast as possible. There's no time to pause and reflect – any passenger who freezes at the door is pushed out onto the slide. That's the theory.

Behind me, one of the pilots asked why we weren't doing an emergency evacuation. It was a good question. We looked at all the threats and considered all our options, and we ultimately came to a conclusion and I made the decision. My decision was simple: where are the passengers safest right now; inside or outside? Given the current situation with no fire I thought the passengers and crew were safer inside the fuselage than evacuating down the slides onto the dangerous runway.

The QF32 flies the Kangaroo Route from London to Australia. We had wheelchair passengers and babies on board, and I knew that elderly passengers would be injured descending the slides and some would break their legs or hips as they slid to the bottom of the steep evacuation slides. Other passengers in a panic would jump from the aircraft, down the same slides, then concertina into the injured. I figured that 5 per cent of the passengers would have fractures escaping from the lower deck slides, 10 per cent from the upper deck slides; that would equate to 30 fracture cases with our 440 passenger-load. But it gets worse. The passengers who survived the slides would run the risk of slipping over on fuel or foam, or could become confused and walk in front of Engine 1 that was still running and be sucked into it. Passengers who had survived to this stage might walk through jet fuel, creating a spark or taking flash photography and igniting the fuel. Even if all the passengers did get off safely, then we would have the dangerous situation of all the passengers being outside and all the supervising staff being inside the aircraft. Who would be monitoring the passengers at this time? A friend of mine commanded an evacuation of his aircraft in Osaka. After the passengers cleared the slides they ran away from the aircraft and some ran onto an active runway where a Boeing 747 was making another emergency landing.

We had a discussion rather than an argument about it. Harry pointed at the last images to display: the wheels on the left body landing gear had reached 900 degrees Celsius – they were getting hotter. But there was no fire.

It was a surreal feeling sitting on that tarmac. We had 440 passengers sitting patiently behind the bulkhead, while aviation fuel fell around a 900-degree ignition point.

Although we didn't know it at the time, Michael von Reth and his cabin crew were working hard to control the passengers. They'd just been through a harrowing flight, now they were in sight of the terminal but they were still sitting on the aircraft, and I hadn't given the cabin crew any information to impart.

Michael would tell me later that the passengers were fully aware of the amount of fuel pouring onto the ground and were equally – loudly – aware of the lack of fire fighting crews or water or foam. In this fuel-soaked environment, Michael's standing order to his troops was to be vigilant in not allowing anyone to start up a phone, a camera or any other personal electronic device. He would also express his frustration at the lack of communications between the flight deck and cabin during our wait for the fire trucks.

The passengers had become a part of the team. On the lower deck a passenger's phone rang. Before it could be answered, every passenger within earshot yelled, 'TURN THAT PHONE OFF!'

Finally the firefighters arrived and we breathed a sigh of relief as we watched six fire trucks surround the left wing. But as we watched, we noticed something: they weren't hosing down the plane.

CHAPTER 26

Evacuate!

Four hectic minutes after we'd stopped on the runway, we finally made radio contact with the fire controller. The first thing the fire controller said was, 'Shut down Engine 1!'

I looked at Matt, who shrugged. We had shut down the engines – we were electrically 'cold'. We looked at our engine display; no engines were running.

Matt keyed the radio. 'We have shut down all engines!'

'Repeat,' said the Changi fire controller, 'number 1 engine is still running!'

Matt and I were confused. Of the ten flight displays only one display was operating normally. We scanned it for something we may have missed. We could see that Engines 3 and 4 had shut down correctly, but the Engine 1 indications were all crossed ('X'), the same as the indications for Engine 2 that had failed. The fire controller obviously thought Engine 1 was still turning. This is why they'd been standing clear. But we could see nothing to suggest that Engine 1 was running.

The dispute about Engine 1 running went back and forth a few times until the fire controller got annoyed. I opened the A380's cockpit window and stuck my head out the window. Engine 1 was indeed running – I could see it turning and I could hear it!

I went back to my crew, asking Matt and Mark to cross-check our systems to see if we could shut Engine 1 down. But we couldn't switch it off and the fire crews still wouldn't approach us. Matt recycled the engine fire switch – no joy. I found that incredible as I knew there were two independent wires running from the switch to the engine. Both must be broken. But there was another independent path.

I looked up at the 'Engine Fire' pushbutton on the overhead panel. Matt's eyes followed mine. Pausing, I then asked everyone if there was any reason they could think of why we shouldn't use it. There was no response. 'Hit it, Dave,' I called. Dave lifted the large clear cover then hit the big red button in the middle of the console between the two front seats. Clunk! The switch popped out as it sent commands using scores of separate wires to close different valves to kill the engine.

But nothing happened! Two of the most critical control switches for the engines had failed. I wondered what had happened to that wing. I asked if anyone had ideas for how to shut it down.

'You could fire a bottle,' said Harry.

Matt's and my eyes drifted up to the overhead fire panel. Next to the 'Engine Fire' switches are buttons that explosively discharge two bottles of toxic and corrosive agent around the engine's housing. The agent would damage the engine components, but I also knew it would not enter the engine's core and so would not shut the engine down. But we were plum out of other ideas.

I told Matt to press the button.

Nothing happened. The first fire extinguisher was inoperative.

'Hit the other one, Matt,' I called.

He pressed the other button – but it failed to discharge. Nothing was working.

*

Meanwhile, back at Qantas headquarters in Sydney, Allan Rowlandson (Rowly), the deputy fleet manager, had been monitoring our progress and, once we had landed, called Coral at home. For Coral, Rowly's call was the first news she received of our crisis in the air. Rowly said, 'Coral, Rich has been in an incident, an engine exploded but I wanted to tell you that he is safe and on the ground. Don't believe anything you see on TV.'

A little overwhelmed at this sledgehammer news, Coral turned on the TV to see reports that we had crashed. She managed to keep her composure long enough to call my father, Alex and Sophia, but then collapsed into tears in front of the TV for the next half an hour.

*

At this point it finally dawned on me that multiple wiring looms in our wings must have been destroyed. So many wires must have been cut! The damage to the wing must have been enormous – it was extraordinary we'd still had thrust control of Engine 1 inflight.

No one, not even aviation fire crews, approach a jet engine that is running, because people get sucked into them. We had to find another way to deal with the fact the engine was still running. The firefighters thought that perhaps the engine could be extinguished by spraying water into the intake. But in over 100 years of aviation, there has never been a procedure anywhere in the world detailing how fire crews might shut down an engine using water.

It wasn't, however, the first time rescuers had been confronted with recalcitrant engines. In September 1993, Air France 72, a Boeing 747–400 flying from Los Angeles, overran the runway while landing in Papeete (Tahiti) and ended up in a lagoon. Due to an electrical fault, Engine 1 ran for three and a half hours before it could be shut down. Passengers evacuating the aircraft from the forward left doors were lucky not to have been killed as they waded to the shore and passed too close to the running engine. In another accident, in November 2007, an

The team: Captain Harry Wubben, First Officer Matt Hicks, me, Captain Dave Evans and Second Officer Mark Johnson.

Me and the indefatigable Matt Hicks in the A380 cockpit, March 2011.

Most of the QF32 crew. *From bottom left, clockwise*: Sandy Lam, Paul Weson, Freddie Monte, Annie Jostsons, Julie Hart, Vahid Jasaragig, Aldo Calleja, Jordan Lee, Jaay Hayward, Craig Bax, Simone de Mario Henry, Nicolle Sirelles, Trentan Jurkans, Mark Hyland, me, Michael von Reth, Simon Murray, Deborah Berghofer, Ian Madison, Sarah Zemek, Luka Morton, Harry Wubben, David Evans, Matt Hicks and Mark Johnson.

'The Manager': Customer Service Manager Klaus (Michael) von Reth and me at the Qantas eXcel Awards 2011.

Unlike many big jets, the A380 has two openable cockpit windows that were a great asset during our event. They provided the only access to view the engines from the cockpit, and were also used to enable contact with the engineer and firefighters on the ground. Bubbles would be relieved to know that these windows may be opened at up to 250 knots in-flight.

Nancy-Bird Walton at her 90th birthday party, with the model of the A380 that was named after her.

Airbus Experimental Test Flight Engineer Pascal Verneau and me in MSN004, Toulouse, 2008.

Nancy-Bird Walton taking off after dust storms in Sydney on 26 September 2009.

Right: The mighty 6.4 tonne Rolls-Royce RB211 Trent-900 engine (US$18.5 million).

Left: The tips on these Trent-900 fan blades travel faster than the speed of sound. Every eight seconds, the four engines suck in the same amount of air a human breathes in 100 years!

Right: 'Fly the nipple' – the A380 sidestick. The red button disengages the autopilot or takes control away from the other sidestick.

Coral in the A380's cockpit in 2010.

Automation: being one of the new big jets, the A380 has a fully integrated and coordinated flight deck. Its human-machine interface permits the machine (which is 6900 times more powerful, 1700 times heavier, flies 1400 times higher and carries 853 more passengers than the 1903 Wright Flyer) to be operated with only two times the number of pilots!

This night flying eastwards over northern France reminded me of 'High Flight' by John Gillespie Magee, Jr: 'Oh! I have slipped the surly bonds of Earth, And danced the skies on laughter-silvered wings ...'

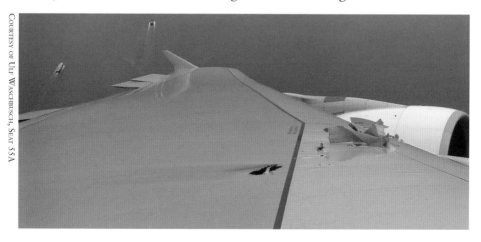

Passenger Ulf Waschbusch's photo of the upper wing damage, fuel leaks, Engine 1 damage, two floating (uplifted ailerons) and one uplifted spoiler (middle left).

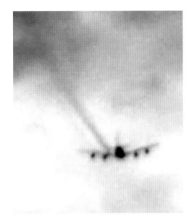

Left: Everyone thought we were dumping fuel, unaware that our jettison system had failed and that we were leaking fuel from at least ten holes.

Below: Qantas Crisis Centre 'think tank'.

Left: Within minutes of the explosion, tweets from Batam about our demise spread around the world: @jezzaround: 'Airplane crash/xplode at batam, Indonesia~!!' and @foxheadlines: 'WORLD: Plane Crash Reported in Western Indonesia'.

Right: Diagrams from Neil Armstrong's (and G Matranga's) 1959 NASA research memo of the 270-degree glide spiral descent. NASA's Space Shuttle flew a Heading Alignment Cone (HAC) which was derived from Armstrong's research. I submitted details of this 'Armstrong Spiral' to Airbus in 2008 with my suggestion for an engine out profile for Airbus's new A350. I positioned *Nancy-Bird Walton* to be able to intercept this spiral on 4 November 2010.

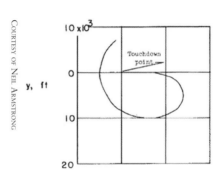

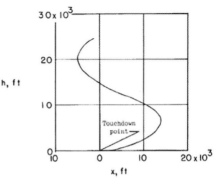

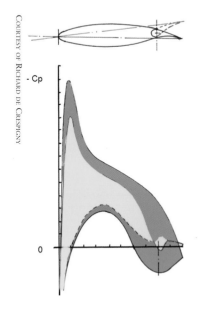

Left: For the more technically minded, this diagram shows the pressure along the chord of an aft loaded supercritical wing tip such as the A380. The yellow and green areas represent the lift for the normal wing tip. In *Nancy*'s case, 65% of her ailerons floated up, resulting in a significant loss of lift (green area) over that portion of the wing. Only the yellow lift remained. Even worse, this loss of lift creates a rolling moment, that must be countered by equally damaging aileron or spoiler deployment on the opposite wing, and perhaps even rudder (with its secondary effects). Safety margins that prevent the wing stalling are lost if the approach speed is not increased to mitigate this loss of lift.

Photos showing the normal engine (*top*), scale of the turbine disk (*centre, yellow line*), and QF32's uncontained turbine failure (*bottom*), showing the nacelle has been cleaved from the engine, and the exhaust is held on by only the low pressure shaft.

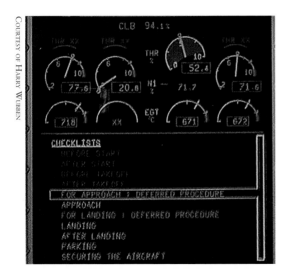

This is Harry's in-flight photo of the engine display. Most people who see this photo think we only had one engine operating normally – in fact we had none. Engine 2 failed, Engines 1 and 4 were operating in the unrated-degraded mode, and Engine 3, which appeared normal, was operating in an alternate mode with a reduced maximum thrust.

Foam and water surround four deflated left body tyres.

Trent-900 engines are certified to ingest three tonnes of water per minute and not fail. This attempt to snuff the engine (with water) failed.

Three hours and 39 minutes after we landed, Engine 1 was finally stopped after water-foam was sprayed down its throat.

Left: An engine that ingests foam requires 100 per cent disassembly and a total rebuild.

Below: Damage to the top and bottom of the wing, Engine 2 and Remote Air Turbine (lower left).

ENGINE #2 FAILED ON CLIMB OUT AROUND 4000 ASIR TO FOLLOW

This is the text that we entered into the aircraft's technical log (and the Air Safety Incident Report) to explain the problems we experienced on 4 November 2010. The repair was probably the longest and most expensive in aviation history.

All passengers and crew safely disembarked QF32.

Debriefing the passengers after the flight in the boarding lounge; closing off four hours of extensive passenger addresses with full and open disclosure and my personal guarantee.

From left: Harry Wubben, Dave Evans, me, Matt Hicks and Mark Johnson after receiving IFALPA's Polaris Award in Chiang Mai, Thailand, April 2011.

From left: Matt Hicks, Nicole and Mark Johnson, me and Coral, Liz, Natalie and Harry Wubben and Kate and Dave Evans at the IFALPA dinner in Chiang Mai, Thailand, in April 2011.

Old habits die hard: 'Kick the tyres ... light the fires ...'

Breaking out of cloud just before touchdown.

Etihad A340–600 aircraft crashed in Toulouse during a ground engine test that went foul. Engines 1 and 2 shut down normally, but Engine 4 ran for two and a half hours before the firefighters managed to drown the engine with foam. Engine 3 ran for nine hours before it ran out of fuel.

I asked Dave to call the Qantas engineers and ask how we could shut down the engine. Dave asked for a phone number. I knew the phone number was stored in the A380's flight deck computer systems (because I had helped build that system) but the main screens to view it had failed. So I pulled out my iPad and passed Dave the phone number. It was a sad day for the A380. *Nancy-Bird Walton*'s information systems, with all their redundancies, had collapsed down to an iPad!

Fire crews do not pump high-pressure water directly into the core of jet engines unless requested. But our situation was desperate, our multiple methods to shut down the engine had failed and so more desperate measures were needed.

I leaned out my left cockpit window again, to see what was happening. Nothing had changed. So many shutdown systems had failed and the engine was still running!

Matt radioed the fire controller and instructed him to spray water over the hot brakes and foam over the fuel. We were very worried about the 1000-degree Celsius reading on the left-wing wheels. The temperature gauge stopped at 1000 degrees and so we assumed it was well over that. Anything combustible could be set on fire by simply going near a structure at 1000 degrees and we were very focused on what would happen if a gust of wind whipped jet fuel off the concrete and onto the super-heated brake callipers. We were lucky with the weather: it was calm.

The twenty firemen started pumping 3600 litres of foam and 60,000 litres of water onto the landing gear and ground around it.

The time was 11.55 am, and we had been stopped for seven minutes. Dave called the Qantas Crisis Centre to bring them into the loop.

While we were confronting the challenges of electrical and radio failures, a runaway engine and trying to coordinate firefighters to deal with the leaking fuel, the ECAM was continuing its barrage of checklists. Matt was calling the checklists out, but by this stage I'd shifted focus from anything which was not safety related. Matt clearly hadn't lost his sense of humour, crying out in the middle of a checklist: 'I bet they can't put this into a simulator session!'

As the water and foam effused from the fire trucks, I asked Matt to pull up the emergency evacuation checklist so they were handy if we needed them. I knew the aircraft was certified to evacuate 853 passengers and twenty crew out of half (eight) the doors in the dark in just 78 seconds. We had all the slides available and only 440 passengers, so I reckoned I could comfortably have all of the passengers off QF32 in less than 45 seconds.

Passenger evacuations are very dangerous. Even in airline training exercises, when all of the pretend 'passengers' are cabin crew and other employees, a broken leg or badly sprained ankle is not unusual. The video of the A380 certification trial can be viewed on the internet. It shows young, fit and prepared people evacuating the aircraft – and it's a mess. One person broke his leg during the test. Ours was a complex situation and there were many reasons why it might not have been best to evacuate the aircraft. I knew there was an engine still running, and people might act irrationally around the aircraft and wander off or turn on mobile phones, and I knew those hot brakes could have ignited the fuel on the runway while people were trying to get themselves to safety. What's more, we had many passengers with wheelchairs, veterans, babies and children on board. If anyone was injured on the slides, then others coming down behind would concertina into them. The slide is designed to bounce the person off their bottom into the air so they land on the ground in the running position. If people did not fall at the base of the slide, they might slip on the foam or the fuel. And if they didn't slip on the fuel they might take a flash photograph, light a cigarette or walk in front of Engine 1 and get sucked into it. So I wanted to see if there was another safer way of getting people off this aircraft.

We could evacuate now, run a precautionary slow evacu-ation, or we could wait for stairs and de-plane the passengers directly into the buses. I decided we were safest on board, but that we should keep the cabin crew in the alert phase ready to evacuate on any call of fire. I am happy with my decision not to evacuate the passengers. It was made after consulting the other pilots, considering every threat we could see and imagine.

I then jumped on the public address and told the passen-gers everything we had just discussed in the flight deck. The passengers were safer on board, and when they realised this they started to relax.

Matt and I sat in the cockpit for two hours with the 'passenger evacuation' checklist ready to go; the cabin crew were at the 'alert phase' and had been ready to evacuate at the blink of an eye for two long hours – the longest alert phase in Qantas's history.

The threat of fire was high, but it did not eventuate. And with every passing second the threat diminished as the firefighters hosed the brakes and the fuel was covered by foam. The situation was stabilising and we waited for the fire crews to give us the 'safe' call.

After twenty minutes of this highly stressful situation, the brakes had cooled and the fuel was thoroughly covered in foam and water – I thought the worst was over. The fire controller told us that Engine 1 was still running, but he was much more relaxed than he'd been in our first conversation.

Dave Evans had turned on his mobile and was talking to the Qantas Crisis Centre in Sydney to give them an update. I assumed they'd be pretty worried. At the same time, Harry got on his phone to the engineers in Sydney to see what we could do about the engine.

The Qantas engineers told Harry to go out and walk around the engine, and have a look. When Harry said the environment wasn't conducive for a walk right now, they suggested we transfer fuel from Engine 1's feed tank to Engine 2's. But that had been our nightmare for almost an hour and half – the fuel pumps didn't work and the transfer galleries were busted.

Harry was dispatched to pull circuit breakers in the upper electronics bay, and to try and transfer fuel from the fuel panel under the aircraft, but none of these ideas worked. There was even an attempt to open the engine's cowls and manually shut a fuel valve, but alas the cowls are electrically operated and the left wing was electrically dead. This Rolls-Royce engine that worked flawlessly in the air kept to its creed – nothing stopped it then, and nothing would stop it now.

We waited for another few minutes while the engineers in the Crisis Centre spoke to the appropriate people. A team of Changi ground engineers were sent out to try and shut down Engine 1 but they couldn't stop it. And then the word came back: we were cleared to ask our fire crews to turn their water pumps into Engine 1.

The firefighters pumped as much water as they could into that engine, at one point training two nozzles into it. They couldn't deploy more than one fire truck to kill the engine as the firefighters' primary function is to stop the escape slides and passengers catching fire during an evacuation. They almost won. The engine had faulted, wound down and almost died. But then the fire truck ran out of water at the last second and, in a final testament to Rolls-Royce resilience, the igniters kicked in and that big Trent 900 just started up again. As far as indefatigable machinery is concerned, it's worth mentioning that the engine was designed to ingest 3 tonnes of rain and hail per minute – that's a lot worse than the heaviest rain showers.

We couldn't shut Engine 1 down: we couldn't starve it of fuel and we couldn't drown it in water.

By this stage the brakes had cooled and the foam had smothered the fuel. Matt and I were in the flight deck guarding the aircraft. Matt said, 'Nice landing, Rich.' I replied, 'This aircraft is buggered for a month!' No one could argue with that.

CHAPTER 27

Qantas is Not Going to Like This!

I had decided we would disembark the passengers from the aircraft via stairs and buses, as it was less dangerous. The stairs had arrived but the buses were not forthcoming. In frustration, David used his phone to call the Qantas office in Singapore and then the Qantas Crisis Centre in Sydney.

We were still very busy. At this point all of us on the flight deck were working as a very efficient team. Matt and I were in the front seats ready to action the evacuation checklist if a fire broke out. I made PAs to the passengers about every ten minutes updating them with what was happening. Harry was working with the Sydney engineers to try and extinguish Engine 1.

Dave was trying to get buses to the aircraft. Mark was on a continuous loop around the aircraft talking to the passengers and keeping them informed.

The APU's air duct had been severed so the APU was unable to power the air conditioners. The lack of airconditioning on the dead plane was starting to distress some of the passengers. It was 30 degrees Celsius outside in the midday sun, and it was getting hot and muggy on board. So I got on the PA – still our only communication channel with the cabin – and told the passengers, 'Sorry about the delay to de-plane and the lack of airconditioning. We're currently not in comfort mode, we're in safety mode and your safety is our only priority. We are waiting for buses to arrive before we de-plane.'

I didn't blame them for being annoyed. Everyone on that plane was hot and sweaty. Michael von Reth sent a messenger to the cockpit to say that passengers needed to go to the toilet but they were being kept in their seats. I said, 'Let them go but keep the door areas clear in case we have to evacuate.'

So they went to the toilets and they clogged the doorways, and I had to go back on the PA and warn the entire plane of the situation: we were in safety mode and no one could block the exits. If they didn't follow my instructions and keep the doors clear, then I would turn the seatbelt sign back on and force everyone to stay in their seats. Our approach worked.

The engineers back in Sydney still wanted a personal account of what the engine looked like, and our first set of stairs had arrived on our right side. Dave went out and made the first inspection: 'Oh, it was a total shock. Unbelievable, it was unbelievable. To look at that engine up close was just gobsmacking. It's the only way to describe it.'

Matt took the next look: 'I didn't expect the whole back of the engine to not be there. I mean the only thing holding the back section of the engine on was the shafts, the turbine shaft. The whole intermediate pressure turbine was gone. To look underneath and still see fuel leaking out of the fuel tanks, and just be walking around, it was actually a bit surreal. There's all this, you know, retardant foam blowing around through the air, and I'm just sort of wandering around under the plane and fuel leaking everywhere, and it, it's weird.'

Dave Evans took my seat and I walked through the entire aircraft talking to passengers. Some of the passengers called out to me. One said that I should open the rear doors to let some air in. I told them I didn't want to do that without either stairs or a slide attached to it. An open door is one less door that can be opened to deploy an escape slide, and there was no way we could guarantee that a person or child might not fall out of an open door. But I also told them that if anyone felt close to fainting or collapsing, that the local cabin attendant was authorised to bring them forward in the aircraft for additional care. The passengers now understood my reasoning and so started to relax and accept their predicament.

With the passengers secure, I walked outside into the warmth and haze of the Singapore tropical noon, then down onto the runway where I saw for the first time the scale of the damage. I briefly met some of the firefighters who had covered the ground in foam and cooled the brakes. A fire officer guided me under the plane towards the left wing. I was shocked by the amount of damage I saw, and my first thought was how remarkable the aircraft was to stay together and fly so well when so much had failed, and how lucky the 469 of us had been to make it back to Singapore alive. The wing was opened up like a sardine can with impacts and holes everywhere. Fuel was gushing out of multiple holes. I was dumbstruck to see Engine 2 from the side, with the gaping hole exposing the engine's core right down to the low speed rotor. It's a view I don't think any pilot had ever seen before, and it's one I'll certainly never forget! Remarkably, the engine pylon was twisted and the engine was hanging off the wing by just two bolts yet it hadn't fallen away. The belly was sliced, four tyres had overheated and deflated (a thermal fuse prevents them exploding), and fuel and foam covered the ground.

The passengers would have panicked if they saw this view, so I was even more resolute now to unload the passengers from the right-hand side, from the stairs directly onto the buses so they did not see the damage I was seeing.

It was a smorgasbord of destruction. A total mess. But we were alive! We were all so very lucky. The events that day could have transpired so very differently. I would have many months in front of me to read the investigators' and engineers' reports on what damage had been sustained and how fortunate we were that the aircraft kept flying. The reality is that most events where the turbine discs fail end in disaster. So the residents of Batam Island were lucky we were flying an A380 that day, for if it were a lesser aircraft, there would have been a lot more collateral damage.

Climbing back into the aircraft, I told Michael von Reth to disembark the passengers methodically and carefully down the steps when the buses arrived. I then made my way back to the cockpit.

I keyed the PA and thanked the passengers for their cooperation, and told them the aircraft was now stable and that they'd be leaving the aircraft shortly. I handed them over to the care of the cabin service manager and his crew, and said their instructions were to be carried out to the letter and no one was to carry any luggage off the plane; it was all to be left behind. I also requested that, once in the terminal, they were to stay assembled in the areas they were directed to by the airport management. I signed off by saying I would follow them back to the terminal building where I would conduct a full debrief and explain everything. The standing order in an emergency evacuation is that passengers may take no luggage. And that means no luggage except what you can carry in your pockets. The last thing we needed after all our efforts to secure the passengers' safety was for someone to trip while trying to carry a bag down the stairs. I explained this very carefully to everyone, and only a few complained.

Matt's wife, Georgie, called too. I didn't hear any details but I remember him saying afterwards: 'Georgie says we're all over CNN. No wonder she was crying . . .'

It was 12.40 pm, 52 minutes after we stopped, when the first passenger stepped off the aircraft, and down the stairs into the waiting buses. It was a great relief. The aircraft brakes had cooled, but there was still tonnes of fuel on the ground and so the crew were still at high alert, and Harry was still trying to shut down Engine 1.

At this stage, with the aircraft stabilised, the stress was easing and I found myself with a moment to reflect. I was proud of the teamwork displayed by the crews. I gathered my thoughts, and then I put my hand on Matt's shoulder and thanked and then congratulated him on the way he had handled such a stressful event.

During our otherwise orderly evacuation, one passenger tried to leave the plane with a roller bag. Michael von Reth, who was monitoring every passenger movement, stopped the passenger and said, 'I told everyone not to take any luggage.' The passenger, an Aussie, said curtly: 'Well, the bag is here with me, so what are you going to do about it?' Michael grabbed the bag and threw it with full force through the air right across to the other side of the aircraft and said, 'That's what – now get off!' No one appeared at the door with any luggage after that.

At 1.20 pm Singapore time I got a text message from Coral: 'Holy cow – that was close. It's all over the news. Rowly called me just before the news broke. So glad you're safe. Call me when u can. Love u, Coral.'

I wouldn't reply until 1.48 pm, when I sent a reply: 'Can't call yet – still have probs shutting eng down.'

Michael carefully counted every passenger as they disembarked – he had counted 440 souls when the last passenger exited for the bus. We could tell the Qantas Crisis Centre to now write 440 against the passenger count on the right side of their white board.

Michael and I knew well that a very large whiteboard was mounted on the back wall of the Crisis Centre in Sydney. The board was split into two columns: in the left column were spaces where the crisis staff wrote totals for men, women, children, infants and crew, and a total at the bottom. I knew someone had already written a large '469' at the bottom of the left column. The right-hand column contains similar spaces, but also lines for 'uninjured', 'hospitalised' and 'unaccounted for', and a 'Total Souls Onboard' at the bottom. I knew everyone in the Crisis Centre would be watching that total slowly creep up as news flowed in, praying for it to match the left – so was I. These thoughts were foremost when I spoke to the passengers in the aircraft on the ground. My sole motivation now was to get a 469 into that right column – and everything else was irrelevant.

Ideally, an airline wants to make the two totals match. But you can't make them match if the people you want to count are wandering around Changi Airport, talking to the press, looking for a beer, a sandwich or a Valium! We would have some help from airport management, in that the passengers could be escorted into certain lounges and not allowed to pass through customs. But it's a big airport and my colleagues' experiences had reminded me that after a crisis such as this the passengers would not act rationally. So we needed to keep the group together until Michael and his people had done their counts and reported them to me. The passengers had done nothing wrong – they couldn't be physically restrained by airport security or the police.

With most of the passengers off, the tension eased in the flight deck. We started to think about the investigations, interviews and the analysis of every detail of this flight that would come. Matt told Dave that when he filled out my route check form, he could create a new check for 'degree of difficulty' and mark it as 'extreme'.

Mark asked me what I wanted written into the technical log. *Nancy-Bird Walton*'s big red technical log is a sort of captain's log that must be annotated at the end of every flight, listing the flight details and any aircraft unserviceabilities. Mark's question made me revisit the events that we had just grappled with over the last four hours. An exact log report would fill many books. After reflecting for a while, and to Mark's surprise, I asked him to write down this short and succinct summary: 'Engine 2 failed on climb out around 4000.' Our Air Safety Incident Report that is sent to the Australian Transport Safety Bureau would report just the same.

It was 1.40 pm when the last passenger disembarked the aircraft – that's one hour and 52 minutes after we stopped on the runway, and three hours and 39 minutes since the engine exploded. I swung immediately into the next mode – passenger debriefing. I handed over my command of the aircraft to Dave to stabilise the aircraft with the engineers. Before I stood up from my seat I grabbed the summary sheet that contains my private notes for conducting the flight. It was remarkable – I had not written one word on the page since the engine had exploded;

the Airbus computer systems had displayed everything I needed to know during the flight. It was a wonderful testament for the Airbus information systems. I grabbed my Qantas hat then circled the entire cabin, checking with the cabin crew that all zones were clear of passengers. When I finally arrived at main door 2 right, ready to leave the aircraft, I looked at my watch; it was about 1:50 pm. The cabin crew had been at the alert phase for a whopping two hours since we had landed – a record for any airline.

I descended the aircraft stairs and located a policeman, who took me to the passenger terminal. As we left the runway and crossed over the runway's holding point, I looked back through the car's rear window. I squinted as I caught the enormity of the sight of the sad and dishevelled *Nancy-Bird Walton* dowsed in the Singapore midday sun. Beneath her, rivers of dirty foam flowed around her deflated tyres and the six fire trucks administering intensive care.

It struck me that I had been wrong when I'd told Matt the aircraft would be buggered for a month; it would be wrecked for a year. And it wasn't going to look good on the news.

It was an emotional moment for me. Watching that huge, battered bird sitting there, surrounded by firefighters, police, ambulances and airport personnel, I felt guilty, like I was running away from the scene of a crime that was somehow my fault. But just as I was starting to feel overwhelmed another thought lifted my spirits. I recalled meeting the aircraft's namesake, Nancy-Bird Walton, ten years before, and then again at the naming ceremony in October 2008 when the first A380 was delivered to Qantas. She was a spritely, short, 93 year old with piercing pale blue eyes, who had been taught to fly by Charles Kingsford-Smith when she was seventeen. She'd then gone on to create the air ambulance service in outback New South Wales. She smiled and told the audience, 'I was asked if Qantas could name this plane after me, at my 90th birthday three years ago, and I made it my decision to stay alive.' When a bottle of champagne was cracked to christen the aircraft, Nancy cried, 'Don't scratch my aeroplane!'

Nancy-Bird had died a few months after that ceremony, and now, two years later, here was her plane, deciding also to stay alive until she had returned 469 souls to safety. I'm not a religious person, but if Nancy was watching us from afar I am sure she would have been so very proud of how her aircraft performed and to have her name emblazoned on that wonderful machine.

It was an eerie and silent fifteen-minute drive to the terminal. It was the first silence I had experienced in the last four remarkable hours. My phone beeped. My daughter Sophia had texted me: 'Just heard what happened. U OK?'

I replied: 'Fine Soph, but busy. Luv U.'

She came back: 'Love U 2.'

I then called Dad. My 'wicked stepmother' answered. 'I think I've wrecked an A380, Mariea!' I said. She replied, 'I think they will understand'. I then hung up.

I needed time to reflect on what I was about to tell the passengers.

At the end of the fifteen-minute drive I was dropped at bay Charlie 32 (C32), the gate we'd departed from more than four hours earlier. My first stop was the main lounge where the Economy and Premium Economy passengers were assembled, all wide-eyed and waiting. I walked to the counter, grabbed the PA and started talking. I knew what I was about to say would probably be uploaded to YouTube within 30 minutes, and so I spoke carefully, explaining what had happened, why it had happened and what was about to happen to the passengers. I could see Ulf Waschbusch, the passenger from seat 55A, holding up his mobile phone, still recording every word.

The passengers had de-planed on the right side of the aircraft, so they hadn't seen the terrible damage to the plane, even though I would later learn that so many of them had seen the explosion, the fireball and the debris flying out of the engine while inflight. So I kept things simple, explaining about the failed Engine 2, the holes in the wing, the fuel leaks, and Engine 1 that would not shut down after we landed. I spoke about the engine and the degraded systems, and explained how wonderfully the aircraft performed. As I spoke, someone pointed up at a TV screen where CNN was broadcasting a Qantas press conference at which Alan Joyce, our CEO, announced that Qantas had grounded all its A380s. This was the first word I'd heard from Sydney, and it confirmed my confidence that the Crisis Centre had convened early and was looking after the interests of my passengers. There was a hubbub among the passengers, who were all starting to ask, since the A380s were grounded, how they would get back to Australia. I said to relax, and told them that, at that very moment, there were a thousand people running around organising their accommodation, meals and transport. They liked that.

But there was a growing sense of tension in the air. The passengers didn't seem so fussed about the flight, but suddenly realised all the attention on CNN meant they had to inform their friends and relatives back home that they were safe. People's phones began ringing and the tension was mounting as they spoke to people who thought they had died. I could see the passengers' perceptions were beginning to change and the incident was starting to seem worse. Also, there was every chance the media would spin the details of our flight into such a feeding frenzy that the passengers' stress would be elevated hours after the event, when everyone had adjourned to their hotel rooms. I felt the only way to counter this escalation was to provide full and open disclosure, and to offer the passengers some sort of personal guarantee to ensure I could follow up later and provide assistance if required.

So I spent fifty minutes debriefing the passengers, describing what had happened and answering their questions. I explained that jet engines only fail about once in every 300,000 hours, so that everyone should feel comforted, having experienced this engine failure, that statistically they should never see another engine failure.

I didn't tell them this was my fourth engine failure.

One passenger asked me why we hadn't evacuated the aircraft. I answered, 'The decision not to evacuate was mine, and I based it on the simple notion of where you would be safest.

Are you safest hurting yourself during an evacuation, or are you better off inside a stable cabin with experienced cabin crew looking after you. I continually re-evaluated this decision. After fifteen minutes, when the brakes were cool and the fuel covered in foam, I think you were absolutely safer inside the aircraft than outside. With the benefit of hindsight I think I made the right decisions.'

Up until this point, I was the captain in charge of the flight and responsible for the passengers' welfare. But now I was passing the passengers over to an unknown group of Qantas and Singapore staff, and I was unsure if the Qantas standards could be maintained. So I then said something very unusual: 'Qantas is not going to like this – but I want you all to grab a pen and be ready for information that I give you. Qantas is a value-added airline, we are not a no-frills airline. You paid more to fly with us than you would have for a no-frills airline, and although I have not delivered a good service to you today, I want to make amends. So here is my personal guarantee. If you don't agree with how Qantas is treating you or if you think Qantas doesn't care, then call me on this number.' And then I recited my mobile number several times.

I was well aware that the passengers, and in fact the media, had no idea just how severe the incident was and how many systems had failed. But I did know the media would have amassed outside the terminal and would try to paint the passengers into a position where they would think that they might have died. I told the passengers that they now knew more about the incident than the press, and that they could tell the press exactly what had happened because I had just given them an accurate account.

'Don't let the press suggest we were on fire – we were not,' I said. 'Don't let the press suggest the crew were scared, because we weren't. We were busy, but we were never scared.'

A US Embassy official in Singapore cornered me, wanting to know if there were US nationals on board. I didn't know, so I used my mobile phone to call Sydney Crisis Centre, and Captain Peter Probert told me he'd call the embassy official and take it from there. Finally, a passenger thanked me for my efforts. I replied that many teams had worked brilliantly to bring them home, so although I refused to accept their thanks personally, I would be proud to accept thanks on behalf of all the pilots, cabin crew, air traffic controllers, police and firefighters who had worked so effectively.

Finally, after 50 minutes of debriefing, I found myself standing alone in the centre of the room surrounded by 300 passengers who were all happy, smiling and talking to each other. There were no more questions.

By this time the cabin crew had started to arrive at the terminal, so I took the opportunity to start to debrief them, telling them I thought they'd done a fantastic job. When you have a crisis in the air, the pilots have to grapple with machines and the laws of physics; the cabin crew have to deal with hundreds of people, all of them responding differently and unpredictably to the danger. After a ten-minute crew debrief it was time to debrief the 62 Business Class and fourteen First Class passengers in their respective lounges.

The adrenaline was wearing off and I was starting to feel fatigued. I had to contact the Crisis Centre over the phone, so I asked Matt and Harry to debrief the Business Class passengers. Mark and I then went to the First Class Lounge, spending another 45 minutes answering every question until Mark and I found ourselves again standing like totem-poles alone in the centre of the room.

The decision to hand out my phone number to passengers wasn't unprecedented – I'd done it four months earlier on 7 July 2010 when QF32 from London to Singapore had been delayed overnight. I had felt so bad about the way it had gone that I announced my phone number to the passengers and asked them to call me if they were not happy with the way Qantas was treating them or if they thought we didn't care. I travel with my own kids a lot and I knew the disruptions that are caused when there are delays and long periods of sitting in stationary aircraft. I thought it was the least I could do. In response, many passengers sent positive emails and letters to Qantas's Head Office, and the flight crew and cabin crew of that 7 July flight would be honoured with the 2010 Qantas eXcel Service Award. So I knew that giving full and open disclosure generates trust in the minds of the passengers. Everyone feels vulnerable in these situations; they just want to be given the truth and be treated with respect.

After the debrief, we were ushered by airport management and Qantas crisis managers through immigration and then into a side alleyway used for consular and VIP passengers. The media were prepared for us, lined up along the 30 metres of paparazzi barriers that bordered the concrete walkway to where our bus was waiting. I estimate there were 200 media people there, pushing so hard on the barriers that we had to walk single file. The flash guns went off, the cameras clicked and the reporters yelled questions at us as we walked that gauntlet.

I don't remember the bus ride back to the Fairmont Hotel. There was little chat, just lots of exhausted people lost in thought, recounting the event in their minds. Coral's phone recorded me sending her a text at 5:49 pm: 'In bus to hotel.' She was keen to talk to me but knew I was distracted so left me alone. She replied: 'Let me know what room you're in and I'll call you.'

I was proud of the care we provided to the passengers that day. We provided continuous communications, with full, open and honest disclosure, hiding nothing, answering all questions, and providing phone numbers for a personal guarantee. We also empowered the passengers to meet the media throngs outside. The proof was in the pictures that quickly circled the globe. When the passengers departed the airport for the hotels, their smiles conveyed the happiness and gratitude they felt for Qantas that day – our passengers had become Qantas devotees, and every Qantas employee is grateful for their understanding in tough circumstances.

Our passengers had smiles on their faces because all their questions had been answered, and they had my personal guarantee that Qantas would care for them. I am not aware of images of any passengers crying or in distress as they left the terminal. The press looked for criticism of Qantas, but the passengers refused to play along, only offering praise. I could not have asked for a better outcome. It's a privilege to be part of such a wonderful mega-team.

CHAPTER 28

Deja Vu

A police guard protected our path from the waiting press into the Fairmont Hotel. I asked the hotel manager to cordon off a section of the main bar and close the curtains so the cabin and technical crews could talk privately among themselves after the day's events. I also asked if hotel security could be posted around the bar to block the media.

Michael von Reth had already received authorisation from Qantas to spend $400 at the bar, and he began to take orders. I received the following SMS message from Captain Murray Crockett, the A380 fleet manager:

Richard, please pass on my sincere thanks to all of the crew on a job well done. All of you appear to have handled a very serious event in the best tradition of Qantas pilots. Please buy a celebratory drink for everyone on me. Look forward to hearing the details on your return. Best regards, Murray.

Murray was on holidays and so, like most other people in Australia, I didn't think he knew all the things that had gone wrong on our flight.

I approached Michael at the bar and said: 'Murray has just given me permission to buy a drink for everyone. Bugger that – these people need to de-stress!' I told Michael to put the $400 back in his pocket and said to the barman it was my shout. 'Give all the crew whatever they want for as long as they want it. And please bring lots of plates of snacks!'

The 29 of us were in the bar until midnight, debriefing each other while the enormous wall-mounted TV shared continuous surreal coverage of our flight, with amazing graphics re-enacting the explosions and images of our aircraft rolling around. My bar bill was just over $4000 that night; money well spent to help everyone unwind. These people had done a remarkable job under incredible stress for the passengers and Qantas, and they deserved to have a couple of drinks without having to reach into their own pockets.

By 10.28 pm I was conscious Coral was still keen to contact me, so I texted her: 'I'm still in the bar getting the crew relaxed. I'll call when I get to the room.'

I went to my room at about midnight. It was the same room I had had the night before. I called Coral and spoke to her for two hours, and then I tried to go to sleep, but (cortisol) energy was still coursing through my body, keeping me awake. I was very concerned about the whole incident: Did I carry out every activity correctly? Were the passengers okay? Did I embarrass Qantas? Was there something else I should have done? Who should I have called?

I knew I had to sleep, but my mind was racing and I couldn't relax. I am not sure how much sleep I got that night, but I was certainly not rested in the morning. I was tired, I had no clean clothes or toiletries (my suitcase didn't arrive until 6 pm the following night) and I felt dirty.

I'd arranged with the four other pilots to meet for breakfast and go over things. As I was making my way to the restaurant at 8.30 am I received a call from Peter Wilson, the chief pilot at Qantas. Peter congratulated us on handling a very challenging event, but he was also concerned about our wellbeing. He'd seen the data feeds from QF32, and he told me we'd processed 58 checklists from the ECAM and that we had handled the complex incident very well. But I think many more checklists and alerts that we actioned were not logged by the aircraft data systems, and that we had cancelled the master warning bell about 100 times in flight and about twenty times on the ground. It was possible our ECAM checklist tally was in fact closer to 120. However, I appreciated Peter's comments and his praise for the crew, for it was an extraordinary team effort.

The phone call only took about two minutes, and in retrospect he was probably probing my mental state and deciding whether I was in a fit mood to take a call from Alan Joyce, Qantas's CEO. Sure enough, two minutes later Alan Joyce rang, congratulating me and the crew, and saying that Qantas was proud of the team effort.

I went out and bought a phone charger and some toiletries, and I had slightly shaking hands as I shaved back in my room. I was starting to experience the memories of the flight with unnerving clarity in a sort of video loop.

I was still in one piece and so was everyone on that flight, but I was finding it hard to process all the information: the wing damage, the landing gear damage, an engine explosion, two speed warnings below 500 feet and a stall warning as we flared for landing. *A stall warning, how could we ever have got close to the stall!* And then, as we'd sat on the runway, we'd watched, horrified, as 3 tonnes of jet fuel had poured out of the holes in the wings and around a set of wheels that was at least 1000 degrees Celsius, and the aircraft electrics, radios and systems collapsed.

I should have felt elated: I was the captain on a severely damaged aircraft with 469 people on board, and I'd brought it down without a single injury – not even a broken toenail. But I felt overwhelmed, exhausted and melancholy. And beyond the stress was confusion about what had happened: it couldn't really have happened, could it?

It was dawning on me that QF32 might be talked about as a 'black swan' event – an unforecast event that has significant consequences. I decided to write down what we'd dealt with on that flight. The list went something like this:

Engines: Engine 1 degraded, would not shut down on ground; Engine 2 failed; Engine 3 alternate mode; Engine 4 degraded. One less thrust reverser for landing; runaway Engine 1 on ground (two shutdown systems faulted); Engine 2 failed then fire warning; no over-thrust protection on Engines 1 and 4. Three out of four fire extinguishers inoperative on left wing.

Hydraulics: 25 per cent pumps operating – GREEN system failed, and YELLOW system operating on two of four pumps.

Electrics: two generators failed in flight; 50 per cent AC buses failed in flight; 1 per cent emergency services available on ground; ram air turbine failure.

APU: pneumatics and electrics failed.

Flight controls: operating program degraded to alternate law; 60 per cent less lift devices (slats, ailerons); 64 per cent roll control lost; wing damage – about 10 per cent lift lost; 50 per cent spoilers lost. Spoilers reducing stall margin.

Landing gear: half computers failed; reduced sensors; gravity extension; no retraction available.

Brakes: auto-brakes failed; anti-skid failed; wing gear on emergency accumulator only; 64 per cent braking.

Fuel: a mess. Two lateral imbalances; one longitudinal imbalance; six fuel pumps failed; no transfer; no jettison; more than fourteen fuel leaks; eight out of eleven tanks unuseable; both fuel computers failed.

Weight: centre of gravity well aft for landing; 42 tonnes over maximum landing weight.

Flight instruments: probe heating failed; air data computer failed; incorrect minimum speed calculations and pilots' displays; speed and stall warnings activated.

Auto-flight: auto-thrust failed; no auto-land capability; autopilot disconnected many times.

Pneumatics: 50 per cent failed (leaks isolated). APU backup pneumatics failed.

Avionics: both Ground Proximity Warning Systems failed; system overheat. On ground: six out of seven radios failed; nine out of ten screens failed.

Cabin: multiple lighting failures; indication failures; management computer failures.

Performance application: incorrect stall speed calculations, incorrect speed margins; incorrect approach speed.

Airframe: greater than 70 penetrations under wing; seven penetrations on top of wing; about 500 impacts on fuselage.

All up, there were at least 130 minor faults logged and about 120 master caution alarms (perhaps checklists) spread over two hours.

But in addition to the horrific list of damages to the aircraft was my lingering memory of what had happened as we were about to touch the runway. The speed and stall warnings lurked in my imagination like a monster, and by the time we'd been on the ground 24 hours and I was readying to return to Sydney, I'd gone through the approach and landing a million times in my mind: the computers and flight instrument displays were wrong! They let us approach at too slow a speed, too close to the stall. This issue haunted me, and continued to haunt me for a number of months.

I knew I had to pull myself together and get some sleep as, prior to the accident, I had volunteered to help Qantas celebrate their 90th birthday in Sydney on Saturday 6 November (the next day) by talking about the A380 as guests watched our A380 take off for Los Angeles.

Having fielded calls from friends and media all Friday (nearly all the passengers protected my number and refused to give it to the media), I took the hotel bus to Changi to catch the QF6 night-flight into Sydney. I was given a comfortable seat on the 747–400, on the upper deck next to the right emergency exit door. I remember looking around me and seeing Matt Hicks to my left, and I believe Michael von Reth was behind me somewhere on the upper deck. We barely made eye contact with each other – we were spent.

We took off and I could feel the stress leaving my body as we climbed into the night sky. Then, at 2000 feet, there was a loud bang and a brief shake of the airframe. A flame shot out of a left engine for a few seconds: it was a compressor blade failure. The blade failure was not dangerous but the engine would have to be repaired. So we'd take an hour to dump fuel to get our landing weight within limits, then make our approach to land back to Changi. There'd be an hour sitting on the tarmac, and then we'd be taken back to the Fairmont Hotel.

I looked to my left, where Matt simply rolled his eyes, pulled his eye-shade down, reclined his seat and went to sleep. Somewhere in the plane I could hear a female yelling. My heart sank, not because of the yelling woman, but because I wouldn't be going to the Qantas birthday party and I doubted the airline would be able to host a big birthday party just after two engine failures in two days. This was a PR disaster for the airline. We couldn't win a trick and I felt so tragically sorry for everyone involved. I found out later that they de-rated the birthday party, cancelled the interviews, called off the press and shredded all the PR material. It was a washout.

It didn't go very well on board QF6 either. In the back of the plane, a female cabin attendant had flipped out and started yelling, 'BRACE, BRACE!' to the passengers after the engine failure. She shouldn't have done it and no one else in the crew knew what she was doing, and sitting at the back of the Jumbo was a big group of Germans who had no idea what she was talking about. In these situations, one person makes the call and the other cabin crew repeat or relay the message down the plane. The other crew simply ignored her until a more senior person could get down the back and disarm the situation.

After the passengers had left the plane at the terminal, I joined the cabin crew from QF32 on the lower deck. Many of my crew were already in a stressed state when they boarded the QF6, but then they had been sitting in the back, spread out around the cabin among the confused Germans, and they were either upset with the incident or angry with the attendant who had freaked out. One of our passengering QF32 crew members was crying, so I sat and held her hand and had a chat with her. Another male attendant was not responding to conversation – the whole thing had made him shut down. We were all affected one way or another; some were depressed, all of us were exhausted. Unless you have experienced it, you just can't appreciate the different ways people respond to severe stress. I could sense rapid mental deterioration from many of them. Michael could sense it too and he told me that his crew weren't flying anywhere until they'd had some professional psychological help. That was a great call.

Michael – who was staying at the adjoining Stamford – called Qantas and demanded that the crew spend an extra day in Singapore and be given access to a psychologist specialising in trauma. Qantas was fantastic. They had already dispatched a team from Sydney to assist the crew, and that help was gratefully received. I asked to stay behind in Singapore and support the cabin crew, but I was ordered to fly back to Sydney on the next plane. So that's what I did. As I dragged myself onto the flight that Saturday morning, I felt I was abandoning my crew – I felt absolutely deflated.

*

I have never been in the public eye. I had no idea how to handle journalists and I really didn't understand the extent of emotion that would be around after the QF32 incident. Even before I flew back to Sydney, Singaporeans who had seen me in the newspaper and on TV would point at me in the street. I had no idea how to respond to that since I saw myself as a person just doing his job.

I sent Coral an SMS message at 8.46 am on 6 November. It read: 'Looking forward to coming home. As per normal coming home checklist, please have mattress strapped on back!'

Coral replied to my SMS at 9.03 am: 'Acknowledge normal coming home checklist: mattress strapped on back. Please ensure you are the first person through the door!'

By the time I flew in to Sydney on 6 November (on another flight named QF32), Coral had been fielding calls from journalists and they'd camped outside our house – this at a time when she'd been half-crazy with worry. She'd had a tip-off from a friend at a newspaper that the photographers knew I was coming in on QF32, as when I'd been checking in at Changi a photographer had walked up close to me and started taking photos – one right in my face, which made me wince with the flash.

Coral rang Qantas and warned them that I was going to be ambushed, and, with all the media already around the house, had said she wanted me protected. They didn't believe her but she argued strongly, and so when I arrived, Qantas security escorted me out the consular exit and into a car. I'd flown with Qantas for 25 years and finally I got to see how the diplomats and politicians arrive and depart Sydney Airport without being seen by the media. They drove me along airside roads to the

Qantas building where Coral, Dad, Mariea, Alex and Sophia, and our good friends, the Ford family, were waiting for me.

Coral was very happy to see me. As the wife of a pilot she lives in dread that something like QF32 will happen, and now she'd had to deal with me on two failed-engine flights, two days in a row.

I knew from Singapore there was some interest in me because of the flight, but nothing like the scrum that had apparently assembled at Sydney Airport and around our house. I was not feeling well and I didn't want to feel trapped in my house, nor did I want my family becoming stressed. So we took refuge with our best friends Julie and Simon Ford, and their daughters (Alexandra, Erin, Kirsten and India) for four nights until our neighbours reported the coast was clear.

We had a great low-key evening with friends; a few wines and a bit of a chat. But when I rose in the morning, I sprinted for the toilet and threw up. It was a post-stress reaction, and I knew that it was something that would happen for a couple of days as the cortisol slowly left my system and my sugar (energy) levels subsequently plummeted.

But the day got worse by the hour, ebbing to a terrible low. I had no energy and no optimism, and there was a wretchedness hanging over everything. I wanted to get my thoughts on the record, so I recorded a conversation with a journalist friend about the flight. It didn't help.

I thought rest and the presence of my family would be enough, but when Monday morning came around the stress of the situation had taken its toll. During the flight, and in the terminal and then at the hotel, I was concerned about either the passengers or the crew or both. Even on the aborted QF6 flight on the Friday night I'd been settling into deep relaxation when the engine surge forced me back into the role of worrying about everyone else's welfare. And then, on the Saturday morning flight into Sydney, I'd been concerned about Coral.

By Monday I was starting to take some interest in my own welfare. I felt deflated, exhausted and unable to concentrate. I was kidding myself that this was an extended adrenaline–cortisol come-down, but it was more than that – I could feel it.

My mind was running in a two-hour continuous loop, replaying that flight. I couldn't stop the loop. It was debilitating.

Dad and Mariea were also staying at Simon's, which was great because, Dad being a pilot, I could discuss things with him.

*

I realised that I was too stressed to fly. With deep regret I picked up the phone and rang fleet manager Murray Crockett. I was due to make a delivery of the latest A380 from Airbus headquarters in Toulouse, France, in three weeks' time. It was a privilege I'd been extended because of the handling of the delayed QF32 flight at Heathrow on 7 July 2010. I really, really wanted to make that delivery flight. However, I told Murray I wasn't in a suitable state and he told me to take it easy.

I was on a roller coaster: manic about details and research one minute, and then completely mentally exhausted the next. I realised the severity of my unpredictable emotional state the next day, on the Tuesday, when I went to the Australian Transport Safety Bureau (ATSB). They'd planned to interview me for only one hour, but when they started off by asking, 'Richard, tell us what happened after you arrived at the counter to check out of the hotel that Thursday,' my answer to that simple question took over four hours.

Experience shows us that there is a need for post-crisis management (PCM) for every person who experiences a crisis or traumatic stress. Good PCM identifies the symptoms and acknowledges the human after-effects from a significant event, deals with them and ensures that the sufferer is fully supported and assisted along their journey back to full health. PCM prevents emotional 'broken wings'.

Those who are fortunate to never experience a crisis usually underestimate the significance and duration of the effects to the victims. Some critics volunteer that those who suffer stress after an incident should simply toughen up. Most people do not realise that even for people who do not show overt symptoms of stress, these symptoms exist but are masked or submerged only to resurface up to decades later with severe consequences.

Here is my PCM story.

My recollection of events at the ATSB enquiry was fine and controlled until I recounted the episode twelve minutes after the engine failure, when I had asked to turn back to Singapore and got clearance to climb to 10,000 feet. As I approached this element of the story, I lost composure and cried for about fifteen seconds. I was shocked at my response. I didn't know why I was crying, it had totally ambushed me. I was choked up, unable to continue, needing a minute to gather myself before I could resume the conversation. This was the first time I had cried since my mother died 37 years prior, when I was seventeen and in my final year at school. So I was unprepared for my emotional response with the investigators and confused when it happened.

This emotional unpredictability wasn't a one off. Immediately after the ATSB interview, I visited the Qantas Crisis Centre to meet and thank the staff who had assisted us during the crisis. During my address to the twenty support staff, just as my discussion turned to describing the inbound path, I broke down and I had to leave the building. I soon discovered that every time I recalled that specific part of the flight I would choke up and cry. I found it very confusing and I was worried why I was reacting so unusually.

I was embarrassed about it to start with. I worried that someone at the ATSB or Qantas might think I had gone nuts, report me, ground me and finish my career; I worried about what people would think of me and I worried that I was losing my mind.

I'd always seen myself as an alpha male – a sportsman, motorcyclist, military man, pilot, father and husband, someone with 'the right stuff'. Now I didn't know where to put myself, and in my panic I decided not to confide in Coral.

It was a mistake.

Steve Anderson, the Welfare Officer at AIPA (the pilots' union), recommended I contact a psychologist who deals with pilots and with trauma and stress-related disorders.

The psychologist helped me understand that when I broke down and cried that I was returning to the point in my memory when my emotions had been overwhelmed. He told me it was natural and the best solution was to accept my reaction, and that its effect would gradually reduce.

Over the next month I found myself revisiting the sensitive spot in my memory and reacting. But the reaction diminished, and soon I wasn't crying any more. However, the entire episode was still 'looping' endlessly in my mind.

I remember driving with Coral from Sydney to Dungog and back in one day, a three–hour journey each way. For the entire time my mind was in a furious, intense replay of the two-hour loop of the QF32 flight. For those six hours in the car alone with Coral, I spoke to her only once, and then it was briefly. Coral was frustrated but knew she had no power to get me out of this loop. She was very worried for me.

I heard 'SPEED, SPEED' and 'STALL, STALL' warnings on the approach – warnings that should not have triggered, warnings that indicated to me that there were errors with our performance data and flight instrument presentations. I was worried that news of these warnings would be released to the media and would cause additional concern in what was an already very delicate situation.

Confused and exhausted, I finally told the psychologist about the loop. With his help and advice, I eventually managed to extract myself from the loop. Today I consider myself healed psychologically. I think it took two months; Coral thinks it took five.

I volunteer my experiences and I share them happily so that readers might learn from them and seek professional help if they find themselves in a situation similar to mine: it's called post-traumatic stress. It's real and there is a way to fix it.

CHAPTER 29

Stub Pipe

The Australian Transport Safety Bureau (ATSB) is planning to release its final Transport Safety Report into QF32 towards the end of 2012. It will be the ATSB's largest investigation, involving up to half of the ATSB's investigators and many teams from the United Kingdom and France. I think I know the sequence of events that lead to the engine failing and exploding.

In June 2011, I heard from other pilots that Airbus had simulated our loss of systems.

'What happened?' I asked, wondering how you simulate cutting and shorting almost 600 wires and damaging most systems.

'They couldn't simulate your wiring failure,' said the pilot. 'But they simulated the flight and said there were no problems controlling the aircraft.'

I thought this was a joke when I first heard it: if you can't simulate the damaged wiring and the damaged wing, then how can you simulate the flight?

I was told that the Airbus test pilots thought that there was plenty of stall and manoeuvring margin during the approach and that I'd got it wrong and overreacted.

I don't think so. After landing, Matt Hicks approached me and said: 'Rich, during the last control check, I felt the aircraft shuddering when we rolled left and right. Should I have told you that?' I told him it would have been useful, because I would have increased our approach speed and tried another control check. But there was a practical limit to increasing our speed because, with only 100 metres of surplus runway remaining, we would have only been able to speed up by up to three knots before we faced an overrun situation.

The ATSB employed four people for a one-year period, dedicated to uncompressing then decoding and analysing the gigabytes of data from QF32's computers. I believe that we dealt with about 100 ECAM checklists in the air and another twenty on the ground. Whatever the true number of ECAMs really is, I'm sure it's a world's record and one that is unlikely to ever be attempted again let alone broken.

The final ATSB report will detail the exact technical causes of the QF32 engine failure, and it's guaranteed to be a fantastic read with many surprising revelations, but it's not bedside reading for most of us. So here is my perspective.

*

But firstly, some background about the engines. The Rolls-Royce RB211 engine was originally developed in the late 1960s and was immortalised by powering Boeing 747s since 1973 as well as 757 and 767 aircraft. The Rolls-Royce Trent engine is derived from the RB211 design. Five versions of the Trent engines power aircraft such as the Boeing 777, 787 and the Airbus A330, A340 and A380 aircraft. The new Trent XWB will power the Airbus A350.

The Rolls-Royce Trent 900 engine was designed for the A380. The Trent 900 has over 34,000 parts made from one-third of the elements in the periodic table. Four thousand air foils in the engine enable an astounding compression ratio of 39:1. Each engine weighs 6.4 tonnes and costs US$18.5 million; that's over two times its weight in silver. Compared to the earlier RB211 engines, the Trent 900 produces half the noise for 60 per cent more thrust, with 23 per cent more fuel efficiency.

The RB211's three-spool design provides performance benefits, but it also presents engineering challenges. One issue is that the rear bearings for two of the spools must be located near the hottest part of the engine. This Achilles heel would play a part in our engine failure.

An oil-feed pipe supplies lubricating and cooling oil to a bearing support in the turbine section of the engine. This pipe enters the engine from outside the core, just forward of the intermediate turbine disc. The pipe extends radially towards the centre of the engine, where it connects to the bearing housing via a short 'stub' pipe. Here was our problem. Through a manufacturing fault, the installed stub pipe was found to be out of tolerance.

Here is my best guess on the events that *led* to the failure: it appears that the stub pipe fractured three minutes after take-off, or one minute before the engine failed, as we climbed through 5000 feet. When the stub pipe fractured, oil under pressure sprayed into an air cavity that was ventilated by 'cooling' air (coming from the high-pressure compressor) at about 800 degrees Celsius. The leaking oil immediately ignited and a flame of approximately 2600 degrees Celsius surrounded about half of the turbine disc, overheating and weakening it. The oil fire might also have overheated the bearing housing. For the one-minute period while the symptoms of the oil leak became apparent, the oil temperature (of all the oil returning to the oil reservoir) started to increase and the oil pressure started to decrease, though these changes were insufficient to trigger any warning or reports to the pilots or to the flight recorders.

As the combusted air leaves the combustion chamber, its temperature cools from 2200 degrees Celsius down to about 1520 degrees as it impacts against the high-pressure turbine (producing 63,000 horsepower), and then down to 1170 degrees Celsius as it impacts against the intermediate pressure turbine.

The intermediate turbine extracts 51,000 horsepower from the flow to turn the intermediate shaft (and compressor). It was probably the heat of the oil fire that did the damage. With the extraordinary torque produced by the turbine blades and the turbine disc being softened by fire, it was inevitable and only a matter of time before the disc sheared itself off its shaft. With the turbine disconnected, the intermediate compressor was now unpowered and slowed down. This action starved the high-pressure compressor (at the front of the engine) of air, causing the engine to surge (or backfire).

'BANG' number 1.

Meanwhile, further aft, the fire was still alight in the combustion chamber and the engine continued to introduce more fuel. There was plenty of heat and gas flow. The high energy exhaust flow engaged with the free-wheeling intermediate turbine and the result was obvious.

The intermediate pressure turbine, disconnected from its shaft, then accelerated rapidly. The normal limit speed for this disc is 8300 RPM, and it is certified to survive when over-sped by only 25 per cent, to 11,200 RPM. But the disc had been superheated and was weakened. There are three other defences designed to de-power a runaway turbine, but they might all assume the turbine is not overheated and weakened. The overheated turbine disc overstressed and exploded before the defences de-powered the turbine.

Within one second: 'BANG' number 2.

The 1-metre diameter, 160-kilogram turbine fractured into many pieces that punctured their way through the engine housing, exiting the engine faster than 1.5 times the speed of sound. These pieces then impacted with the engine cowl, fragmenting into smaller pieces, creating a wall of shrapnel – a 'cluster bomb' that cut through the wing like it was butter and sprayed the fuselage with pieces of steel, alloy and carbon fibre. Shrapnel even hit the top of the 24 metre–high (eight-storey) tail section.

One large chunk pierced straight up through the top of the wing, ripping out flight controls and obliterating every wire in the leading edge. Another large piece flew horizontally across the underside of the fuselage, slitting through the plane's belly and cutting at least 400 wires and numerous services. The third significant piece travelled back, splintering into five pieces that holed the forward wing spar, creating devastating shockwaves and carnage within the fuel tanks.

It was surreal. It all happened so fast and with such destruction that our flight deck indications could never give us the real picture. In quick succession ECAM displayed that we had an Engine Turbine Overheat, followed by an Engine Fire, followed by an Engine Turbine Overheat. It all happened so fast that I never saw the engine fire warning. It was as if the plane was in shock; it knew it was hurt but, like a human being when badly injured, it just lay there and slowly 'felt' and assessed its systems one at a time.

The rest is history. Six hundred-plus wires cut, hundreds of holes in the wing, 100 impacts on the leading edge of the wing, flaps and tail plane, 200 impacts along the fuselage. At least fourteen holes in multiple fuel tanks, cut airconditioning and pneumatic pipes, severed electric generator cables. Engine 2 was a wreck. Engine 1, that could not be shut down, nor be drowned with water, was eventually extinguished three hours and 37 minutes after QF32 landed. Spraying foam into the engine stopped it, but also committed it to a 100 per cent disassembly and overhaul.

The aircraft was in a hazardous state for five days after being towed to the airport maintenance area. It was in too dangerous a condition to power up. Fuel continued to leak from the aircraft for the first two days, after which the frustrated engineers had only been able to transfer 13 tonnes of the 72 tonnes of fuel away from the aircraft. Fuel was flooding over the ground, with the added problem of thunderstorms spreading the fuel afar and lightning igniting it. In the words of one engineer: 'You just couldn't believe it! The aircraft was a wreck and no one had ever seen damage like it before. All the problems we had, we couldn't work the fuel system either. We threw our recovery and refuelling manuals out the door. It beggared belief!'

It was both an unlucky and a lucky event. It was unlucky because the engine's many defences failed. And it was lucky that no one was killed.

This is the first turbine disc failure in an RB211 engine. The first failure in 40 years and over 200 million engine hours. Each hour of every day, Rolls-Royce engines fly more than one million miles; that's two times to the moon and back every hour! At this very moment there are 200,000 people sitting atop Rolls-Royce engines, and up to 400,000 in peak hours. Finally, the most stringent certification standards require engines to fail not more than one in every 50,000 engine hours. But this standard is not a constraint, as I have researched engine failure rates for my technical book and found them to fail at about one in every 300,000 hours – that's six times better than the most stringent standard.

In the end, the Rolls-Royce RB211 family, which includes the Trent 900, is one of the safest ways to fly. In an industry measured by fuel costs, hours and dollars, the facts and safety record for the RB211 speak for themselves: they are remarkably safe and this accident does not skew the statistics.

I calculate the odds of this accident happening again are ten to the power of minus fifteen, or one in a million billion. That's one million times less likely than the most unlikely event that certifiers and aircraft manufacturers consider.

Frank Ogilvie (Director of Aerodynamics – A380 Program) sent me this message shortly after the QF32 flight:

Dear Richard,

Heading up the A380 aerodynamics team, our job was to make sure that the aerodynamics of the wing combined with the weight of the airframe provided the best possible performance for the aircraft, consistent with meeting all the certification criteria. The Airbus Handling Qualities people wanted an unusually high level of residual control in the event of systems failure cases, thus providing more resilience, but which would result in a heavier airframe. Having struggled to get close to the weight and drag targets, I was reluctant to accept this philosophy. After your incident I am very proud that I was overruled and that the Handling Quality people got their way.

I was fortunate to discuss details of the QF32 flight with Claude Lelaie, the former Senior Vice President Flight Division at Airbus, and one of the two captains on board the A380's maiden flight on 27 April 2005. I asked Claude for his opinion for what things we might have done differently. Claude's response was telling:

> Richard I have no suggestions; we never tested the A380 with the failures that you experienced. You were on your own – outside the 10^{-9} safety envelope that certification provides. We designed the A380 to be strong and resilient; you proved it. Everyone at Airbus is proud that our aircraft performed so well.

The cause of the QF32 engine explosion was a badly fitted oil pipe that was supposed to supply oil to the bearing unit but instead separated and leaked oil onto very hot metal. The industry and regulators identified the problem and came together to fix it.

I'm still flying the A380, and I take Coral, Alex and Sophia with me whenever I can. I believe the combination of Qantas, Airbus and Rolls-Royce is still one of the safest ways to travel.

CHAPTER 30

Wash-up

On 4 November 2010 Qantas's brand new Crisis Management Centre in Sydney swung into immediate overdrive – pooling every resource to manage the unravelling disaster. Engineers, customer care, public relations, safety, security, executive management, Rolls-Royce and Airbus experts bunkered down in locations around the world to establish what had just happened, and what needed to be done to avert disaster and get all crew and passengers home safely. Volunteers appeared at the airport and hotels to assist and support the passengers. The Singapore air traffic controllers, emergency staff and ground staff were also on hand to help throughout the emergency.

But we were on our own in the air. We were oblivious to the ground support swelling for us as we prepared the aircraft to land, because most of our communications with the outside world were severed save for a radio connection to Singapore air traffic control and fire services.

In the cabin, our 24 cabin crew, despite their own fears, kept all passengers informed, calm and composed. They had trained extensively to be ready for the worst possible event, while probably thinking they would never experience it. They excelled when handling every challenge.

Carolyn and Derwyn Jones, passengers in seats 80A and 80B, recounted that a cabin attendant, Luca Morton, sat in his crew seat directly in front of them and facing them at the time of the explosion: 'Luca didn't have such a clear view of the rear of the engine so Derwyn asked him to phone the pilots and inform them that smoke was pouring out of the engine. Luca made the call immediately. Senior crew members also arrived very quickly to check what was happening to the engine for themselves. Luca didn't panic, but initiated a routine he had been trained to follow, and in doing so I believe he significantly contributed to our overall safety and the eventual successful outcome that was achieved by all the pilots and crew.'

Another passenger described how they became suspicious regarding the severity of the incident because Michael von Reth kept adjourning his team behind 'drawn curtains for extended discussions . . . When they emerged from these talks they appeared unruffled and cheerful.'

In August 2011, Leigh Clifford, the chairman of Qantas, awarded all 29 QF32 crew members the 'Chairman's Award':

> For valour and/or selflessness so extraordinary, that the reputation of the airline has been enhanced in the eyes of other Qantas staff and the Australian travelling public.

Other extraordinary awards have included the Polaris Award (International Federation of Air Line Pilots' Associations), the Hugh Gordon-Burge Memorial Award (Guild of Air Pilots and Air Navigators), and the Professionalism Award in Flight Safety (International Flight Safety Foundation (FSF)). This last award is remarkable because it included Michael von Reth in the citation, the first time a cabin crew member had ever been recognised in the FSF's 65-year history.

I admire and am grateful to all the passengers who expected nothing more than a safe and smooth ride, good views, and food and entertainment, but who quickly found themselves involved in this crisis. Many witnessed the explosion and aircraft damage and most viewed the damage on their inflight entertainment systems yet, despite the opportunity to panic, all passengers remained calm. They even functioned as a team to assist us on the ground.

Most people live without ever knowing how they will perform under pressure. The crew and passengers of QF32 all had the potential to panic, but no one did. The outcome was evidence that good teams are greater than the sum of their parts, and every person should be proud to know that they remained composed in the face of danger.

Teamwork is everything! As mentioned previously, I don't think great teamwork is an accident. It's the result of knowledge, training and experience. As the leader of the QF32 team that day, I believe my approach was never that of a hero, but that of an experienced leader who absorbs and gains from the wisdom of those who know more than I do and who are willing to share and work as a team.

The upshot of this is that, after the accident, I felt the need to bring together all of the Qantas teams who assisted in ensuring QF32 ended well. Qantas didn't want an official function so I organised one of my own and invited 200 people to thank the teams involved that day – crisis, operations, cabin crew and technical crew – as well as numerous individuals who helped make the incident manageable. After the crisis I had worked out there were more than 1000 people involved in and around the actual event. The Changi response team alone incorporated hundreds of personnel.

The QF32 party felt like a closing event for the whole incident. I had crystal vases engraved and high-quality A380 books sent over from France, which I handed out to the guests of this party. It was a hugely emotional and cathartic night, with many amazing speeches. All members of the teams – from flight crew to crisis management, and cabin crew to the maintenance engineers – had their say, and every discussion was extraordinary for the emotion and passion that underpinned what was a remarkable response. The cabin crew discussed how they were preparing for passenger evacuations across a lake of fire; the crisis management teams in Sydney were preparing for hundreds of phone calls to next of kin; the engineers in operations back in Sydney were frantically trying to find stairs and buses and do 'workarounds' after we landed. Everyone was communicating to prevent what looked like an imminent aviation disaster.

It doesn't matter how well trained you are for these incidences; when they actually occur it leaves an emotional scar.

*

How I led the team was unfortunately lost on many friends as they started to unfold this drama immediately after we landed. Their questions and the conversation turned to who argued for what, who wanted to kick who out of the seats and who had which opinions. These were fair enough questions to ask, since they had a right to know what the 'dynamic' or the 'culture' was during that flight. I answered their questions as best I could, stressing that an aircraft's flight deck is not a committee, and that there is a pilot-in-command. I admitted that I wanted to go to 10,000 feet so we had a chance of setting up for an Armstrong Spiral, but bowed to the majority opinion against it; I also admitted that they had wanted me to not flare at the landing, but I had done it anyway; and I confirmed I had performed control checks prior to landing, which was commented upon in the ATSB preliminary report.

One of my friends asked me why I'd ignored the advice to not flare, and before I could think I said, 'Because we all would've died.' But these discussions were blown out of proportion. I told the ATSB investigators that the flight deck atmosphere was very quiet, calm and professional. I asked if there was anything in the cockpit voice recorders that suggested otherwise.

They looked at one another and back to me. 'Actually,' said one of the interviewers, 'there is no cockpit recording of the event.'

'Why not?' I asked.

'Because the cockpit voice recorder only records the last two hours of a flight finishing when the last engine shuts down. Your Engine 1 didn't shut down until three hours and 39 minutes after you had landed, so the voice recorder kept recording, overwriting your flight audio with the last two hours of ground audio.

So, to this day, the ATSB can decide how the plane was piloted from the data recorders, but it sadly can't reveal how the human factors, management and leadership contributed because the voices on our flight were scrubbed. The investigators, therefore, have the opinions of the other pilots to rely on, and my own observations.

So from my perspective and having made it through the toughest challenge of my professional life with no injuries or deaths, I can honestly say that everyone on board was lucky that they had a crew full of knowledgeable, case-hardened, experienced pilots who worked effectively as a team as we wrestled to keep *Nancy-Bird Walton* in the sky then bring her back to earth. My brother Michael agreed with me. He texted me after hearing of the flight: 'Well done, Rich, but please don't do it again!'

I needed Matt Hicks in the right-hand seat that day; not just because he was indefatigable and calm and professional, but because, when our brains had turned to mush as we calculated and recalculated our almost impossible landing performance, he immediately ruled out a 145-knot landing. Indeed it was a payback of sorts, for Nancy-Bird Walton had helped Matt, fifteen years earlier, by providing a character reference for him when he applied to join Qantas. An FO like Matt makes every captain look good. You get a first officer like Matt because the airline recognises his role as a professional, as a 'safety and profit centre' not a 'cost centre', and therefore actively develops his excellence.

I'm very focused on teams achieving outcomes, but teams need excellent members and excellence doesn't emerge from pilot factories or cut-cost licensing regimes. So thank you, Qantas. You've been around for 83 per cent of the time since powered flight, and the standards set by the directors Paul McGinness and Hudson Fysh over 91 years ago have been maintained and developed to produce a record sheet we can all be very proud of. The QF32 was a great flight, but we were only one of thousands of flights that take off every day, each of which are manned with excellent crews. Now that's a remarkable 91 years of team effort.

*

I have tried to be factual in presenting the many stories in this book. Some things I have documented may not have been ideal for me or my employer, but that's life and I can't and won't hide it. There is more to be gained from the QF32 experience by providing full and open disclosure than to hide behind the pretence that I and my employers are perfect. Everyone is fallible, everyone makes mistakes and we can all improve. We should all learn from other people's mistakes, not ridicule others for them. So I've presented honest stories of my past, my employers past and my personality. But I am happy to present the QF32 story 'warts and all' so that you can learn from my experiences, my mistakes and hopefully we can all become wiser and safer in the process.

And just so no one thinks I'm above it all, an old-fogey who's too perfect to be questioned, I leave you with this story.

On 10 November 2010, six days after the QF32 flight, when Qantas had cleared us all back to go flying, I rang David Evans for his verdict on the route check I'd been undergoing when we flew out of Changi on 4 November 2010. Although Harry was checking me he was undertaking training, so it was David who determined whether I passed or failed. The outcome?

I didn't pass.

APPENDICES

Appendix 1

Letters and Emails Richard received from Passengers on QF32

SMSs

Adrian Freer, 31 December 2010

I would like to take this opportunity in wishing you and your family a happy new year. I was on board the QF32 flight with my partner and our two young sons. We are ever so grateful for what you did that day and myself and my family thank you for that. Again good luck and god bless you.

(Footnote: Richard also received an invitation to Adrian's wedding in the UK in December 2011 – unfortunately Richard was not able to attend.)

Dr Derwyn and Carolyn Jones, 5 November 2010

Now that we have had more opportunity to process more of what happened to us we have become increasingly aware of the high level of professionalism and competency you demonstrated at a highly volatile time – we just want to thank you personally at the most profound level for all you did for us.

Mick, 4 November 2010

Great job. Earned your stripes today. Thanks

Mick, 3 December 2010

Rich, owe you a beer. Just read the Preliminary Investigators Report. Thanks for allowing me to spend Xmas with my family this year.

Patricia Giller, 6 November 2010

I would like to thank you for your efforts on Thursday. Although I know you would say you were doing your job, you did it with absolute professionalism. Your grace & patience were very much appreciated.

Claire Ryan, 4 November 2010

Hi Captain Richard. I was on your flight today and wanted to thank you for getting us back safely. Your communication was great along with the fantastic cabin crew in my area.

Claire Ryan, 1 January 2011

Thank you so much for your message and a very happy new year to you too. I can't thank you enough for getting us all down safely. I was in seat 74A and could see everything happening out the window, but with your constant and calming communication it helped to keep the panic at bay. I wish you a year of safe travels.

Prue Carlton, 7 November 2010
I was on the QF32 on Thursday, just want to say thank you for the fantastic job you did getting us back safe and keeping us informed.

Letters

Dear Captain Richard,

I was a passenger on QF32 Singapore – Sydney on 4th November.

I would like to firstly, thank you very much indeed for your incredible skill in bringing QF32 safely back to Singapore and secondly for your graciousness in returning my phone call, on my query regarding the length of our wait back on the ground.

You showed amazing gifts by keeping the passengers calm, as well as informed of the circumstances.

With that number of passengers – it was most surprising that there was no audible panic – and that can be credited to your tone of voice. You were rightly credited in the newspapers as being a hero.

It was especially considerate of you to come to the Boarding Area for that length of time to answer questions, when your expertise and presence would have been needed with the technical staff – and most thoughtful going 'beyond the call of duty' to give us your mobile number for any further questions.

I am visiting my daughter here in Sydney and return to Dublin on Tuesday. Thank you again for your gifts and skill in the safe return landing without injury or loss of life – and also for your kindness. With all good wishes to you.

Marion Carroll

Dear Captain de Crespigny and the crew of QF32.

My name is Lee Cavanagh and I was a passenger on QF32 on 4 November 2010. I just wanted to say thank you to you and your crew for getting us safely back on the ground last Thursday.

Even though it was a very serious situation, you and your crew managed to keep us all informed and calm. I will try and forget the events of 4 Nov, however, I will never forget how you and your crew saved the lives of 465 people. I am scheduled to fly on the A380 in January, and hope that you will be at the wheel!

Best wishes to you and your family,

Regards Lee Cavanagh (20J)

December 6 2010

Dear Captain Richard,

I fly (a lot) for my work and I 'happened' to be on QF32 out of Singapore on Nov 4.

When the latest Australian Air Safety report was released last week I felt it was high time I wrote to tell you how grateful I am to you. Actually I need to add – I'm also expressing the gratitude of my wife, my family, and my friends. Nov 4 was my daughter's birthday – hard to imagine how she would ever again have been able to celebrate that day if I and the rest of us on board the Airbus had ended up in a heap on a lonely Indonesian island!

My thanks is not just for the skill which you obviously demonstrated in managing to land our 'flying wreck.' I also want to thank you for the hundreds of hours you must have spent in the flight simulator to fully prepare you for the unexpected. As I recall, you told us you went into the simulator every three months and you always came out sweating. It's that sheer effort and energy expended on our behalf that I am very grateful for. You also displayed great sensitivity to your passengers' feelings by reporting to us so regularly via the plane intercom and also coming to speak to us personally on the plane and in the Changi airport gate lounge.

Although I live in New Zealand I have flown Qantas by choice for over twenty years. I think I will continue to do so although my wife is not so convinced. However if we ever have another incident in flight I will call up your personal mobile phone number which you gave to us in Changi airport and ask for your assistance!

I don't know how Qantas has rewarded you for the way you handled that event. I hope they give you a big bonus and an all expenses paid holiday to wherever you and your wife want to go in the world! Feel free to let me know if they haven't done something really nice for you and I will take it up with your CEO.

I do wish you, your wife, and family a wonderful blessed Christmas and happy New Year.

With kind and very grateful regards,

John A. Watson

08 November 2010

Dear Mr. Champion de Crespigny,

I would like to thank you for your very professional, well-considered and peaceful action at the very serious incident of the A380 on 04.11.2010. The most important and best thing I have, my daughter Alina, was on board and sat right on the window next to the destroyed engine. She was scared to death and cried all the time. You and your crew is due to the fact that no panic broke out.

Thanks again
I wish you all the best, especially health
Thomas Hinzpeter

4th November 2011

Dear Captain de Crespigny

Qantas Flight QF32 – November 4th 2010

As two of the passengers on board the QF32 flight on that memorable day of November 4th 2010 and its emergency landing at Changi airport in Singapore – we would like to extend our heartfelt thanks to you, your fellow pilots, your crew and all the ancillary services who worked together so seamlessly to produce an eventual safe landing for all the passengers on board. Our special thanks go to you, for spear-heading the operation on the flight on that particular day. It has subsequently become clear that, without your clear minded and focused decision-making strategies, the final outcome would have been likely to have been very different.

There is a public perception of the pilots who routinely inhabit our skies as being – in a sense – disembodied entities in which we entrust our lives from time to time. We take for granted the expertise and wisdom that the flight deck team are expected to possess. Our long held perceptions changed dramatically on that fine day one year ago. We had never felt so *consciously* dependent on the judgement, skills and expertise of pilots in our lives before. Since that time we have become aware that the successful outcome of this critical event was also facilitated by a wide range of other personnel from several countries who worked collectively and collaboratively in bringing the flight safely to ground. It appears that the number of these personnel could well be in excess of 1,000 individuals overall who rallied to the aid of our particular flight by the time we landed – if the security, maintenance and emergency response teams are included.

In particular, we want to express our gratitude and admiration to those heroic fire fighters on the ground who risked their lives for us in dire circumstances. We were amongst the relatively few passengers who had a clear view of the precise circumstances in which these people were operating, and we could appreciate firsthand how close we had all come to being reduced to ashes. Words would be inadequate to thank them for the contribution they made in saving so many of our lives. Whilst it would be impossible to extend our gratitude personally to all these people and agencies involved in our plight, the contribution of each and every one of them in relation to the safety of the flying public should never be minimised. As the anniversary of our flight passes, we remain acutely aware of our ongoing debt to them for the skill, professionalism and humanity they each exercised for our benefit.

Aside from all these pivotal people, and the formidably impressive track record of aviation experience of the co-pilots on board with you, it needs to be documented that you – Captain Champion de Crespigny – provided the senior leadership and facilitated the effective alignment of communication between yourself and the crew. We wish to document our own debt of gratitude to you as the key individual who lead the enterprise, and for your faultless professionalism whilst managing a potentially dire situation. From the moment the engine exploded, through to our safe landing and beyond, you showed us an exemplary level of care and consideration, whilst managing the situation with great expertise. With the passage of time, and with the knowledge we have subsequently gained about the extent of the systems failures and difficulties you and your crew were experiencing, we can only marvel at your achievement.

We were particularly amazed that you should speak to us so soon after landing in the transit lounge of the airport, and felt it showed an extraordinary level of care and concern for our well being on your part. What you did that day went above and beyond what any passenger could expect of a pilot – even within the stringent boundaries set by the aviation industry. Your personal leadership – both on the flight itself and afterwards – came across to us, as passengers, as being very personal and compassionate in a potentially threatening and highly technical environment, as the significance of the events we had experienced rapidly began to unfold before us. Furthermore, you took the unprecedented step of giving us all the opportunity to record your personal mobile number so that we had an ongoing point of contact with you if we needed to ask you any further questions in the future. We felt that this was a uniquely humanitarian gesture – the value of which should not be underestimated.

As passengers, we were treated exceptionally well by Qantas Airlines throughout our ordeal. We can only hope that the senior personnel within the organisation will afford you and your crew the same care, consideration and recognition of your remarkable collective achievement. In our opinion each of the many individuals involved in this critical event deserves commendation – even though there are so many of them. Nevertheless, *you* were the lead pilot who signed off the plane that day and the individual who took responsibility for it. You provided unique, personal and ongoing attention to your passengers and – in doing this in your own distinct way – provided a singularly caring and pivotally human interface for Qantas.

We trust you and your crew will get the recognition you so richly deserve in your exemplary management of this crisis. This could provide Qantas with a unique opportunity to publicly proclaim and amplify the high level of professionalism of so many individuals within their organisation for the benefit of the comfort, convenience and safety of the flying public everywhere – whilst at the same time recognising and acknowledging the contribution of the diverse range of people and agencies who played a pivotal role in averting a potentially catastrophic disaster.

With kindest regards,

Derwyn F. Jones   Carolyn M. Jones

Appendix 2

A380 Specifications

Additional information is provided at http://QF32.Aero

Typical Weights (Tonnes)

242	Manufacturers Empty Weight – to which is added:
	45 tonnes – typical cabin fit out (5 galleys, 16 toilets, 450 seats)
287	Basic Weight – to which is added:
	8 tonnes Catering
	2.5 tonnes Crew
	2 tonnes Water (hand basin drain water is jettisoned inflight)
300	Dry Operating Weight – to which is added:
	Passengers (maximum 853), Luggage & Freight
369	Maximum Zero Fuel Weight – after which only fuel is added
575	Maximum Take-off Weight

394	Maximum Landing Weight
–2,200 / +900 kilograms	Weight change due to the slingshot effect: Sydney – Los Angeles – Sydney

Typical Speeds

127, 135, 128 knots (235, 250, 237 kilometres per hour)	Vr (Rotate),V2 (Initial Climb) and Vapp (Approach) speeds at lightest 310 tonnes weight
157, 163, 143 knots (290, 302, 265 kilometres per hour)	Vr, V2 at (Maximum Take-off Weight) and Vapp at (Maximum Landing Weight)

Fuel System

200 kilograms (approx. 250 litres) per minute	Fuel flow at normal cruise (12 tonnes per hour)
2.5 tonnes per minute (or 50 litres per second)	Fuel Jettison rate
1.2 tonnes	Maximum fuel imbalance between the outer tanks (QF32 was 200% over this limit)
310,000 litres (approx. 254 tonnes)	Maximum fuel load (enough to fill 5600 family cars)

Crosswind Limits

35 knots (65 kilometres per hour)	Take-off
40 knots (74 kilometres per hour)	Manually flown landing
30 knots (56 kilometres per hour)	Autoland

Acceleration

–1 G to + 2.5 G	Clean – flaps and slats retracted. The aircraft is certified to a Factor of Safety of 1.5 above these limits

Cockpit

2	Pilots – Aircraft certified to be flown by a minimum of 2 pilots. (Additional pilots added to crew for long flights)
10	Cup holders (for 5 seats)
51	Light switches / dimmers
Other	Dedicated bathroom, 2 rest seats, 2 bunks (flat single beds)

Airframe

845 metres²	Wing Area (62% more than the Boeing 747-400 (525 metres²)) Big enough to park 70 cars.
79.75 m	Wingspan (equivalent to a 27-storey building)
673 kilograms per metre² (or 1 psi)	Maximum wing loading. Lower than A340, 747, 767, 777, 787
72.7 metres	Airframe Length (A380-900 is 79.4 metres)
2.3 metres	Wing tip (bottom to top)
7.3 metres	Cockpit height above ground
5.3 metres	Main Deck doors (base) (2 stories) above ground
8.0 metres	Upper Deck door (base) (3 stories) above ground
24.1 metres	Tail Fin height above ground (8 stories)
853	Maximum certified passengers – QF32 was configured for 450
16	Doors (10 lower deck, 6 upper deck)
6.4° roll	Roll angle above which inner engine scrapes ground
7.1° roll	Roll angle above which outer engine scrapes ground (3° pitch)
7.4° roll	Roll angle above which wing tip scrapes ground (7.7° pitch)
11.5° pitch	Rear fuselage scrapes (oleo compressed)
70%	In cruise, supersonic airflow exists over more than 70% of upper wing
0.5%	% Trim drag of total drag (remarkably low)
2%	% (Shock) Wave drag of total drag (remarkably low)
3600 litres	Paint applied by 24 people in 16 days covering 3200 metres²
US$37,500	Cost to wash & polish an entire A380

Altitudes (Feet)

43,100	Maximum altitude
28,000	Maximum guaranteed height for Trent-900 engine restart
20,000	Maximum altitude to start Auxiliary Power Unit Maximum certified altitude for flaps and slats extended

Airspeed Limits (Knots)

340 / M0.89	Vmo/Mmo maximum speeds (310/.89 Alternate Law; 310/.86 Direct Law)
7.8 nautical miles (14.4 kilometres)	Turn radius at 500 knots and 25 degrees angle of bank, which creates an additional 10% G loading on the passengers.
263	Max speed: CONFIG 1 (with first stage slats)
250	Max Landing Gear extension/retraction Max window opening speed Minimum speed for windmilling engine start Maximum operating speed for windscreen wipers
196	Max speed: CONFIG 3 (with full slats, stage 3 flaps)
182	Max speed: CONFIG FULL (with full slats and flaps)
118	Vmca 3 – Minimum speed (airborne) with one engine failed
117	Vmcg – Minimum speed (ground) with one engine failed. The A380 is the only aircraft I know that has a Vmcg < Vmca. This will be analysed in my *Big Jets* book

Autopilot

100 feet	Minimum engage altitude after take-off (and 5 seconds after take-off)
80 feet	Minimum disengage height if Autoland active

Temperatures (Celsius)

300° C	Maximum brake temperatures before take-off
900° C	Maximum Exhaust Gas Temperature (measured at the rear of the engine, just before the low pressure turbine)
–40° C	Minimum (freezing) Fuel Temperature (USA Jet A fuel)

Pressurisation

8.7 psi	Maximum normal cabin-atmosphere differential pressure
7,500 feet	Maximum cabin altitude (cruise)

Visibility

125 metres	Minimum visibility to take-off (airline limit)
75 metres	Minimum visibility with Autoland (airline limit)

Electrical Power Sources (910 kVA)

4 × Engine Driven Variable Frequency Generators (115VAC, 150 kVA each)

2 × APU Generators (115VAC, 400Hz, 120 kVA each)

1 × Ram Air Turbine (powers 70 kVA generator)

4 × 50 Ah NiCad Batteries

Landing Gear

18 tonnes	Weight of landing gear
2	Nose landing gear tyres. At maximum weight, each tyre loaded to 20 tonnes (static). May re-tread once
20	Body and Wing Tyres, each inflated to 218 psi and at maximum weight, loaded to 27 tonnes (static). Average of 180 landings per $6000 tyre.
16	Wheels with brakes
Nitrogen	Tyres inflated with this inert gas. Minimises explosion risk from 'isoprene' liberated from tyre at high temperature

Flight Controls Surfaces (52)

6 Ailerons (bank control)

2 Rudders (yaw control), 4 Elevators (pitch control)

2 Trimmable Horizontal Stabilisers

12 Slats (extra lift)

4 Droop-nose panels (extra lift)

6 Flaps (extra lift)

16 Spoilers (spoil lift)

Independent Yellow and Green 5000 psi hydraulic systems

Two independent electric backup systems.

RB211 – Trent 900 Trivia

8 seconds – the time for the four engines at take-off thrust to exhaust all the air that is breathed by a person throughout their 100 year life.

7.6 million – The number of people needed (blowing out a candle over a one-second period) to produce the thrust of the Trent 900 at maximum (72,000 lb) thrust.

98 billion, or 15 times world population! – The number of people's energy (blowing out a candle over a one-second period) that must be harvested to equal the kinetic energy of an A380 flying at 500 knots.

1000 beats per minute – the heart rate of a hummingbird.

Trent 900

General	High compression, air-cooled, counter-rotating, twin turbo-charged, fuel injected, electronic ignition, 0 overhead camshaft, 0 valve, single chamber, 84,000 pound thrust (82,500 hp) engine. 6:1 thrust/weight ratio. Air start (no hand, electric, kick or push starting)
1 million miles (1.85 million kilometres)	Distance all the world's Rolls-Royce engines fly every hour: two times to the moon and back!
200,000	People atop Rolls-Royce engines flying now (400,000 in peak hours)
US$18.5 million	Published list price (each)
34,000	Parts
4000	Air foils
8.1 to 8.7	Bypass Ratio
33%	Contains 33% of the elements in the Periodic Table
42:1	Pressure Ratio
20,000 hours	Planned life on wing (between overhauls)
6.5 tonnes	Weight (dressed: including nacelles, accessories)
8.36 metres	Length (nacelle to exhaust)
3.87 metres	Exterior diameter
2.95 metres	Fan diameter
1.17 metres / 2.37 metres	Ground Clearance (inboard/outboard)
8.8 metres / 70 metres	Minimum safe distance (front/rear) to be from an idling engine

8.8 metres / 548 metres	Minimum safe distance (front/rear) to be from engine at full power
70,000 pounds	Maximum Thrust (selected by most airlines)
72,000 pounds	Maximum Thrust at 30°C (Qantas)
78,300 pounds	Maximum Thrust (A380 Certified) – i.e. + 12%
84,098 pounds	Maximum Thrust (Trent Certified) – i.e. + 20%
93,000 pounds	Maximum Thrust achieved on Rolls-Royce test bed – i.e. + 33%
3000 revolutions per minute	N1 (Low Pressure shaft or Fan) max revolutions per minute (counter clockwise) 24 hollow wide chord titanium blades Tip Speed 1668 kilometres per hour or Mach 1.3
8300 revolutions per minute	N2 (Intermediate shaft) max revolutions per minute (counter clockwise)
12,200 revolutions per minute	N3 (High Pressure shaft) max revolutions per minute (clockwise)
High Pressure Turbine blade	70 blades extract 63,000 horsepower (900 per blade) to power the High Pressure Compressor 2,000 kilometres per hour – Tip speed 800° C – internal cooling air 1000° C – operating temperature 1200° C – melting temperature 1580° C – exhaust air impacting against the blade
51,000 horsepower	Extracted by 126 Intermediate Pressure Turbine blades to power the Intermediate Pressure Compressor
82,500 horsepower	Extracted by 120 Low Pressure Turbine blades to power the fan
5.6 seconds	Time to accelerate from 15% to 95% of take-off power
Fuel System	1750 psi fuel pressure provided to 20 fuel nozzles
Testing / Certification	The engine must not fail under the following tests: 2.5 kilogram bird ingested (the weight of an average Seagull) 3 tonnes per minute rain ingestion 1 fan blade explosively released at full power
2	Thrust Reversers (fitted to inboard Engines 2 & 3 to save approx 800 kilograms)

Acknowledgements

Of all the people who assisted during our crisis in the air, I owe the most profound gratitude to Matt, Mark, Harry and Dave, and to Michael von Reth and his cabin crew for their overwhelmingly remarkable accomplishments that day. Everyone worked 'outside the square' that day, defiantly staring down adversity, and everyone performed brilliantly. Many people train for disasters yet few are ever challenged to put that training into practice. I hope everyone on the team can take comfort in the knowledge that they have been stressed to the max, managed themselves through an incident that was one million times less probable than the most stringent aviation certification requirement, and performed exceptionally and lived to tell the tale. Life's other challenges should be easy after this! Thank you from the bottom of my heart – we share a common bond and I shall always be indebted to you.

The professional pilot's job is a life's quest. Family, friends, colleagues and industry experts have mentored and morphed me into my current form. My deepest knowledge came from my decade of research for my (next) technical pilots' book about big jets. My search for knowledge took me to all corners of the industry, giving me confidence to remain calm during the events on 4 November 2010. To all of you, thank you:

Airbus: Wolfgang Absmeier, Richard Carcaillet, Ann de Crozals, Tom Enders, Claude Lelaie, Frank Ogilvie, Terry Lutz, Stephane Vaux and Pascal Verneau.

Artists and photography: Lee Gatland and Jaak de Koninck.

Australian Transport Safety Bureau.

Boeing: Dave Carbaugh, Bill Roberson and Frank Santoni.

Family: Coral, Peter, Mariea, Michael, Alexander, Sophia, David and Rafe Champion de Crespigny. Roy and Betty Ford. Simon, Julie, Alexandra, Erin, Kirsten, and India Ford.

Pilots: Neil Armstrong, John Bartells, Martin Buddery, Jimmy Buffett, Dave Cassebohm, Peter Cleary, Murray Crockett, Eddie Foo, Ben Holland, Christopher Orlebar, Steve Padgett, John Pickhaver, David Princehorn, Duncan Pudney, Bruce Simpson,

Bob Small, Mike Sterling, Sully Sullenberger, Kevin Sullivan, Warwick Tainton, Peter Wilson, Richard Woodward and Steve Wright.

Mentors and support: John Connolly, Brent Espeland, Peter Ford, John and Nick Fordham, Peter Harbison, Sally Loane, Stewart McAlister, Larry Robertson, Sir Ninian and Lady Stephen.

Qantas: Doug Alley, Tim Gent, Alan Joyce, Paul Kirby, Alan Milne, Wes Nobelius, Alan Rowlandson, Ros Wheatley, Olivia Wirth and Tom Woodward.

Media: Steve Creedy, Christine Negroni, Andy Pasztor, Paul Sadler, Elisabeth Sexton, Stephen Taylor and Geoffrey Thomas.

Passengers: Prue Carlton, Marion Carroll, Lee Cavanesh, Adrian Freer, Johanna Friis, Patricia Giller, Thomas Hinzpeter, Carolyn and Derwyn Jones, Claire Ryan, Maja Stenegard, Ulf Waschbusch and John Watson.

Publishers: Mark Abernethy, Jace Armstrong, Catherine Drayton, Tom Gilliatt and Emma Rafferty.

Research: Dr Paul Barach, Carl Bergman, Dr Leo Davies, Mitzie Derks, Geof Fethers, Bob Hawke, Andy Schuster, Sir David Smith and Gayla Solomon.

Rolls-Royce: Simon Beevers, Andrew Dudgeon.

Special thanks to Peter Ford and Sally Loane for not only helping with editing this book, but also for the many hours spent tutoring and mentoring Coral and me for the press and media.

For More Information

For more information about flight QF32, please visit

http://QF32.Aero

A Note from the Author

About Big Jets

My other book is a technical guide to the new big jets A320 up to the A380, and the B737 up to the 747-8. The book will suit pilots studying for a career in the airlines as well as providing current pilots with in-depth analysis of human factors and new technologies, such as fly-by-wire and modern aircraft design and performance.

To register your interest or suggestions for the book and receive updates, please visit http://QF32.Aero